THE BIG EAST

Inside the Most Entertaining
and Influential Conference
in College Basketball History

DANA O'NEIL

BALLANTINE BOOKS
New York

Published in the United States by Ballantine Books,
an imprint of Random House, a division of
Penguin Random House LLC, New York.

BALLANTINE and the HOUSE colophon are registered trademarks
of Penguin Random House LLC.

LIBRARY OF CONGRESS CATALOGING-IN-PUBLICATION DATA
Names: O'Neil, Dana Pennett, author.
Title: The Big East: inside the most entertaining and influential
conference in college basketball history / Dana O'Neil.
Description: New York: Ballantine Books, 2021. | Includes
bibliographical references.
Identifiers: LCCN 2021007352 (print) | LCCN 2021007353 (ebook) |
ISBN 9780593237939 (hardcover) | ISBN 9780593237946 (ebook)
Subjects: LCSH: Big East Conference—History. |
Basketball—East (U.S.)—History.
Classification: LCC GV885.415.B54 O64 2021 (print) |
LCC GV885.415.B54 (ebook) | DDC 796.3230974—dc23
LC record available at https://lccn.loc.gov/2021007352
LC ebook record available at https://lccn.loc.gov/2021007353

Printed in Canada on acid-free paper

randomhousebooks.com

2 4 6 8 9 7 5 3 1

First Edition

Book design by Alexis Capitini

To George,
for two-plus decades of love, kindness,
and, above all else, patience

CONTENTS

AUTHOR'S NOTE

On a chilly January morning, I walked into Carnesecca Arena and headed to a small room generally used for academic advising. I spent the next several hours in the spartan space, decorated with just a table and four chairs, as the man for whom the building is named and his boss took me on the journey of their careers, from the humble beginnings to the legendary finishes. That day spent with former St. John's coach Lou Carnesecca and athletic director Jack Kaiser, ninety-five and ninety-three years young respectively, began what can only be described as nearly a year's worth of enlightening, entertaining, and oftentimes hilarious research for this book. When I started covering Big East games some thirty years ago, I never imagined I'd write a book on the league's storied history. Yet in some ways, my career led me here. All of those seasons of reporting helped me establish the contacts, the relationships, and the luck necessary for this endeavor. I interviewed more than sixty people for this book, from the bit players to the superstars. Unless otherwise noted, all of the interviews included were conducted by me with this book in mind. In some cases I asked people to retell stories they'd shared with me earlier, but most of it was new, with the goal of telling the story of the Big East. I am grateful to everyone who shared their stories, and indebted to the basketball gods, who graced me with the good fortune of a few more phone calls with John Thompson, Jr., before he passed.

THE BIRTH OF THE BRAWLING BIG EAST
"It was Camelot with bad language"

His head aching, a dazed Mike Tranghese walked out of the locker room and shuffled back toward his courtside seat at Madison Square Garden, knowing his boss would be calling soon. It was March 1984, the year before the NCAA Tournament expanded to a sixty-four-team field, and as chair of the tourney selection committee, Dave Gavitt was holed up in Kansas City. In a day's time, the committee members would reveal the bracket. Those duties meant Gavitt, the Big East commissioner, couldn't attend his own tournament final.

But he was watching intently, and phoned regularly to check in with Tranghese, his right-hand man. After watching Syracuse and Georgetown nearly come to blows on the court, Tranghese knew Gavitt would be looking for a full report.

Just five years old, the Big East already owned a reputation as a physical, and occasionally brutish, conference. Fights and in-game extracurriculars were commonplace, with game officials often forced to restore order after tempers flared. It didn't matter if one team was 10–0 and the other 0–10; this was a Northeast basketball turf war, and everyone got into it.

Fueled by their hotheaded coaches and burnished by their early dominance in the Big East, Syracuse and Georgetown held a special dislike for each other. Their rivalry was primal, a mutual hostility that established the league's image more than any other. The two met in the very first Big East Tournament final, and between them owned three of the first four championships. By 1984 the enmity was near its apex when the two came together for the tournament championship in New York.

Though Georgetown ranked number two in the nation and the Orange were unranked, Syracuse held a 3-point lead late in the game when the Orange's Andre Hawkins and Georgetown's Michael Graham fought for a rebound, their arms tangled around the ball. Hawkins gained the momentum, but as he fell backward Graham appeared to swat at the big man with his left hand. Game official Dick Paparo charged into the melee, hooking his thumb over his shoulder, seemingly tossing Graham from the game for the would-be sucker punch. But after conferring with his other game officials, Paparo called off the hook. Graham remained in the game. Already furious and fuming at the reversal, Syracuse coach Jim Boeheim neared blinding rage as Georgetown not only rallied to force overtime but won the championship in the extra stanza.

Hoping to calm Boeheim afterward, Tranghese made his way to the Syracuse locker room. But there was no placating the Orange coach. He was fuming mad, convinced his team had been robbed of its rightful title. Gesticulating wildly as he retold his side of the story, Boeheim then headbutted his assistant commissioner. Stunned, Tranghese turned and left the room, his forehead bleeding slightly from the conk on the head. "So Dave calls and says, 'How's it going?'" Tranghese recalls. "I screamed,

'How's it going, Dave? Jimmy Boeheim just headbutted me. That's how it's going.' Dave just laughed. It was crazy, but it's also what made the whole thing so great. I mean, some of this stuff, you can't make it up."

No, you certainly couldn't make up much of what happened in the Big East Conference. It is almost too preposterous to believe. Years later, mention of the conference conjures up a well of sentiment, a heavy dose of yarn-spinning, and more than a little awe at what everyone got away with. This was a conference perfectly named. Everything about the Big East was *big*—its teams, its players, its games, its coaches, and, it turns out, its staying power.

Because it's more than basic nostalgia that fuels Big East memories. It is genuine fondness and appreciation for a basketball league that transcended even fan allegiance. Grads always hold their alma maters close to their hearts, able to recount the minute details of glorious plays past. The Big East somehow spans school allegiances. "Shoot, I'm fifty-seven years old and I'll be walking down the streets of Manhattan and people will stop me to talk about certain games," says St. John's great Chris Mullin. "It's unbelievable."

It really was unbelievable. The players too good, the moments too magical, the personalities too oversized, and the tales too crazy to possibly be real. And yet it all happened, the ridiculous and the sublime, the sweet shots and the flailing fists, the hijinks and the histrionics.

Built from the vision of one man, Dave Gavitt, the Big East grew into a national power, partnering with an equally spunky sports network, ESPN, to become the most formidable and influential conference in college athletics history. The symbiotic TV partnership introduced national branding to a sport that previously had contented itself with mastering the local markets, and with ESPN as megaphone, the Big East introduced a whole different attitude to college basketball. From its physicality to its playground style, its fashion to its fuming coaches, the league knocked the civility of college hoops on its ear, bringing instead a whole new appeal with its urban street cred that still lives today. Today's posterizing dunks and posturing after made threes—it all stems from the snarl and style of the Big East.

And thanks largely to the Big East's parity, which strengthened rather than weakened its appeal, a sport once comfortably housed on the cushy campuses of its bluebloods exploded into the game for Everyman.

"It should have been called the Gavitt League," Boeheim says. "None of it happens without him." But Gavitt's dream and vision would only take him so far. It was the people—the on-court talent that played second fiddle only to the off-court personalities—that lifted it to another stratosphere. "What's that old song?" the late Georgetown coach John Thompson, Jr., says, reciting from memory the lyrics to "Doin' What Comes Naturally" from *Annie Get Your Gun*. " 'Folks are dumb where I come from; they ain't had any learning. Still they've gone from A to Z doing what comes naturally.' We were naturally good theater. We didn't have to fake it."

From its inception, what happened behind the scenes was nearly as incredible as what happened in the games. Between arguments over boardroom tables and near fistfights in hallways, the coaches fumed and fussed to try to get an edge in a league blessed with the good fortune to come of age with a collection of eventual Hall of Famers. "A lot of the personalities were, what's the right word? Experimental?" says former Big East referee Tim Higgins. "They were, uh, junior personalities when the whole thing started." In a short time they'd grow into legends, fueled by competitiveness and combustion, and craft a league that changed the face of college basketball.

The Big East redirected the epicenter of basketball, shifting the power base firmly to the Northeast. Before the Big East came into existence, the East Coast suffered a thirty-year drought without a national champion. Since the league's inception in 1979, nine national champions have come from the Big East. Five of its coaches are members of the Naismith Memorial Hall of Fame, and seven of its players are enshrined as well. But what makes the league truly special can't be summarized in a statistic. It's the reverence in which it's held by anyone associated with college basketball. NCAA honchos, coaches who lost to Big East foes, and others who watched the league from afar all practically gush when they discuss it. They marvel at the talent and the competition, of course, but also about how the Big East led college basketball away from a neighborhood, parochial sport and into a national event. Maybe college basketball eventually would have grown into the popular sport it is today without the Big East, but there's no denying that the league shoved it into the mainstream.

There is also, among insiders and outsiders, a real awe and appreciation for the collegiality that fueled the Big East's success. The greater good was not necessarily a concern to leagues already long established. They could succeed with the bulk of their teams riding the coattails of the few. In the Big East, beneath the cussing and the name-calling ran a river of respect. The coaches bickered like siblings, but maintained the same protectiveness as a family. It was OK for them to call each other names, but no one else could. At its core, the national conference was exceptionally parochial, intent on standing up for its turf. Everyone understood how good they had it in the Big East, and the league's needs always would come before their own. "It was Camelot," says former UConn coach Jim Calhoun. "Camelot with bad language."

In King Arthur's tale, of course, Camelot itself cannot continue, existing in the end only as an ideal. So goes the song:

> Don't let it be forgot
> That once there was a spot,
> For one brief, shining moment
> That was known as Camelot.

The Big East would be pushed to the brink of extinction, undermined, not unlike Camelot, from within. Were it any other conference, it might have caved, fallen victim to realignment and greed, or at best continued only as a shell of its former self. Instead, people quite simply refused to let it die, fighting to remake the Big East essentially in its own image, guided by the same principles Gavitt used to establish it.

They recognized what Tranghese could see, even if Boeheim's headbutt clouded his vision, and what Mullin still finds on the Manhattan street corner: The Big East is more than a mere collection of teams.

"It's heaven," former St. John's coach Lou Carnesecca says. "It's something that was made in heaven."

THE BIG EAST

CHAPTER 1

GAVITT'S FOLLY

"There would never be a Big East without him."

Giddy with success, Dave Gavitt and Mike Tranghese stepped outside and into the din of New York City. It was September 16, 1981, and the two men had just put the finishing touches to a $1 million deal with Madison Square Garden. In two years, their fledgling Big East Conference would play its tournament in the world's most famous arena. The move was audacious, maybe even borderline harebrained. Then again, only a few years earlier some had thought the same of the very idea of the Big East Conference. But Gavitt, the league founder and commissioner, was undeterred, convinced a tournament in New York City would give his conference the verve and legitimacy it needed. With Tranghese, his aide-de-camp, at his side, he spent three meetings negotiating the deal with Sonny Werblin, the MSG president.

After the two sides finally hammered out the last of the details, Werblin invited the pair to stay the night as his guests.

Tommy Hearns and Sugar Ray Leonard were meeting that night in a welterweight fight dubbed "The Showdown," and Werblin had a spot to watch the fight. Gavitt preferred to head home to Rhode Island, but Tranghese, a huge boxing fan, begged his boss to stay. Gavitt agreed, and after the meeting the two wandered to the curb to hail a cab for a quick ride back to their hotel. Whereupon Gavitt, who had just brokered a $1 million deal, turned to Tranghese and asked, "Do you have any money?"

Some forty years later, Tranghese shakes his head as he recalls the memory. "I had $11 on me," he says. "But this is Dave. Dave never had any money. He borrowed money from me all the time, and at the end of the month I would tell his wife, Julie, and she'd send me a check. Dave didn't do details. Only big ideas."

The man with the big ideas once concocted a doozy that changed the shape of a sport. It is impossible today to imagine college basketball without the Big East Conference; in 1979, it was equally impossible to imagine college basketball needed the Big East Conference. Only one man believed it did—Dave Gavitt. "There would never be a Big East without him," says Syracuse coach Jim Boeheim. "I don't care what anyone says. We were all against it. All of us. Only he could see the bigger picture."

Gavitt was universally praised as brilliant, but his real gift lay in his people skills. Everyone loved him, and everyone trusted him. He was intelligent without being elitist, a networker but not a user, and a charmer but not a used car salesman. "A common man" is how Gavitt's son, Dan, described his father, recalling a man who spoke with his hands and an Italian flair, despite his Irish and French Canadian heritage. He had a knack for talking to people, cajoling them almost. "Huddling"—that's how Georgetown coach John Thompson, Jr., described Gavitt's methods. Connecticut head coach Jim Calhoun says every time he saw Gavitt walking down the hall, he'd think, "Look at this, look at this, he's coming down here and he's smiling. I don't want to hear what he's going to tell me, but I know I'm going to say yes."

The world felt smaller then, and certainly simpler. The basketball circle was especially tight, more like two degrees of separation than six. Gavitt came up in it, forging relationships and connections that carried him a lifetime, able to call on friends when he needed a favor. Dee Rowe, for example, would become UConn's athletic development fund director and help steer the state school into the Big East. Long before that, though, he hired Gavitt as his assistant coach at Worcester Academy because Gavitt had played baseball at Dartmouth College for Tony Lupien, who just so happened to have been Rowe's college coach at Middlebury. Similarly, as an assistant to Joe Mullaney at Providence College, Gavitt took an African American star out of D.C. under his wing, helping the big man ward off homesickness and an initial wish to transfer. Years later, as the congregation made its way to the gravesite for Gavitt's funeral, that player—John Thompson, Jr.—pulled Gavitt's son aside and told him, "One guy made me comfortable at Providence, and Joe Mullaney was not that guy. Your dad made me feel safe. He's the only reason I stayed at Providence."

Born in Westerly, Rhode Island, and raised in Peterborough, New Hampshire, Gavitt grew up with a ball in his hand. If he wasn't the best player, he was the hardest-working. He played baseball and basketball at Dartmouth, a point guard and critical sixth man for Doggie Julian, the former Celtics coach, who headed up the Big Green. Teammates called Gavitt "The Mayor" because he gathered everyone around and led them, a skill set that would come in handy in adulthood.

The title Gavitt loved best was coach. Alongside his headstone in a Rhode Island cemetery sits a marker that reads "Coach

Dave Gavitt." "At the core, that's who he was," Dan Gavitt says. No surprise, then, that after graduating from Dartmouth, he immediately embarked on a coaching career, spending two seasons as Rowe's assistant at Worcester Academy before joining Mullaney at Providence, and then doubling back to his alma mater as Julian's assistant coach. Midseason Julian suffered a stroke, which propelled Gavitt into the head-coaching chair. The following season the new head coach was named New England Coach of the Year.

After Mullaney took the Los Angeles Lakers job in 1969, Gavitt jumped back to Providence, where he'd stay for ten seasons. He led the Friars to five NCAA Tournaments, including a memorable Final Four run in 1973. That surprising dash to the national semifinals not only affirmed Gavitt's belief that the East Coast could be a player in the national hoops scene but showcased his people skills. Providence reached the Final Four despite troubled forward Marvin Barnes—appropriately nicknamed "Bad News" Barnes—attacking teammate Larry Ketvirtis with a tire iron during an in-season fight outside a dining hall. "Dave Gavitt got to the Final Four with Marvin Barnes, proving he could get along with anyone," says reporter Charlie Pierce, who worked for several Boston-area newspapers in his career.

Gavitt added athletic director duties to his coaching duties beginning in 1971 before segueing into the gig for good in 1979. His background, as much as his abilities to cajole, gave him the credibility needed to get things done. Most of his peers knew him as a coach first—as one of their own—and thereby trusted him, even after he slid into an administrative role. Years later, in fact, when he became Big East commissioner (their boss, if you will), coaches frequently turned to Gavitt for advice on contract negotiations. "Commissioners don't do that, but that's what Dave did," Tranghese says. "He was a basketball coach, and

every guy in that league called him 'Coach,' not 'Commissioner.'
He was Coach."

Having played and coached basketball on the East Coast,
Gavitt long believed his corner of the world would benefit
from a conference to help restore its identity. At one time the
Northeast had loomed large in college hoops, Madison Square
Garden attracting teams from across the country to prove themselves on its court. The local teams, stuffed with local kids who'd
honed their games on the playgrounds, more than held their
own on the national stage. In 1950, City College of New York
won both the NIT and the NCAA Tournament, back when the
schedule allowed for such things.

But a year later, a point-shaving scandal rocked the game,
sullying the city's image. Seven schools would be implicated, including four New York schools (City College, Manhattan, NYU,
and Long Island College), thirty-two players, and eighty-six
games. CCNY would go from the highs of the double championship to banishment from the Garden, eventually dropping out
of the Division I ranks altogether.

Into the void stepped schools in the South. The Atlantic
Coast Conference grew as the East Coast declined, robbing
New York of one of its own. After leading St. John's to the Final
Four in 1952, Frank McGuire, eyeing the decline of his region's
impact, left for the University of North Carolina. Players naturally followed. In 1957, McGuire plucked his two star players,
Lennie Rosenbluth and Tommy Kearns, from New York City,
starting a one-way pipeline that the Northeast schools failed to
contain. By the mid-1970s, the ACC Player of the Year roster
was littered with East Coast players—Billy Cunningham (Brooklyn), Larry Miller (Allentown, Pennsylvania), John Roche (New
York City), Charlie Davis (New York City), and Mitch Kupchak
(Hicksville, New York).

Gavitt watched all of this happen in real time and believed

he had a solution. As far back as 1972, when Tranghese first arrived as Providence's sports information director, he told his friend about his dream of an East Coast league to rival the ACC. Former Seton Hall coach and longtime TV analyst Bill Raftery remembers Gavitt doodling on various pieces of paper, kicking up names for a conference only he could envision. Gavitt even casually pitched it to a handful of administrators but never found a receptive audience.

At the time, East Coast hoops operated in a sort of free-for-all, 230 teams glopped together into the ECAC, a messy and unwieldy umbrella organization that loosely governed its disparate members. Some schools committed wholly to hoops, while others were content to play in ratty gyms in front of few fans. Coaches built their schedules largely as they saw fit, ceding only to regional postseason tournaments to determine automatic bid winners for the NCAA Tournament. "There were like different groupings," says P.J. Carlesimo, who worked at Wagner from 1976 to 1982 before moving on to Seton Hall. "In those days, New England got a bid, New York/New Jersey got a bid, D.C. got a bid." Though it was far from streamlined, people liked the setup. Teams won games and earned NCAA bids; best of all, coaches controlled all of it. Why give it up?

But in 1978, with the NCAA prepped to seed teams in its tournament for the first time, the national body mandated a change, requiring teams that competed against one another in postseason tournaments to also play a full round-robin regular-season schedule. On the East Coast, that spelled disaster. Instead of scheduling as they pleased and crossing over their postseason boundaries to play like-minded opponents, coaches would have to build a schedule that included two games against regional foes. Georgetown, for example, would have to participate in a round-robin that included only schools in the Delaware-Maryland-Virginia region, rather than bolstering its resume with bigger games against more accomplished teams such as St. John's and Syracuse.

In the new rule, Gavitt saw his opening. The idea so long percolating in the back of his mind finally had a purpose. The day after the NCAA passed the postseason rule, Jack Kaiser's office phone rang. A baseball star whose college career had been interrupted by a tour in Okinawa during World War II, Kaiser eventually came home to New York, leading St. John's to the College World Series in 1949. Four years later, he took over as the freshman coach, and was promoted to lead the varsity in 1956. He'd spend seventeen years on the diamond, leading St. John's to the College World Series three times. In 1973, the university named him its new athletic director. He knew Gavitt in the same way everyone knew Gavitt—through the small world of hoops. St. John's and Providence regularly played each other back when Gavitt was the basketball coach. Despite their kinship, when Gavitt called that day, Kaiser was slightly suspicious. "My first thought, 'What's he want?'" Kaiser recalls.

Gavitt asked Kaiser if he'd be willing to meet and discuss a possible East Coast basketball league, modeled largely after the ACC. Gavitt made the same call to Georgetown athletic director Frank Rienzo. He was purposeful in his choices, eyeing schools that already enjoyed success and name recognition, but also those parked in big media markets, because he was intent on blanketing the East Coast cities with his future league.

So it was that in 1978, Gavitt, Kaiser, and Rienzo met in a small restaurant just off the St. John's campus, and the first seeds of the Big East were sown. The administrators immediately saw the potential, as well as the solution for the untenable situation the new NCAA rules would present. Their coaches were not quite as excited; they were content with the way things were, and leery of change. "I don't know if skepticism was the word, but it was damn close to it," Thompson said.

By 1978, Thompson already had begun crafting George-town basketball into a power. Hired directly from a head coaching gig at D.C.'s St. Anthony's High School, Thompson used his reach in the area to attract players to a program that had spent decades in anonymity before his arrival. By his third season, Georgetown won the ECAC South Regional, and the coach was hesitant to give up both his autonomy and his dominance for an idea without guarantee. But Gavitt knew his ex-player well, and relied on the strength of that relationship to sway Thompson. "He was smart as hell," Thompson said. "He'd say, 'Hey, we want to show some of those boys we play some ball in the East now, too.' I liked the sound of that."

Gavitt wooed St. John's Lou Carnesecca over a plate of pasta and wine. Back for his second go-round at St. John's (he'd previously left for a bad-fit three-year run in the ABA), Carnesecca followed the same blueprint as Thompson, combing the local high schools to fill his roster, building a team that offered both local appeal and regional dominance. A regular in the NCAA Tournament, St. John's twice made it to the regional semifinal, capturing the hearts of native New Yorkers who loved to cheer for "their" team.

In 1978 Carnesecca was headlining a series of clinics in Italy, and Gavitt went to woo Carnesecca. The two met up in Milan, where, as luck would have it, their flight home was delayed for hours, giving Gavitt more time—and more vino—to sell Carnesecca on his plan. "You could say we had a few glasses," Carnesecca says with a grin. "That is true."

With Georgetown and St. John's on board, Gavitt searched for other schools, inviting his old Dartmouth fraternity brother— and by then the Syracuse athletic director—Jake Crouthamel into the fold. In 1976, a year after a Final Four berth, Syracuse head coach Roy Danforth had left for Tulane. Crouthamel named Boeheim, a young assistant under Danforth, to lead the

Orange. Boeheim immediately signed two pivotal recruits, Roosevelt Bouie and Louis Orr. The "Louie and Bouie Show" lifted Syracuse to four consecutive NCAA Tournaments. But Boeheim was every bit as reticent as Thompson and Carnesecca, while Crouthamel was agreeable. Gavitt worked his magic on Boeheim. "He could take you to the opposite position you were in an hour before, and you'd think you got there on your own," Boeheim says of the snookering. "You'd end up saying, 'I have an idea,' and it was Dave's idea, the one you didn't even agree with at the beginning."

Gavitt believed those four schools—Providence, St. John's, Georgetown, and Syracuse—were essential to his new league's success. After he secured their buy-in, with input from those administrators, he began to strategically cast his net. Soon Gavitt was hosting regular meetings at the Sheraton Hotel at LaGuardia Airport, opting for the locale so athletic directors could fly in and out easily.

He wanted the Boston market, approaching Holy Cross first. George Blaney had built the Crusaders into a strong contender, as well as one of Providence's fiercest rivals. Gavitt thought his friendship with Bob Cousy, the beloved ex-Celtic and former Holy Cross star, would seal the deal. But Cousy couldn't sway Father John Brooks, the Holy Cross president, who thought the move would interfere with the school's academic mission. Holy Cross declined the invite.

Determined to find a team that could one day play in the famed Boston Garden, Gavitt turned to Boston College. The Eagles that season would suffer their blackest black eye when members of the team were accused—and senior forward Rick Kuhn actually jailed—for their part in a Mafia-led point-shaving scandal. But again thanks to lifelong connections, Gavitt never wavered on his commitment to the school. He'd known athletic director Bill Flynn for years and "viewed it as a bad incident that occurred, not a systemic problem," Tranghese says. Boston College was in.

The next school Gavitt eyed was far riskier, and considerably less enticing to his peers. "Nobody wanted Connecticut," Tranghese says. Competing in the Yankee Conference, the Huskies earned regional respect but lacked the bigger draw of the other schools already on board. It also differed in profile, a big state school plopped in the wilderness of Storrs, rather than a private school nestled in the heart of a city. But Gavitt told Tranghese he believed the school was a "sleeping giant," and trusted his lifelong friend Dee Rowe to help wake the giant. Rowe had just left his position as head coach and moved into the fundraising division, a position from which Gavitt thought he could wield even more influence. "Did I help get UConn in?" Rowe says. "I'm sure I did, because Dave was one of my best friends." In an effort to appease the other cynical members, Gavitt opted not to court the school but instead offered UConn administrators an ultimatum—three days to sign up, or he'd move on. Athletic director John Toner took the leap on behalf of the school.

Finally Kaiser pushed to add one more school from the New York area, keying in on Seton Hall. Though they'd played in the NIT in 1974, the Pirates lacked the success of their counterparts— but they did have long-standing relationships with each of the other schools. Raftery, then the head coach, remembers finishing up a practice one evening when a manager told him his athletic director, Richie Regan, wanted to see him. Raftery knew Regan as a go-home-at-five kind of guy—"he'd have his Dewars and water and that would be it," Raftery says. He was stunned, and slightly put off, by the 6:30 p.m. summoning. When Raftery arrived, Regan explained that he'd just come from the Sheraton at LaGuardia, and laid out the plan for the new league. "He names the schools, and I said, 'I'm dead,'" Raftery says. "I also used a word that begins with an *f*."

The six member schools agreed to pay $25,000 in entrance fees, but Flynn, the Boston College athletic director, didn't have the money—the university's budget cycle didn't match up with the new league's calendar. The Eagles that year were scheduled to play West Virginia in a football guarantee game. Flynn asked West Virginia officials to send $25,000 of that money directly to Gavitt. "That's how we got BC's check," Tranghese says.

On May 29, 1979, Tranghese, who by then was both the Providence sports information director and the new league's jack-of-all-trades, issued a formal press release. "Months of speculation ended today with the announcement by the athletic directors of seven of the most prestigious basketball schools in the East, that effective immediately a new basketball conference has been formed."

Note what's missing: a name.

Even before the official announcement, the media had gotten wind of Gavitt's plan, nicknaming the nameless league "Superconference." Their excitement was understandable. It had been decades since such a league came into existence; the ACC, the newbie among the national leagues, had been born in 1953. The other power conferences—the Big Ten, the Southeastern Conference, and the Pac-12—dated back to the turn of the century. Tranghese suggested they run with the media's title, but Gavitt wanted something more personal, a name that reflected the league's real identity. At meetings, the group bandied about a list of suggestions, trying to capture the geographic significance of the new membership. The Mayflower Compact gained little traction. The Empire Conference, Galactic East, and Seaboard Seven also were shot down. By then, Gavitt had brought in David Duffy, of Duffy and Shanley marketing, to help promote the league. Like everyone in Gavitt's orbit, Duffy went way back with Gavitt, to 1964, when Gavitt arrived at Providence as Mullaney's assistant and Duffy, a PC alum, worked as the university's public information director. Both left on the same day in 1966, Gavitt to Dartmouth and Duffy to start his own company. When Gavitt came back as head coach, Duffy helped market the program via a Holiday Classic tournament, the two developing a lifelong friendship.

Best of all, Duffy understood Gavitt maybe better than anyone else in the room, and knew what his friend was looking for in a name. A week after the formal announcement, he pitched something a little less grand but equally powerful, and it stuck: the Big East.

Fittingly, the league's style guide put the first word in caps: BIG.

Three days later, Tranghese was sitting in his Providence College office when Gavitt popped his head in. There was no time to celebrate all they'd accomplished. The league existed, but in name only. It had no schedule, no championship plan, not even an office, so Tranghese was more than ready for whatever his boss tossed at him. Except... "I'm leaving for a few months," Gavitt announced. He explained he was headed overseas, to tour with the Olympic team. He told Tranghese he needed him to get "a few things done." "I need you to find an office space, organize all of our championships, and oh, by the way, we've gotta be on TV this year." Shell-shocked, Tranghese, who wasn't even officially on the Big East payroll, stared at his boss. The league staff, aside from Gavitt, consisted of secretary Diane Woods. "Chaos?" Tranghese recalls. "If the members knew what a mess it was . . . oh my God."

Gavitt shooed his deputy on his way, telling him to negotiate his salary with Kaiser, who was representing all of the ADs, and get to work. The negotiation went as follows: "Tell me what you're making," Kaiser requested. When Tranghese responded with a number, Kaiser said, "We've got to give you more than that. What do you think about this?" and he named a figure. Tranghese agreed.

That was pretty much how every big decision went in the early days of the Big East—handshake agreements or Tranghese using Gavitt's name for collateral. He found, for example, office space in Providence, but with no actual money in the league coffers to pay the rent, he pushed the lease date back to September, promising that "Dave will take care of it."

Tranghese asked Duffy to sign on more formally and work with the league, but offered him no contract, parroting Gavitt's response: "We'll work it out later." He also met with all of the other coaches in the other sports in June, vowing they'd have a schedule by September, even if he wasn't exactly sure how they'd pull it off. Though the Big East came together because of basketball—an oddity, as the other conferences aligned traditionally over football—Gavitt and the other athletic directors remained committed to providing the same level of care to all of their sports. It was a good thing, too—by 1981, UConn would deliver the first two national championships to the league's trophy case, winning it all in men's soccer and women's field hockey.

Office space, marketing, scheduling—those were easy compared to Tranghese's most critical charge, which was to get Big East games on television. Television in the 1970s was more Wild West than stuffed-shirt boardroom, with deals bartered as much as brokered. Cable was in its infancy, as was live sports programming. The ECAC included more than two hundred teams, but a grand total of six games were televised. In fact, when ABC agreed to a deal to launch *Monday Night Football* in 1970, plenty thought it would be the demise of the network. But as *MNF* grew in popularity, insiders saw the exposure and marketing television could offer.

Duffy was among the early converts. Before the Big East came into existence, he helped Georgetown develop a marketing plan, meeting with Rienzo at a Chinese restaurant off the Beltway. At the time, the Hoyas played second fiddle to Maryland, unable to gain traction even in their own D.C. backyard. Duffy called on local stations, offering to pay whatever it took to get Georgetown on the air. WTTG Channel 5, an independent station in D.C., took three games. "The ratings were great, and we never paid a dime after that," Duffy says.

Still, the Big East essentially sold a dream and a vision, hoping that TV execs could see in the league's geography the promise for lots of eyeballs. But again, things were different then. It wasn't just about going to some big national outfit and negotiating a deal. "The way it worked, you'd go to individual stations around the country, sell the game, or buy your way in, or barter it," says Tom Odjakjian, who worked as an ESPN executive from 1981 to 1994. "'Give us free commercials instead of a fee'—that kind of thing."

Which is where William B. Tanner came in.

"A barterer" is how Tranghese describes Tanner. "No," says Duffy. "He was a bullshitter." Parading around Memphis in fancy suits and even fancier cars, Tanner was billed as the "Sultan of Swap." Years later he'd serve eighteen months in federal prison for mail fraud and filing false tax returns, but in the 1970s, he was known as a man who got things done. Just how? Well, that was a little murkier. Originally he created jingles for local radio stations, and if the stations couldn't afford the jingles, he'd take airtime in exchange. That led to a broader bartering business, Tanner eventually supplying everything from office furniture remodels to credit cards in exchange for commercial airtime. "Tanner Co. got commercial time at a rate usually half of what it would have cost. And advertisers, in turn, got that time at cut-rate prices—with Tanner Co. earning its profit on the difference, plus whatever it could make reselling or trading the goods and services—and a commission to boot": That was how *The Washington Post* described Tanner in 1985, two years after federal agents raided his office in the investigation that would send him to prison.

But if you wanted the business of television done in the late 1970s, you wanted Tanner. Duffy knew Tanner from his Georgetown negotiations, and brought him into the fold.

While Tanner worked the syndication market, Tranghese and Duffy decided to take a ride up to visit with a man developing an idea considered even crazier than Gavitt's.

Bill Rasmussen grew up a die-hard baseball fan in Depression-era Illinois, playing ball during the day and listening to the Cubs on the radio at night. A forward-thinker like Gavitt, he fearlessly followed his instincts, quitting a job at Westinghouse to start a shipping company, and leaving the shipping company at its peak to pursue a career in sports. His first sports-related job, at an Amherst, Massachusetts, daytime radio station, paid him $150 a week to be its advertising salesman and sports director. But it got him in the door, and soon he was working as a news anchor and news director in Springfield, Massachusetts. He parlayed that into a gig with the New England Whalers, but when he and the team ownership came to loggerheads, Rasmussen was fired.

That was in May 1978. Happily untethered but also uncomfortably unmoored, he memorably hatched his idea for a cable sports network with his son, Scott, while stuck in a Connecticut traffic jam. He knew about as much about cable television as Gavitt did about running a league: just enough to have the nerve to pull it off. By July he'd incorporated his network under the name ESP-TV.

A little more than a year later—on September 7, 1979—Rasmussen sat in a closet-sized room and watched the launch of ESPN, an all-sports cable channel lampooned as lunacy. If the birth of ESPN depended on equal parts nerve and luck, the marriage of conference and cable network ranks as the nerviest piece of luck of all. Each dogged by critics, Tranghese and Rasmussen visited in a trailer in the middle of a mud-soaked field in Nowhere, Connecticut, also known as Bristol. They'd met years earlier in Springfield, when Rasmussen worked in news and Tranghese, a Springfield native, worked at American International College as sports information director.

Rasmussen saw the value in college sports, well aware that his upstart network wasn't likely to infiltrate the pro ranks. By the time he met with Tranghese, he'd already negotiated a two-year deal with the NCAA, happily agreeing to take all of their "scraps"—any games not already promised to one of the big networks. He understood the allure of college basketball. Weeks after Rasmussen and the NCAA agreed to their deal, Larry Bird and Magic Johnson squared off in the 1979 national title game. NBC scored a 24.1 rating for the game, an estimated 35 million people watching.

The Big East, not promised to another network, essentially was offering Rasmussen unlimited programming in a sport that had already captured people's attention. He knew better than to say no. "College basketball helped put us on the map, as much as we helped put it on the map," Rasmussen says. Ultimately, the two would grow up together, the Big East becoming a monster league and the network an international goliath. "My fourth-grade class was the first class to take a tour of ESPN," says Steve Pikiell, the Rutgers head basketball coach who grew up in Bristol and played at UConn. "It was like a gas station with a bunch of TV monitors. That's it. One single building. I think the whole tour took forty-five minutes. Now when I go back to Bristol, it's an entire campus. It's taken over the entire city."

Between ESPN and Tanner's wheeling and dealing for a syndication package, the league scored thirty-two games on either regional or national television in its first season. Almost all of them were on tape delay, the local affiliates at the mercy of the local station for scheduling. Some games didn't tip off until 11:30 at night, and no one had a clue what kind of deals Tanner had cut. "We had no idea what the advertising would be," says Duffy, who watched one of the first televised games from the production truck. "We crossed our fingers. Here comes d-Con rat killer. The second was for a casino in Vegas." Opting for better production in lieu of more cash, the league received just $75,000 in TV revenue that year.

Tranghese and Gavitt sought out the advice of Billy McCoy, a producer/director who worked ACC games and *Hockey Night in Canada,* for direction, and hired Len Berman, a Syracuse grad who was based in New York, to do the play-by-play. Berman was working part-time with a CBS station and sent a memo to his boss to let him know about his new gig. "The Big East, I didn't know how to spell it," he says. "Was it one word or two? I thought it was kind of . . . I don't know, it didn't roll off the tongue." In need of a color analyst, the league decided to go with the man who knew the teams best—Gavitt himself. "People killed us for it," Tranghese says. "I got all the crap."

The critics might have crowed and the doubters hedged their bets, but against all odds and, really, against all rational reasoning, the Big East had in a matter of months gone from concept to ready for launch.

Ever the marketer, Gavitt asked Tranghese to put together a preseason tabloid newsletter to trumpet the league's arrival. He mass-produced 15,000 copies, sending most to people he eyed as potential ticket buyers, but setting aside a bunch for media, high school coaches, athletic directors, and other college coaches. "He wanted them all to know what we were doing," Tranghese says. "He wanted them to know that we were here to stay. This wasn't some little operation that was going to fail." (Shortly thereafter, the NCAA put the kibosh on the newsletter, writing legislation against it after several coaches complained that it was a recruiting advantage.)

Finally, on December 11, 1979, in the otherwise undistinguished Walsh Gymnasium on the Seton Hall campus, the Pirates hosted Boston College in the first official Big East basketball game. As debuts go, it was a rather inauspicious start. Neither team was exactly destined for greatness—BC trounced the home team, 82–61, but finished 19–10 that year and Seton Hall went just 14–13.

The league needed a headline to truly proclaim its arrival.

A little more than two months later it found its moment. On February 12, 1980, in a game that, by dumb luck, was scheduled to be aired live in every Big East market, unranked Georgetown headed to number two Syracuse for the last game played at Manley Field House.

CHAPTER 2

A RIVALRY IGNITES A CONFERENCE
"Manley Field House is officially closed"

The place smelled, and the lighting stank. The wooden bleachers, the old-school sort that uncurled from the wall with a key, were hard, but the court flooring was soft, even warped in spots. Some places effuse quaint charm in their decrepitness. Manley Field House was not one of them. But the ugly old place did its job. Teams walked in for games against Syracuse and promptly withered, frazzled by fans so close they could catch the ball on a fast break and an atmosphere that bordered on manic.

Officials who whistled unpopular fouls crossed half-court trailed by the thuds of frozen oranges tossed from the seats in their wake. If Syracuse started slowly, a soda-bottle-meets-court splash provided a conveniently timed break in the action, allowing the home team to regroup. "The first time I walked into Manley, oh my God, I was so happy I went to school there," says Roosevelt Bouie, who'd become a Syracuse All-American. "I remember thinking, 'This place is scary, and they're cheering for me.'" In the seventeen years of Manley's existence, Syracuse lost just 28 games there.

Not even the dominance of Manley could stymie progress, though. Confronted by lousy weather and a decaying football stadium, the university built the perfect solution—a 30,000-seat, state-of-the-art dome that would house both basketball and football, a facility unlike anything else on a college campus. The Carrier Dome, set to debut in the fall of 1980, rendered Manley obsolete. And so it came to pass that on a typically snowy February night in Syracuse, Manley took its final bow. At the time, in 1980, the Orange, ranked second in the nation, owned a 57-game win streak in the building. At a more pedestrian 14–5, Georgetown was set up as the ideal sacrificial lamb to the Manley altar. Fans happily packed the place, ready for a win and the perfect send-off to the gym that had served the home team so well.

That Syracuse had ascended to such a level that it could consider the audacity of a 30,000-seat basketball arena speaks to the uniqueness of the place, and the impact of the man who would become synonymous with both city and university. Jim Boeheim arrived as a freshman at Syracuse University from nearby Lyons, New York, in the fall of 1962. He essentially never left. It is not necessarily an easy place to stick. The cripplingly cold winters send plenty of people packing, or at least create a flock of Florida snowbirds, but ask Boeheim to talk about his town and he speaks as if it's Shangri-La. He toyed with leaving just once, in 1986 when Ohio State came calling. The interview lasted ten minutes, and ended when Boeheim told the school it should hire his buddy Gary Williams. (The Buckeyes did.)

His loyalty has been returned in full, the people of central New York rewarding Boeheim with undying devotion and a filled Carrier Dome. He has achieved what few can in the peripatetic world of coaching—staying power. Through struggles both personal and professional, he's endured. Boeheim has survived cancer and weathered NCAA scandals with stoicism, and always with the steadfast support of the people of Syracuse. "I shouldn't say this, but I've seen him get out of like nine speeding tickets," says Mike Hopkins, who played for Boeheim and then served as his loyal assistant and coach-in-waiting, until the waiting part took too long. "Police pull him over and it's, 'Oh, Coach. How's the team this year?' Syracuse is different. It's a big family, and he's the father."

Had he not found his spot on the basketball court, Boeheim probably would have returned home after college, to the house that doubled as the family business. Boeheim's great-grandfather started the Boeheim Funeral Home in 1854, and future generations kept it going through Boeheim's childhood.

Like most central New Yorkers, the Boeheims were loyal Syracuse fans, listening to the games on the radio, and when Jimmy, who grew up shooting on the driveway hoop until the neighbors complained, had a chance to walk on to the team, he jumped at it. By his senior year, Boeheim would become a scholarship player and team captain, and alongside his roommate, All-American Dave Bing, he would lead Syracuse to a 22–6 record and the school's second NCAA Tournament bid. After graduating in 1966, he split his time working as a Syracuse graduate assistant/golf coach and playing on the weekends for the Scranton Miners, an Eastern Professional Basketball League team. His future good friend, Seton Hall coach P.J. Carlesimo, used to watch the games on the weekends, a fact he loves to razz his older buddy about to this day.

Neither job was exactly making Boeheim millions. The $2,000 he got from Syracuse was for his golf duties, a gig he didn't exactly treat with the same attention he would later devote to his basketball coaching career. "I would send them out on the front nine, and I'd go out on the back nine," Boeheim says. "When I finished eighteen, they finished, and I'd ask, 'How'd you do?' Everybody thought we were undefeated because I only called the scores in when we won." After three years, he shelved his links work and became a full-time basketball assistant, making a whopping $8,000. The first year he worked with the freshman team, leading them to a 16–2 record, before becoming Danforth's top recruiter.

With Boeheim at his side, Danforth led Syracuse to its first Final Four in 1975, but that success, coupled with a 20-win season the following year, made Danforth a sought-after coach. In April 1976, he left Syracuse for a job he deemed "too good to be true," taking the head-coaching gig at Tulane. (It paid $30,000.) Boeheim was scheduled to interview at the University of Rochester, but with the backing of former players and a powerful booster club, Syracuse tapped the thirty-one-year-old for the job. His starting salary was $25,000.

The ink barely dry on his contract, Boeheim drove to Manhattan to woo his first recruit, albeit not the player version. Rick Pitino, a brash New Yorker, had spent three seasons working at the University of Hawaii and was earning attention back east. Wagner College expressed interest in hiring him as its head coach, and several other coaches were talking about adding him to their staff. Desperate to scoop up Pitino, Boeheim called the young coach, begging to meet him in the lobby of the Americana Hotel. It was Pitino's wedding night. He took the meeting anyway, agreeing to forgo the trade winds of Hawaii for the snowbanks of Syracuse.

With Pitino's assistance, Boeheim secured the foundation for Syracuse's future in his first month on the job. Together Roosevelt Bouie and Louis Orr, two of Boeheim's first recruits, would lead Syracuse to 100 wins and just 18 losses in four years, the two combining to score more than 3,000 points and yank down some 1,800 rebounds. Both took a leap of faith on the young and unproven coach.

Orr, a skinny 6'8" kid out of Cincinnati, was getting looks mostly from Midwestern schools, but a friend of a friend of a friend got hold of Pitino, suggesting he take a look at the gangly player. Pitino loved Orr's raw talent, and Orr liked the idea of playing for a team just two years removed from the Final Four. "I didn't know a whole lot about Eastern basketball," Orr says. "But not a lot of schools were recruiting me, and that bothered me."

Plenty were homing in on the 6'11" Bouie, and he enjoyed the courtship. Raised in the tiny town of Kendall, New York, Bouie attended a high school with just 250 kids, so when given the opportunity to see the country, he took it. He visited Santa Clara, Georgia Tech, and Duke, and though he loved the allure of the warm-weather campuses, he worried if he'd be able to concentrate. "I remember thinking I'd be flunking out in two weeks," he says now. "I knew my limitations." Instead he turned to the more familiar misery of cold upstate New York, concentrating on St. Bonaventure . . . and then Boeheim got the Syracuse job.

Bouie had attended Syracuse basketball camps growing up, and knew Boeheim well. He liked the coach's no-nonsense demeanor, and when his high school coach came to Bouie's house, informing him that not only had Boeheim just been named the Syracuse boss but he wanted to come for a visit, Bouie switched his allegiances automatically. "He came out on a Thursday," Bouie says. "I signed my letter of intent that day."

Bouie and Orr were like country mouse and city mouse. Bouie, effusive and chatty, loved the outdoors, content to pass his time fishing. A bit more reticent, Orr was an urban kid, who figures he might have touched a fishing pole once. Both arrived on campus borderline scrawny for the college game. Orr checked in at around 170 pounds, and Bouie at 190. At their first Syracuse practice, they walked into a gym with Billy Keys (6'6", 225) and Reggie Powell (6'5", 230). "Keys, he had a beard as long as his hair, and I don't think I got facial hair until I was twenty-one," Bouie says. "You talk to him, the glass on the shelf would shake. He had this baritone voice."

This, of course, was long before strength coaches and nutritionists became regulars on staff, so Boeheim put both on a high-calorie diet that included Nutrium shakes at 800 calories a pop. "Wake up, drink a shake," Bouie says. "Walk through Manley, some coach hands you a shake. I needed it. You held me up to the light, you could see through me."

Skinny or not, the tandem proved powerful. As freshmen, Orr averaged 9.4 points and 6.5 rebounds to Bouie's 10.9 and 8.1 and helped launch their first-year coach into the NCAA Tournament. Though barely older than the guys he coached, Boeheim commanded their respect.

Not many coaches are more misunderstood than Boeheim. Because he always looks aggrieved, people assume he is a misery to play for. He's actually far less of a screamer than people would expect, and prefers efficient practices to interminable ones. He expects his players to honor the game and one another, and to own their mistakes rather than blame others.

Not that he didn't work his players hard. Bouie insists there was never a chair anywhere in the gym during practice, and drink breaks only seemed to come when players were at the opposite end from the water jug, forcing a dead sprint to get a gulp out of the crappy pointy paper cups that maybe held a few ounces of water. "You drink too fast, it came out your nose," Bouie says. "I remember Marty Headd taking three drinks as a rookie, and on his third cup, he blew two streams out of his nose. He wiped his nose and got down on defense. Coach yells, 'That's what I'm talking about.'"

Canadian import Leo Rautins, who played for Boeheim from 1980 to 1983, recalls only one time that Boeheim really got after him and his teammates. Syracuse lost to Georgetown on the road and played poorly in the process. Boeheim laid into the Orange so loudly after the game, the media could hear him through the doors. The rant made the news the next day, and when weeks later the two teams met up again in the Big East Tournament final, Boeheim made sure his players knew the same effort wouldn't be tolerated. During a practice at an area high school, Rautins says, they worked the three-man weave for ninety minutes straight. "Oh my God, I'm going to lose a lung," Rautins remembers thinking.

Ask people about Boeheim, and to a person they'll bring up his high basketball IQ. In his early years, the Orange played man-to-man and loved to score. They averaged 86.9 points his first season and 87.8 the second, thrashing opponents in the old ECAC configuration who couldn't match their athleticism or high-octane offense. Orr and Bouie grew into unstoppable forces, helping build that seemingly unbreakable Manley win streak. But years later, after losing to LeMoyne in an exhibition game playing man-to-man and beating North Carolina by 20 playing zone, Boeheim switched his entire philosophy, Syracuse's zone becoming near synonymous with both program and coach. It was a riddle few opponents could solve.

But with that intelligence comes almost intolerance for those who can't match it. Boeheim has been known to be combative with the media, and can sometimes sound downright snarky. He's gotten into it with student reporters and national ones, dismissing questions he doesn't want to answer and even arguing topics he believes to be irrelevant. It's produced the image of a nerdy whiner—"The Accountant," Lou Carnesecca called him—which is fair, if not entirely accurate.

But for those who get to know him, they find a man with a caustic wit and quick retort. Former player Eric Devendorf likens him to Ben Stein, the old lawyer, comedian, and actor known for his monotonous delivery. "That voice," he says. Devendorf remembers needling Boeheim for appearing in a Nike commercial with his star player, Carmelo Anthony. Standing in the huddle after a practice, Devendorf chided his coach: "I see you in that commercial. You're looking real good." To which Boeheim replied, "Yeah, $100,000 good." "And then he has that laugh. 'Hehheheheheh,'" Devendorf says.

Boeheim and Carlesimo, the odd couple, forged a friendship in the league that lasted long beyond their Big East days. During summer golf trips with Tranghese and Gavitt, the pair roomed together, Boeheim the perfect foil for Carlesimo's pranks. At a golf outing during a Big East meeting, the two were partnered up and Carlesimo needed only to make a three-foot putt to ensure they'd cash out. Before approaching his shot, Carlesimo asked Tranghese how much his side would win if he made it and how much it would lose if he missed. He missed intentionally, busting on Boeheim as he did. "Jimmy, you're so cheap, I wanted to see you lose and have to pay!" he yelled.

Like his fellow coaches, Boeheim was at first hesitant about joining the Big East. He liked the advantage he'd built in the ECAC, and could see no reason for a change. But his administration eyed the business end of the deal. The Dome was coming, and better opponents meant better crowds. History would prove them more than right. Those crowds would become part of Syracuse's lore. The Orange are the only game in town, the nearest pro city a good three-hour drive away. People came through the turnstiles in droves, the school breaking its own attendance record year after year.

What not even the most optimistic administrators could envision, though, was how the Big East would take what Boeheim built and make it even grander. Debuting at twelfth in the nation in 1979–80, the inaugural Big East season, Syracuse rose all the way to number two as it built a 21–1 record. Literally unbeatable at Manley, the Orange were equally effective on the road. By then the Louie and Bouie Show felt more like a barnstorming event, the two seniors captivating crowds with their skills, and nearly identical in their domination. Bouie that year would average 16.1 points and 8.1 rebounds, while Orr chipped in 16 points and 8.5 boards.

In a nationally televised showdown at tenth-ranked Purdue, the then number five Orange staked a claim for Big East basketball, roaring back from 12 down. Pressing like mad, Syracuse made the Boilermakers look nearly flat-footed, going on a 23–7 run to win the game, 66–61. Somewhere in the mayhem of the comeback, an enthused Boeheim not only shed his plaid sports jacket but tripped over a chair. "He's limping around, but coaching the whole time," Orr says.

A game later, Old Dominion gave Syracuse a dose of its own medicine, pitching a comeback with a full-court press to upset the Orange on a tip-in at the buzzer and stop their win streak at 13 games.

Speed bump notwithstanding, few could match Syracuse that year, and certainly no one among the Orange's new league partners. They beat UConn by 10, Providence by 20, and Seton Hall by 23. So good was Syracuse that down in Washington, D.C., John Thompson III, the son of the Georgetown coach, named his middle-school intramural squad Orange Crush. "I just loved watching them play," says Thompson III. Asked how his father, who would become Syracuse's most hated rival, responded to the nickname, Thompson III chuckles. "He didn't care. He kind of laughed about it."

Ultimately the Orange that year would gobble up all comers save Old Dominion, the season steamrolling toward the perfect celebratory send-off for Manley. That night, fans schlepped through the snow and across the slippery roads, determined to fete the old building as well as their beloved senior class, the last game doubling as senior night.

Well aware that their overzealous fans might want to create souvenirs out of whatever they could grab, administrators ramped up the security, hiring ninety-five people instead of the usual thirty-five. The pregame festivities worked the crowd into near pandemonium, and lasted so long that Thompson insisted on extra warm-up drills to get his team ready.

The Hoyas knew what part they were supposed to play in the narrative—the saps. They just weren't willing to play it. Though considered an underdog to the Orange, Georgetown was not exactly lacking. John "Bay Bay" Duren and Craig "Sky" Shelton— "the rocks upon which this house was built," Thompson III believes—arrived at Georgetown as two of the best high schoolers in the D.C. area. As teammates at Dunbar High School, they led the Crimson Tide to the nation's number one ranking. A late knee injury scared recruiters off Shelton, but Thompson stuck with him. The coach had known Duren since he was an elementary schooler. As juniors they led Georgetown to the NIT title, and though the Hoyas hit some bumps early in their senior seasons, they arrived at Manley carrying a five-game win streak of their own.

They'd also been talking about the game for days, riling one another up, discussing just how much fun it would be to upset the planned story line. "Coach Thompson, all of us, we talked about how cool it would be to end the streak," says Eric "Sleepy" Floyd, a sophomore on that team. "We wanted to go down in history, not as the last team to play at Manley, but the last team to win there."

Initially, the Hoyas' plans for disruption appeared foiled. They trailed by as many as 16 in the second half, and didn't even reach the 20-point threshold until 15 minutes remained in the

game. The cocksure fans began to sing "Auld Lang Syne" in tribute to their beloved arena. "Never should have done that," Rautins says. "Bad luck. The whole thing just felt off."

Riding the inside work of Ed Spriggs and shooting a blister-
ing 53 percent from the field, Georgetown roared back while
Syracuse conservatively tried to cling to their lead. The Orange,
a lousy free-throw-shooting team all season, clanged their shots
repeatedly down the stretch, allowing the Hoyas to creep closer
and closer. Spriggs also did a number on Bouie, limiting the big
man to just six shots in the game and only one in the entirety of
the second half. Their offense stagnant and their defense exposed, the Orange and their now despondent fan base watched
helplessly as Floyd stepped to the free-throw line with five seconds to play and a chance to give the Hoyas the lead.

From the sideline Floyd heard his coach yelling, "Ice cream!
Ice cream!" "He used to say that all the time—it's as easy as eat-
ing an ice cream cone," Floyd says. The sophomore calmly
drained both free throws. "Never even thought about missing
them," he says of his confidence. "Not once." With one last
gasp Orr, not usually much of a long-distance shooter, launched
a 25-footer, but the shot bounced off the front of the rim, the
ball falling meekly to the floor as Georgetown pulled off the
upset. "We had the lead, and then I don't know what happened,"
Orr says.

As the fans forlornly made their way to the exits, Boeheim
gathered his squad in a private room alongside the locker room,
holding them there for nearly ten minutes, allowing them to gain
their composure.

In the interim, a victorious Thompson emerged from his
locker room and waltzed into the press conference. Before a
single reporter could ask a question, Thompson leaned down
into the collection of microphones and intoned, "Manley Field
House is officially closed."

Decades later, Thompson chuckled at the memory. "I didn't plan it," he said with a bit of a twinkle. "I just captured the opportunity." His own players reveled in the chutzpah—"That was awesome. They were ready to cheer and party, and we just broke their hearts," Floyd says—while the inconsolable Syracuse players left the arena heartbroken. Orr trudged home in the snow, walking the three-quarters of a mile to his dorm room during what he still calls "one of the lowest points in my four-year career." Incensed upon reading Thompson's rebuke the next day, Syracuse fans sent letters to the Big East offices, demanding that the coach be reprimanded, if not suspended.

Those six words ignited what would become the Big East's signature rivalry. "What Coach Thompson said, that stuck with folks," Orr says. It stuck especially with Boeheim. For years the two coaches moved in the same circles but did not exactly care for each other. Thompson chalks up the animosity to competitiveness. "It was not personal hate," he says. "You just don't love the people you compete against. Only ones you love are the ones you beat."

But to Boeheim, it went deeper. "In the beginning it was very real," he says of the dislike between the two. "John wanted it to be us against everybody, and in a lot of ways he was nasty about it. I had to go along with it for a long time." At one point Gavitt insisted the two speak after a game, sending them to the bleachers to at least reach an amicable understanding. The real thaw didn't begin until 1988, when Thompson invited Boeheim to Colorado Springs to serve as a workout coach for the Olympic team Thompson was heading up. "It eventually got ironed out," Boeheim says. "But it was bitter for a very long time."

Bitter rivals, of course, can be good for business. When Thompson's one-liner ignited the feud between Syracuse and Georgetown, he also handed the league its launching point. All of a sudden here sat the Big East, brazen in concept and now equally brazen in reality, complete with vim, vigor, and an upset that reshaped the entire finish of that first season.

A win would have given Syracuse the outright title. Instead the Orange, the number two team in the country, would finish in a three-way tie for first in its own league. On the final night of the regular season in Providence, where St. John's beat the Friars, the league would crown St. John's, Syracuse, and Georgetown as champions, and flip a coin to figure out tournament seeding. Gavitt represented Syracuse, Tranghese stood in for Georgetown, and Kaiser repped for St. John's, the three men flipping a coin on the court. Upon the first toss, they promptly lost the coins in the arena lights, failing to catch them on the way back down. That necessitated a re-flip. This time Gavitt came up tails to the other two heads, and the Orange won the top seed; the Red Storm (who beat the Hoyas in the regular season) earned the second spot.

Of course, the basketball gods didn't much care for seeding. They had a collision course designed by fate and Thompson's declaration. After Syracuse got by UConn and Georgetown topped St. John's, there the two rivals met at the Providence Civic Center, vying for the first Big East Tournament crown— Syracuse versus Georgetown once again.

The game did not quite match the high theater of that Manley meeting, but it still gave the Big East a lovely parting gift. Boeheim earned two technical fouls, Syracuse led late, and once again the Hoyas rallied. After a 6-point Georgetown halftime lead turned into a 6-point hole and the Syracuse faithful roared their approval, Thompson called for a timeout, reminding his team that fans don't win games and imploring them to just play their game. Using a stifling defense to force the Orange into turnovers, Georgetown rallied yet again to top Syracuse, this time winning the game without last-second heroics, 87–81.

It marked the thirteenth consecutive win for the Hoyas, and

their second over the nation's number two team, yet George-town ranked just twentieth. Afterward, Thompson once more poured on the theatrics, displaying his wrists to reporters. "Let me take the place of the Lord," he said. "For all those doubting Thomases, you can come up here and put your hands on our scars, and believe we're pretty good."

So, too, was the league. In just its first year, the seven-team Big East sent three teams to the NCAA Tournament—St. John's losing in the second round, Syracuse in the regional semifinal, and little "upstart" Georgetown in the regional final. The Hoyas missed a chance at the Final Four only after losing a taut game in Philadelphia to Iowa (who had upset Syracuse a round earlier) when Steve Waite hit a go-ahead bucket with five seconds to play. "I remember going back to the hotel room after that game. It was the first time I saw my father cry," Thompson III says. "I remember him saying, 'These chances don't come along. I don't know if I'll get a chance to be here again.'"

Thompson wasn't wrong about much. He was so very wrong about that. Georgetown was on the verge of becoming a near mainstay in the Final Four, their future written a little less than a year after that big game at Manley. On February 2, 1981, a kid in Boston inked his name to a piece of paper, declaring his intent to be a Georgetown Hoya.

Thompson picked up the phone that day and called Gavitt to tell him some news: He'd just signed the nation's top recruit. Georgetown's dominance, the rivalry with Syracuse, and the Big East's feistiness were about to reach another level.

CHAPTER 3

EWING ARRIVES, AND SO DOES THE BIG EAST

"He's the most important player in the history of the league, period"

The middle school kids made fun of the new student with the lilting accent, picking on him because he committed the cardinal sin of being different. He found a little solace in a game he'd never seen before, his size earning him a semblance of acceptance he couldn't achieve anywhere else. But he was raw, unsure of the rules, and completely ignorant as to how to bend his body to his new sport.

On a fall afternoon, Steve Jenkins dragged the boy to a high school gymnasium. Jenkins was the coach at the Achievement School, a Massachusetts middle school housed inside Cambridge Rindge and Latin School, created for kids who had come to town from other countries and needed an assist academically. The boy had just come to Cambridge from Jamaica, arriving on the tail feathers of his mother's American dream. Jenkins thought if the boy could become a basketball player, the whole assimilation thing might go more smoothly. But the boy's thirst for improvement was more than Jenkins could quench; he had a relentless curiosity that Jenkins simply didn't have time to address. The boy begged to work on every nuance of his game nearly every day. So on that fall day, Jenkins brought the boy to his friend, the high school physical education teacher.

Mike Jarvis wanted one thing when he graduated from Northeastern University: to be the head coach at his alma mater, Rindge and Latin. It was, to him, the height of the coaching profession. The school, however, didn't think the twenty-two-year-old was quite ready for the job. Consequently, for nine years Jarvis spent his days at the high school as the gym teacher and his evenings chasing whatever job he could get in basketball. He landed assistant coaching positions first at Northeastern and later at Harvard, good jobs but not enough to pay the bills without the teaching salary.

He was still splitting his time between the two worlds the afternoon Jenkins arrived, the boy in tow. "I never understood why I didn't get what I wanted when I first came out of college," Mike Jarvis says. "Then I realized the reason my journey went the way it did was so that I could coach Patrick Ewing, and so I could help Patrick Ewing. I needed the nine years to prepare myself."

The Big East annals are stuffed with players who need but one name by way of introduction—Mullin, Pearl, Alonzo, Kemba, Allen. None mattered to the league as much as Ewing did. Before he committed to Georgetown, all of East Coast basketball, not just the Big East, had a hard time attracting great players. Roosevelt Bouie, Louis Orr, and Ernie DiGregorio all grew into stars at their respective schools. But the brand-name players, the ones who brought fanfare with them straight from high school, went elsewhere. The pull and safety of the more established leagues were too much to overcome. Of the twenty players named to the first teams of the 1980 and 1981 Parade

High School All-American teams, only Ewing chose a Big East school. From 1955 until Ewing won the honor in 1981, only five Mr. Basketball USA selections opted for East Coast schools— Tom McMillen and Albert King (both Maryland), Calvin Murphy (Niagara), Bill Bradley (Princeton), and Bill Raftery (La Salle).

Simply by selecting Georgetown, Ewing changed the entire course of the Big East. On the day Gavitt learned Ewing committed to Georgetown, he pulled Tranghese aside. "That's it, Michael," he said. "We're going to New York." The conference eventually would do just that, relocating its postseason tournament to Madison Square Garden in time for Ewing's sophomore season. In the big man, the league found its star, its villain, and its persona. In 1984, Ewing would lead Georgetown and the Big East to their first national championships, establishing the conference as a national force instead of merely a beggar at the basketball feast. "Patrick changed everything," Tranghese says. "He's the most important player in the history of the league, period. Nothing close to him."

No one saw any of that coming, particularly Ewing and his parents. "I knew there was pressure," Ewing says. "But honestly, I don't think I knew most of that until I watched [ESPN's 30 for 30 documentary] *Requiem for the Big East*. I think that helped me, not knowing."

Dorothy and Carl Ewing arrived in the United States at Dorothy's insistence, and despite Carl's reluctance. She envisioned a better life for herself, her husband, and their seven children. He thought it best to leave well enough alone, content with his job as a mechanic in Kingston. Dorothy persisted and won, bringing her family one by one as she could afford. She took a kitchen job at Massachusetts General, the family settling into a tiny five-room house on the Charles River. Patrick, only eleven, arrived a year after his mother. He was already tall, much taller than other kids his age, and he didn't fit in. He wore whatever clothes his family had handy—an oversized trench coat, a hat—and loitered around the basketball courts, but he was too afraid to join in until Jenkins got hold of him. Jarvis knew quickly that he was a special player, recognizing in Ewing's motor the secret to greatness. Jarvis, a child reared on devotion to the Celtics, knew of only one comparison for Ewing, telling him early on he thought he could be the next Bill Russell. "I didn't realize it at the time, but he had no idea who Bill Russell was," Jarvis says with a chuckle.

During Ewing's sophomore year of high school, Jarvis's patience was finally rewarded: He was named Rindge and Latin's head coach. By now, Ewing stood seven feet tall, and his raw promise had transformed into pure domination. Fueled by that tireless motor, he played with such intensity that Jarvis had to tell him on occasion to dial it back, lest he burn out before a game was over. During Ewing's tenure, Rindge and Latin would collect three state titles, winning 77 games and losing exactly once (to New Haven's Wilbur Cross in a game that featured 73 fouls, including a technical foul on Jarvis, as well as pushing and shoving between the head coaches in front of 2,000 fans)—despite opposing coaches throwing junk defenses, double teams, and even triple teams at the big man.

Jarvis penned a letter to an old friend, suggesting perhaps he come take a look at the sophomore. Bill Stein had played college ball alongside John Thompson at Providence, and as the backup point guard, he was smart enough to always pass the ball to the star center. The two became good friends, and when Thompson got the head-coaching job at Georgetown, he drove up to Rhode Island, where Stein was working as an assistant coach at Bryant, and asked his old teammate to assist him on the Hoya staff.

The trust between the two, forged originally on the court as teammates, spilled naturally onto the bench as coaches. When

Stein suggested that they sneak a peek at Ewing during the up-coming high school playoffs in Boston, Thompson agreed.

The pair found a seat at the press table in the Boston Garden on March 13, 1979, Thompson flanked by Stein on one side and his old coach Red Auerbach on the other. In a state semifinal against Boston Latin, Ewing blocked a shot, corralled the rebound, ran downcourt, and, when his teammate missed on the offensive end, grabbed the board and dunked the ball in one fluid motion. Thompson looked at his old teammate and in his deep baritone voice said simply, "Get him." "That's how it started," Stein recalls.

Born into the era when dominant big men—Bill Walton, Ralph Sampson, Kareem Abdul-Jabbar—changed the fortunes of college programs, Ewing was an obvious generational talent, intimidating and imposing on the defensive end, where he'd block shots as if he were swatting flies. But thanks to all of that early work with Jenkins, he was more agile than a typical seven-footer. He had decent footwork and was fleet rather than lumbering when he went downcourt. His offensive repertoire didn't include a lot of options—dunks or rebound dunks—but he played against such inferior high school talent, he didn't need to do much more.

Ewing turned into a sensation, stuffing high school gyms everywhere he played, the media flocking to watch the phenom. Pierce, the Boston reporter, palled around with a crew of music critics at the time. They'd go watch the Quincy Chiefs of the Eastern League for fun, and one night Joe McEwen, a celebrated music reporter for *Rolling Stone,* reported back that he'd watched the best high school player he'd ever seen. Soon the crew headed to Rindge instead of the Chiefs games on Friday nights, watching the fervor build around Ewing. "He scared everybody to death," Pierce says. "By his senior year, *60 Minutes* came around and we knew we weren't playing in the same league anymore."

Based nearby in Providence, Tranghese and Gavitt even snuck in to watch him play. The two men, who'd met their fair share of talented basketball players, were near speechless watching Ewing. "He blocked every shot, but the thing that marveled me was how he ran the floor," Tranghese says. "Oh my God. He was a gazelle. I hadn't seen anything like him before."

Nor had anyone else. Ewing's renown spread across the country even without the modern assistance of the Internet. Jarvis knew what was coming—an onslaught of college basketball coaches, all desperate to bring Ewing to their campus—and he also knew that despite his athletic prowess, Ewing remained at heart the same shy, uncertain kid who'd walked into his gym years earlier. He was not naïve; Ewing understood his talents were unique and would merit attention. Newspaper reporters regularly wrote about his exploits, and not just the local ones. The New York tabloids, along with *The Boston Globe,* became regular visitors to Ewing's high school games. But Ewing never grew entirely comfortable with it all.

"He was, even then, intensely private," Jarvis says. "Remember this is a kid who only started to play basketball because he needed to fit in." Ewing also wasn't raised in the American sports machine, where athletic success equates to status, and his parents still saw basketball as a means to an education. So intent were Dorothy and Carl Ewing on their school-first approach, they often held Ewing out of tournaments if it conflicted with his schoolwork. Stein recalls Ewing missing an entire summer league so he could finish an Upward Bound college-prep class his mother had signed him up for, and staying home to do coursework when his team went to California. To Americans hell-bent on getting their kids athletic scholarships, such decisions seemed nearly blasphemous. To Dorothy and Carl, it was sensible.

Jarvis educated the family as best he could on what was

about to happen, but families can't fully grasp the chaos of the recruiting process until they're in it. Even with their limited knowledge, Dorothy and Carl made it abundantly clear to Jarvis that they had no interest in inviting the circus into their home.

Consequently, before the circus could think about pitching a tent, Jarvis and the Ewings pulled up the stakes. The summer before Ewing's senior year, Jarvis penned a letter to every college basketball program in the country. It was actually more manifesto than letter, setting the boundaries for what would and would not be tolerated from anyone interested in recruiting Ewing. Schools interested in formally recruiting Ewing were to write back by the end of the summer. Most important, all communication was to go through Jarvis and Jarvis only. No phone calls to Ewing's house, or to his parents. "Anyone who violated the rules, they would be immediately taken off the list," Jarvis says.

"George Raveling was the first coach to write and say, 'I'm not recruiting Patrick Ewing anymore.'" Jarvis laughs. "He would have loved to have him, but he knew he wasn't going to Pullman," where Raveling was then the head coach at Washington State.

No one violated the rules. Ewing was too precious to mess with. "Half of them would call and talk to my wife, Connie," Jarvis says. "I remember when the recruiting process was over, my wife said to me, 'I used to think I had all these new friends. I don't hear from them so much anymore.'" In return for adhering to the rules, the family promised to cut its list to the sixteen coaches who could come to Boston for a home visit, and eventually to the six schools that Ewing would see in person. "My coach, we kept it simple," Ewing says of the recruiting process. "It never got as hectic as it gets these days."

Ewing eventually whittled his list down to UCLA, Boston College, Boston University, North Carolina, Villanova, and

Georgetown, and his first visit was to UCLA. Coach Larry Brown pulled out all the stops, bringing back some of its greats—including John Wooden, Walton, and Abdul-Jabbar—to lure Ewing. "It was a great trip, a great time," Ewing says. It was also three thousand miles from home.

During a visit to North Carolina, the Ku Klux Klan rallied nearby, scaring Ewing off. Boston College and Boston University remained in the running, and Ewing knew if he stayed local he'd forever be a hometown hero—during his visit to Boston College, students chanted, "We want Ewing!" But he also understood that staying home would come with added pressures—and complications.

By then opposing fans in the city already had unleashed their racial fury at Ewing. In the early 1970s, a busing desegregation crisis consumed Boston, the buses carrying Black children to predominantly white schools under court order often pelted with bottles, eggs, and bricks. The racial tension and unrest found their way into the high school gyms. In a scene that, sad to say, would play out throughout Ewing's college career, opposing fans showed up in gorilla suits to mock the young high schooler. "Jarvis had him on the Jackie Robinson plan, which is to say he couldn't retaliate," Pierce says. "He couldn't do anything." Getting out of Boston seemed wiser than staying home.

John Thompson abided by Jarvis's rules, calling Jarvis's house every Sunday evening but otherwise maintaining his distance. He promised a great education, which appealed to Ewing's parents, but he also promised protection. Thompson had once walked in Ewing's shoes, a big player and prominent recruit trying to fit into a new environment, and a Black man who had confronted his own share of racism. "I remember his mother saying, 'I like you, Mr. Thompson,'" Jarvis recalls. "Because of where she came from, because of who she was, the idea of a strong Black coach leading Patrick was important to his mother."

Georgetown had but one official visit left to offer to potential recruits that year, and a host of choices. Anthony Jones and Billy Martin starred locally, Jones at Dunbar High School and Martin at McKinley Tech. Instead Thompson invited Ewing. "I remember it was freezing that day," Stein says. "He was living in Boston, but he was from Jamaica. I told him it didn't get too cold usually in D.C. Years later when he was in the NBA, I saw him. He was with Spike Lee. He says to Spike, 'Coach Stein, he lied to me.'" Sleepy Floyd hosted Ewing on his visit, remembering a player so shy he had to coax the conversation out of him. But he knew the importance of the recruit. "Coach Thompson kept telling us, 'Help is on the way, help is on the way,'" Floyd says. "He was talking about Patrick."

As Ewing's announcement neared, most predicted the young man would choose Georgetown. Rich Chvotkin, the Hoyas' radio play-by-play man for forty-six years, remembers playing that year at American, days before Ewing was to announce. Gary Williams, then the head coach at American and a year away from taking over at Boston College, sidled up to Chvotkin before the game, having heard that Ewing was a likely Georgetown lean. "He said, 'Go home and tell your wife to take the next four Marches, and mark it all off,'" Chvotkin says. "'You're going to be going to the Final Four every year.'" Despite the strong feeling around the basketball world, Thompson refused to relax. With decisions left to the whims of teenagers and frequently twisted by outside influences, he knew recruiting was never a sure thing. Though they were confident, Thompson and his staff didn't want to assume anything until February 2, 1981, the day Ewing made his announcement.

Michael Wilbon, a new college graduate hired by *The Washington Post,* made the trip to Boston for the announcement at Satch's Restaurant, owned and run by the former Celtic Tom "Satch" Sanders. Wilbon remembers the tension in the room;

even he was unnerved by the amount of pressure heaped on the eighteen-year-old Ewing. Recruiting announcements are the norm these days, with players staging all sorts of productions, some even televised by ESPN, to announce their college choice. Then, though, that wasn't really done. But Ewing was a big deal and Jarvis, a longtime friend of Sanders's, liked the idea of a nice place that also gave Sanders a bit of publicity.

Jarvis arrived early, making sure everything was in order, and immediately was struck by the number of Boston College–leaning people in attendance—not just local reporters, but businessmen and fans who popped in to see if their school could land the hometown hero. Jarvis didn't know officially what Ewing would announce, but he believed in his gut that the young man would choose Georgetown. He could tell in the way his player discussed the school, and sensed the comfort Ewing's parents felt.

Ewing, noticeably nervous and looking uncomfortable in his suit and white shirt, arrived with his parents. When he hoisted a Georgetown pennant over his head, the businessmen actually booed and hissed, and the partisan media filed out pretty quickly. "It was some of the ugliest of Boston on display that day," Wilbon says. "It was so heavy it was crazy. I was scared to death, and I was twenty-two. He was eighteen."

To Ewing, the decision was a no-brainer. He loved his visit to Georgetown, was comfortable with the players despite his shyness, and thought he could be happy in D.C. despite the cold. And above all else, there was Thompson. "The opportunity to play for a Black man who looked like me, who carried himself with class and dignity, he was someone I could look up to and emulate," Ewing says. "Wherever I went, I would have been a great player. But this person, this man helped me become not only a great player but a great man. You listen to any interview I've done. I've always said I came to Georgetown a boy and I left a man."

Months later Stein and Thompson went to Ewing's house so that the player could formally sign his binding national letter of intent. Dorothy Ewing looked at the two coaches and said, "In my country, we sign for land, not people." "My heart just about sank," Stein says. "And then she turns around and says to Patrick, 'Come over here and sign this.'"

The Big East felt the impact of Ewing's arrival instantly. National media, who had previously covered the league in passing, now flocked to Georgetown games, the Hoyas skyrocketing to national fame and bringing the league right along with them. "When people used to ask me who were the most important people in getting the Big East to where it was in those early years, Dave Gavitt was number one," Tranghese says. "And I'm certain Patrick Ewing was number two."

Despite his fame, Ewing did not bluster his way into Georgetown, nor did he act the part of the big man on campus. "He could have very easily said, 'Don't you all try to teach me anything,'" Thompson said. "I tell people all the time, Patrick had more leverage on the school and myself based on who he was, and he never used it. He treated the custodian as well as the president of the college." He was the same with his teammates, never expecting preferential treatment and deferential to his upperclassmen. Ed Spriggs, a senior on the Georgetown team in Ewing's first season, had worked as a truck driver before coming to college, which meant he was a twenty-six-year-old senior, with little to no interest in some freshman sensation. "Here comes this avatar, with all this talent, and Ed could give a fuck," his teammate Gene Smith says. "But Ed was a senior. He was in that Manley Field House game. Ed was history and legacy, and Patrick fell into that. He was not bigger than the program. Even though you and I both know he was bigger than the program."

A year ahead of Ewing, Smith roomed with the big man on campus for two years, recalling a player who could never quite fit in because of his fame and his size, but who tried desperately to be normal. If classmates stopped to chat, Ewing was cordial, content to go about his business as quietly as possible. In their years of rooming together, Smith remembers just one fight between them. Ewing had some sort of Jamaican clackers and whacked his roommate on the head. "Now I was chippy, too," says Smith. "And I went after him." But Smith also gave up 10 inches and 80 pounds to his younger roomie. "He had to lock the door to keep from killing me."

Ewing also was understandably reticent about all of the attention. Since arriving in the United States, he'd been either an outcast or a curiosity. He didn't trust easily, and certainly not carelessly. Taught early by his parents, he was selective with his friendships, keeping his circle tight. In some ways, then, Georgetown was perfect for him. Thompson did not care to go along merely to get along. He crafted his own rules and protocols, never feeling the need to conform. Reporters came to term his approach "Hoya Paranoia," aggravated that covering the Hoyas sometimes felt like an absurd tap dance. The locker room opened for player interviews at exactly the same time that Thompson stepped to the podium to begin his postgame comments; it closed when he stopped talking, leaving sportswriters to figure out how to be in two places at once. Freshmen, including his star freshman, were not available for interviews in their first semester, and when Georgetown traveled, Thompson chose not to disclose the hotel where they stayed.

There was a method to his maddening madness. Thompson felt obligated to protect his players. He'd frequently gripe how unfair it seemed that adult referees never were subject to postgame interviews but his teenage players were. He was especially protective of Ewing, aware of the pressures that came with the klieg lights he lived under. "He afforded me the opportunity to grow and be a normal student," Ewing says. "Coach took the hits for me."

Ewing made his Big East debut at Madison Square Garden against eighteenth-ranked St. John's, with a sold-out crowd on hand to witness the new kid. The Hoyas ran roughshod over the home team that day, building a 41–9 lead in the first half, and Ewing, saddled with foul trouble, didn't have to do much work. He finished with 9 points, 6 rebounds, and 5 blocked shots, but in one play he left the seen-it-all New Yorkers gobsmacked. From *The Washington Post:*

> Georgetown had an 8–2 lead when Ewing blocked a shot by Chris Mullin, knocking the ball to Fred Brown. Ewing then sped up court on the right sideline. Brown took two dribbles and lobbed a long pass that first appeared to be nowhere near Ewing. But he leaped over three defenders, grabbed the ball eight feet from the basket and dunked it, all before any of the startled Redmen even turned around.

So went Ewing's exploits for the entirety of his career, his talents lending themselves to almost cartoonish dominance, even against players meant to be his peers. Stein remembers a 1981 game against San Diego State when three different Aztecs tried to drive from the baseline and score. Ewing blocked each one. "They literally shot over the backboard to try and get the ball over him," Stein says. "I broke out laughing on the bench."

It might have been amusing for those wearing Hoya uniforms, but it was less so for opponents. Led by Ewing, Georgetown was an unapologetic menace to their opponents, as mean as they were good. The league became famous for brawling, and Georgetown figured in plenty of the fisticuffs, developing a reputation as combative as well as competitive. "Coach Thompson had a saying," Smith says. "He'd say, 'We're not looking for a fight, but if it's a fight you want, we can accommodate you.'"

The Hoyas thrived on their ability to intimidate teams and create friction, and they split the fan base: You were either for or against the Hoyas, with no middle ground possible. Ewing never got to play the good guy, even when he wasn't in the wrong. "He was a warrior," St. John's coach Lou Carnesecca says. "But that type of kid, he made everyone else want to fight. It was us against them, let's go." If that had been all it was, Ewing might not have minded. He didn't need to be loved, just to win. "Nobody liked us because we were kicking butts and taking names," he says.

But beneath the casual fan dislike simmered a far more sinister undercurrent. Coached by a socially conscious Black man, with a roster full of Black players at a predominantly white school, the Hoyas served as a cultural flash point. Embraced by the African American community that proudly sported Georgetown gear and supported Thompson, the Hoyas also felt the racist outrage of critics who didn't think they belonged. No one felt it more than Ewing.

When Jarvis created that manifesto for coaches interested in recruiting Ewing, he'd included information about the academic support that he sought for the young man—tutors and advisors to ensure he'd succeed off the court as much as on. It made sense. Ewing had immigrated to the United States less than ten years earlier, and his parents wanted to ensure that he received the full benefit of his college education. To critics primed to pounce, it read as an admission that Ewing lacked the credentials for college, specifically one as highbrow as Georgetown. Fans derided him for his perceived lack of intellect, wearing T-shirts and carrying banners that shouted "Ewing Kant Read Dis."

Others went even further, leaving no doubt about their intent. "Ewing is an ape," they wrote, some wearing actual ape costumes to games. In a game against Villanova at Philadelphia's famed Palestra, fans threw banana peels at the backboard while Ewing took free throws. Following the league tournament in Hartford, Georgetown fielded a death threat that officials deemed credible. Administrators temporarily relocated Ewing and several of his teammates to the Key Bridge Marriott, not far from the Georgetown campus, and notified the D.C. police. Ewing remembers walking across campus with his teammate and friend Ralph Dalton shortly thereafter, wondering aloud "why this white guy was following us." Later Ewing would learn the man was an FBI agent, brought to campus to protect Ewing because of the threats.

"People have no idea how bad it was for Patrick," Tranghese says. "No idea. Everywhere he went. Everywhere Georgetown went."

It counts as the league's biggest black eye that it did so little to protect its star player, punting responsibility to the host schools, who in turn shrugged in a what can we do response. Tranghese attended that game at the Palestra, sickened by what he saw. He reported back to Gavitt in Providence, but the commissioner called on Villanova athletic director Ted Aceto to handle it. Aceto wrote it off as mere hijinks, telling *The Washington Post,* "You have to realize, those kind of signs are common in Philadelphia. You should see all of the signs at the Big Five games [games played between the five colleges located in and near Philadelphia]. It seems like the signs are always about the other team's best player."

Ultimately, Gavitt deferred to Thompson, placing an impossible burden on the coach. Multiple times Thompson pulled his team off the court, refusing to play until the offending signs or fans were removed. Such actions only reinforced the image of Thompson as angry Black coach, unreasonable and difficult to deal with. "People didn't always like the way John dealt with it, but my attitude was, 'To hell with you,'" Tranghese says. "You're not sitting in his shoes." Much as he did in high school, Ewing remained silent. He called Jarvis a few times, more homesick than upset. "Sadly, I think he almost was used to it by then," Jarvis says. "We'd all gone through that stuff his last year in high school."

Indeed, Ewing says it didn't get to him, that he used people's hatred to fuel him. "For all the nasty people who said or wrote things about me, I just decided to take it out on their teams," Ewing says. "It didn't hurt me because I didn't know them. A lot of them, they were just mad I didn't go to their school." All these years later, he's still reluctant to talk about any of it. "I was young" is all he says. "There's a lot of different things that happened, things I don't want to get into." He's grateful to his coach, not only for the protection but also because Thompson never made a big fuss. Though Ewing received the most attention and almost always was the target of fans' nastiness, Thompson never once shielded Ewing and Ewing alone. He spoke collectively about Georgetown, making sure the center never felt like a burden.

But those who know Ewing well wonder about the long-lasting impact on Ewing's psyche. Wilbon now counts Ewing as one of his closest friends. Yet in the span of their nearly four decades of friendship, the two have never discussed how Ewing was treated. Wilbon, embarrassed at how dismissive reporters were of Ewing's treatment at the time, doesn't feel right bringing it up, and Ewing only mentions it in passing—maybe an elbow to his old buddy about "the shit that happened" years ago. "I don't know this, I'm purely guessing, but I wonder if the scarring is too deep, even now when he's comfortable in his own skin," Wilbon says. "So much of his life is on the East Coast. It's home, that stretch of land from Boston to Washington, that's home. It's hard."

And as trite as it sounds, Wilbon believes Ewing did repurpose his anger into fuel, using it to feed what had always been an insatiable work ethic. Combining his talent with his voracious appetite to get better and now a mission to avenge wrongs, Ewing became simply unstoppable. As a freshman, he led Georgetown to its first Final Four in thirty-nine years, defeating Louisville in the national semifinal to set up a championship against North Carolina, a perfect new-blood/blueblood, bad-guys/good-guys story line.

Not working in journalism at the time, Pierce won two tickets to the title game via the lottery, plopping down in section 646, four rows from the top wall in the Superdome in Louisiana, which is also about four steps beneath the heavens. From his perch near the rafters, he looked down on the Tar Heels' basket. At the time, North Carolina had appeared in six Final Fours and three title games but just couldn't get its coach, Dean Smith, over the final hurdle. This team had a star-studded roster that included a freshman by the name of Mike Jordan, and so most thought this was the Tar Heels' game to lose.

Instead, Ewing came out and rejected shot after shot, called four times for goaltending on Carolina's first four possessions. Pierce told his college roommate, seated beside him, that the first was an honest mistake, the second maybe due to nerves. By the time Ewing had swatted away shots three and four, the reporter in him realized what was going on. What he was witnessing wasn't the nerves of an overanxious freshman but the game plan of a wily coach. "Kids don't remember goaltending calls," he says of Thompson's rationale. "They remember getting their shots blocked."

Sure enough, Ewing's defensive prowess did exactly what the coach had hoped, sending a message that the Hoyas wouldn't be a pushover. "Ooh, it was nice to have a seat on the bench," says Gene Smith, who played sparingly after missing some of the season with an injury.

The taut game ended only after Jordan sank the winner with 15 seconds left and Georgetown guard Fred Brown mistakenly passed right into the hands of Carolina's James Worthy. Ewing would finish with 23 points, 11 rebounds, 3 steals, and 2 blocks, cementing his place as more than just the next in line of great big men—he was a legend in the making.

Thanks largely to their larger-than-life player, Georgetown opened the next season ranked number two in the nation in the preseason, the love-'em-or-hate-'em Hoyas the perfect lightning rod to carry the narrative of an entire sport.

And just as Gavitt had predicted all those years earlier, Ewing ranked as the biggest star in the game, the perfect player to carry his league to New York.

CHAPTER 4

THE MAGIC OF MADISON SQUARE GARDEN
"I just knew that was the place to play"

In 1942, a skinny little kid with a mouthful of a last name watched his first game at Madison Square Garden, rewarded with a ticket to a St. John's game after playing his own high school contest in the famous arena. Seven decades and more than 700 games as a head coach later, Lou Carnesecca still sounds a lot like that seventeen-year-old boy when he tries to explain the allure of the Garden. He fumbles for his words like a man still smitten with the blush of a first love, lifting his eyes and hands to the heavens, indicating where the building ought to reside. "It was . . . it was unbelievable," he says. "To play at the Garden, it was just ahh."

In his defense, it is hard to explain the pull. Madison Square Garden offers neither architectural mastery nor old-school charm. It's not Philadelphia's Palestra, Kansas's Allen Fieldhouse, or Indianapolis's Hinkle Fieldhouse, famed basketball cathedrals replete with arched windows and sun-splashed floors. It's not Indiana's Assembly Hall or UCLA's Pauley Pavilion, beloved on-campus arenas stuffed with school history. It doesn't even house all of its own history. The current iteration is actually the fourth version of Madison Square Garden. The first two sat at Fifth Avenue and Broadway at 23rd Street, also known as Madison Square. Carnesecca's first visit was to the third version, on Eighth Avenue between 49th and 50th. In 1968 that gave way to the current Midtown Manhattan model, which takes up two city blocks and is plopped atop a twenty-one-track, seven-tunnel railroad maze known as Penn Station.

People conflate the versions all the time, failing to differentiate that the Garden in which Marilyn Monroe famously serenaded President Kennedy in 1962 is not the same Garden in which Muhammad Ali met Joe Frazier in the Fight of the Century in 1971. It doesn't matter. The Garden is the Garden is the Garden, its appeal universal, its name ubiquitous.

And Gavitt, shrewdly, was very much aware of both.

For its first three postseason tournaments, the Big East bounced from Providence to Syracuse to Hartford, doing well in the safe, smaller confines but hardly matching the panache of its ACC rival, with its self-proclaimed "World's Greatest Basketball Tournament" played annually in North Carolina. Gavitt dreamed of moving to the Garden almost from the league's inception, telling people at the first tournament at the Providence Civic Center he hoped to play in New York in the not-too-distant future. No one paid the comment much mind, and Gavitt didn't mention it again.

Until, that is, Ewing signed with Georgetown. Then playing in New York became a mission. Though the nearby Meadowlands in New Jersey and Nassau Coliseum on Long Island also inquired, Gavitt had his heart set on Madison Square Garden. He wanted the city, not the outskirts, and he wanted the place once considered the epicenter of college basketball. For decades that had been the Garden.

In the 1930s, a sportswriter turned promoter (and eventual president of the Knicks) by the name of Ned Irish lured college teams to the Garden for doubleheaders, the city's rich basketball history making for an easy sell. The events drew crowds of 16,000 or more regularly, and when the NIT was born in 1938, the Garden became the logical place to host it. But with the 1951 point-shaving scandal that embroiled those seven city colleges, New York went from the epicenter of college basketball to the epicenter of corruption. As the NCAA Tournament grew in stature and the NIT became the consolation bracket, the Garden, with its New York address and appeal, still held its allure, but it no longer offered much in the way of inventory.

Until, that is, Gavitt came along, with the promise of a week's worth of games featuring the premier teams on the East Coast. This was more marriage than negotiation, the Big East restoring the Garden as a college basketball hub, and the Garden giving Gavitt and his league the pizzazz he craved. The two sides happily agreed to a three-year, $3 million deal in October 1981.

Some coaches and administrators fretted, worried that the toddler league wasn't quite ready for such a big jump, but they mostly kept their reservations to themselves. Gavitt already had proven his instincts right simply by birthing the Big East. Who were they to doubt him now? "Now here's Dave and his huddling again," said Thompson, using his favorite word to describe Gavitt's technique of convincing others. "We're going to the city. It's going to be great. But this time, of course, I believed him."

By 1981, Villanova had joined the league, bolting the short-lived Eastern Eight to align with its East Coast brethren. That same year the Big East–Garden partnership played a big part in negotiations that would reverberate across college athletics for decades. At the time, Penn State football coach Joe Paterno, who also served as his school's athletic director, was trying to align the East Coast football schools much the same way Gavitt had done in hoops, heavily wooing the Nittany Lions' rival, Pittsburgh. But Gavitt also had expansion and stability on his mind, looking for another team and one with a football-playing background to give Boston College and Syracuse natural opponents in the sport. He, too, set his sights on Pittsburgh.

Gavitt had what Paterno didn't yet—financial backing in the form of a $1.6 million television deal, the $3 million arena package, and, more important, revenue sharing. The Pittsburgh Panthers shunned Paterno and football, signing on with the Big East in November 1981, a month after the Garden deal was finalized. Pitt's decision more or less killed Paterno's football conference dream.

Interestingly, in 1982, Gavitt went back to Paterno. Seeing a future that others could not, he tried to sell his membership on adding Penn State. Though his league was built on the backbone of basketball, Gavitt recognized how big a factor football could become. Paterno's idea had exposed how vulnerable the Big East might be one day. Syracuse, Boston College, and soon-to-be-added Pittsburgh played football; the other six schools did not. Paterno certainly wouldn't be the first visionary to try to woo those schools away.

Gavitt thought adding Penn State would be wise, and though the late Paterno long denied Big East interest, those on the Big East side of things tell a different tale. Tranghese and Kaiser both recall the eight athletic directors voting five times on whether to add Penn State. Each vote finished the same, 5–3, one shy of the 6 votes needed for admission, with Kaiser, Ted Aceto, and Frank Rienzo, representing St. John's, Villanova, and Georgetown, voting no. "They didn't have a big basketball program, and none of our schools had big football programs at the time," Kaiser says.

Eight years later, the Nittany Lions would join the Big Ten, starting the avalanche of conference realignments that ultimately included, just as Gavitt predicted, the defections of Boston College, Pitt, and Syracuse from the Big East. "You don't understand that if Penn State would have come, eastern independent football would have continued just as it was, because everybody had what they wanted," Tranghese says. "The whole face of college athletics would have changed. That decision, in my opinion, in my sixty years of college athletics, that decision changed the face of college athletics."

In 1983, moving to Madison Square Garden did the same for the Big East, with the city, the building, and the conference combining for a splash unlike any other in college basketball. Gavitt orchestrated a bit of a dog-and-pony show to launch the thing, beckoning his coaches to New York for a picture beneath the marquee. He also posed alongside Werblin with one of those oversized checks more often reserved for sweepstakes winners.

In some ways it was a sweepstakes, the long-standing partnership between conference and arena leading to a bonanza and financial windfall for both sides. At the first Big East Tournament in Providence, the final attracted a crowd of 7,500. In 1983, the Garden sold out not just for the final but for all of the sessions. Some tickets were distributed to the member schools, but the rest were made available to the general public, and included admission to every session. By the eve of the first games, fewer than 1,000 of the cheap seats remained, the 15,000 $50 admissions long gone. Not since 1948, when the old Garden on 49th Street hosted the NIT, had the venue welcomed a college basketball sellout crowd through its doors. After that first series of games the demand never waned. Tickets for the Big East Tournament remained impossible to come by for decades in a city that specializes in must-see events. When Tranghese wisely moved the final from Sunday afternoon to the prime-time lights of Saturday night, Big East week felt every bit as big as Fashion Week in New York, albeit with slightly less sartorial splendor.

The hawkers and the buyers would meet out front, transacting at the corner of capitalism and dreams, the former looking to make a buck, the latter hoping for a little bit of magic. Around them, the sidewalks teemed like a walking, talking sporting goods store, nearly everyone wearing a sweatshirt, jacket, hat, or button—or sometimes all of the above—declaring their team allegiance. The grown-ups spilled out of the bars designated for the week as their home team watering holes, arriving just in time for tip-off, properly pre-soused and ready to go. The pep bands marched in through the portico, the echoes of competing fight songs bouncing off the walls, while the mascots pranced around, offering high fives. "With all due respect, the NCAA Tournament is great," says Tim Higgins, a longtime basketball official, "but when you [worked] in front of a sold-out Madison Square Garden, there was nothing like it."

Putting the deal together took some old-fashioned chutzpah. Pulling off the actual tournament required some old-school connections. After negotiating the deal with Werblin, Gavitt and his staff learned to navigate the Garden staff. This was New York, after all, the arena staff governed by the unions, with strict rules. Josephine Traina, a gruff, fast-talking New Yorker straight from central casting, ran the place like a field marshal. Nothing got by Traina, and nothing got done without her say-so.

Before the first tournament, Traina took Tranghese to meet Tony Avalon, the head of security. Union rules made maneuvering the Garden setup tricky—who could do what, when, and where were all left to the union. Tranghese and Traina headed to Avalon's dungeon-like office, where the security chief asked Tranghese where in Italy his family was from. Confused, Tranghese told him about his family, and after exchanging a few stories about growing up Italian, Avalon gave Tranghese the nod of approval. "We're going to get along very well," Avalon declared. "I still to this day have no idea what that meant, but everything was all set," Tranghese says. "Everything I ever wanted at the Garden got done. All of these other people would tell me these horror stories. You couldn't put your hand on a chair. The security had to move the chair. With us, there weren't any problems. If I were Irish, I don't know. Maybe we wouldn't have had a tournament."

In time, the people who worked at the Garden brought as much flavor to the tournament as the teams that participated. Some of the ushers held their same positions for years, recognizing regular faces and even becoming friendly with the coaches and players. "You walk in through the 33rd Street entrance, you'd see these people, these workers, walking around," says former Villanova star Ed Pinckney. "They knew your schedule. They knew who you played. Usually you go into a building, people don't recite, 'Oh, you played Providence and that was a tough game.'" They'd call the coaches by name, and the coaches over time would learn theirs, too. The workers learned over the years that Thompson liked to play the slots, and would jokingly ask when he was heading to Vegas. "No sooner than I'm leaving here," the coach would reply with a grin.

A ticket-taker who worked the media turnstile boasted his own carnival trick, able to rip the stub from your ducat with one hand, flicking his thumb and forefinger at the perforation to perfection. Until his death in 1989, John Condon served as the public address announcer, followed by Ken Werprin, who retired in 2010, both sending chills up the spine of most everyone in the building when they intoned, "Welcome to Madison Square Garden." "The first time John Condon introduces you?" Seton Hall coach P.J. Carlesimo says. "Amazing."

In return, the coaches treated the Garden like their palace. Thompson had a long-standing rule with his players to clean up after themselves, making sure they tossed out the used tape and paper cups that littered the floor after most games; the imposing coach sounded more like a praised child when people recognized the good deed. "The Garden people always commented that they'd come in afterward and it was clean," he said. Such was the reverence for the place, held by virtually everyone who played there, the world-famous as tickled as the Everyman that they got to spend time in the Garden.

Like the people who worked in it, the building offered its own beloved quirks and idiosyncrasies. Accessing the court level required a ride up in a freight elevator that felt more like a cage. "You'd take it down after the game," says former Villanova player John Celestand. "If you won, you'd get in there and joke and it was fun. But if you lost, and you were going home, man, those thirty seconds or whatever in that elevator, it felt like you were making the ride to hell or something."

Lined with pictures of the famous acts who've performed in the place, the hallways snaked around like a maze, just wide enough for two people to pass each other. They led to cramped, utilitarian locker rooms made all the more claustrophobic when stuffed with reporters with notebooks and TV cameras after a game. "Madison Square Garden's locker rooms were dumps," Villanova's Rollie Massimino said before he passed away in 2017. He wasn't wrong. A team knew it had arrived at the Big East Tournament when it dressed in the Knicks' home locker room space, reserved for the highest seed in the title game.

The officials dressed in equally small spaces, just off the loading docks, and the cheerleaders warmed up alongside the arena detritus, practicing their stunts amid forklifts, boxes, and extra baskets laid on their sides.

But the court, blanketed in spotlights with the upper decks dimmed, felt like a performance stage.

Unlike many places of a different era, it never lost its mystique, charming grizzled veterans and rookies alike. Former Big East associate director Chris Plonsky called her father from the press table before her first Big East Tournament, reveling in the pinch-me-it-can't-be-real sensation at her view from half-court. Boston native and Boston Garden snob Red Auerbach once chastised Thompson for referring to the New York arena as the "Mecca," but the Georgetown coach did not apologize for his perceived error. "[Auerbach] said, 'That ain't no goddamned Mecca.' Hell, I didn't know what Mecca meant," Thompson said. "I just knew that was the place to play."

When he took the Garden court for his Big East Tournament, Syracuse star Gerry McNamara tried to gather himself, but failed. "You can't help but think of the storied history of the place, the people who played there. How do I leave my mark? How do I leave my legacy? Any player who played a game in Madison Square Garden will never forget that."

The week sometimes drained players more than the NCAA Tournament itself, the bitter rivalries of the regular season ratcheted up because there was so much riding on the postseason. And unlike the NCAA Tournament, there were no off days, the Big East requiring a night-after-night performance with escalating pressure as it marched to its conclusion. At one point the league swelled to a sixteen-team beast, the tournament beginning on Tuesday night, followed by four-game marathons run on Wednesday and Thursday, the first game tipping off at noon and the last after 9 p.m.

Over time the one-ticket-for-all policy shifted, fans admitted not on one-day tickets but ushered in and out for day and evening sessions. No one complained, using their time off to enjoy some of the city's other splendors, returning with full bellies but unquenchable thirsts, grateful that the Garden sold beer. More than once, a few brazen courtside ticket owners casually grabbed a press row seat vacated by a reporter long since gone, sipping beers and heckling players until ushers discovered the interloper. "The Friday night semifinals, everybody's been in the bars all day, and you come out through the tunnel, you felt like a gladiator walking into the lion's den," says former official John Cahill, who as a kid rode in from his Albany hometown to catch games in the Garden. "You didn't know if the team was going to get you, the coaches were going to get you, or the fans were going to get you. But somebody was going to get you."

On top of it all, outside sat New York, with its cacophony of cabs, crowds, and chaos, all of it combining to create the most beautiful sort of bedlam. The city that never sleeps afforded the basketball insomniacs plenty of options, everyone finding their favorite late-night spot to gather and unwind. The referees frequently gathered at either Frank's on 15th Street or Forlini's on Baxter Street, safe in the knowledge that the owner would give them a table in the back and stay open as late as they needed. "You had to find your own haunts. You couldn't be seen in public, especially with a beer in your hands," Higgins says. "The guys who ran those places, they understood." Rollie Massimino and his Villanova crew had a similar setup at Umberto's, where they could count on privacy and, equally important, fresh pasta for dinner, even if the meal didn't begin until two in the morning. Gavitt frequently held court at Peacock Alley inside the Waldorf-Astoria, the gathering once memorably interrupted by some party crashers looking for trouble. "A bunch of outsiders were trying to get in," Bill Raftery says. "Some guy threw a punch, and the New York guys spent the rest of the week searching for the guys who did it." Jim Boeheim preferred Smith & Wollensky. Thompson? No one knew the answer to that one. Which was just how he liked it.

Staffers, media, and anyone else who could stomach seeing the dawn after a long day met at Runyon's, the fabled sports bar once perfectly described as the frat house for sports people. Rich Chvotkin, the Georgetown radio play-by-play man, called every single Big East Tournament game from 1982 to 1999, convincing a local station that it was a good idea to send him to the tourney back when the league consisted of just nine teams. By the time 1999 rolled around, his days included noon-to-midnight marathons. He'd show up at Runyon's just the same, order a steak and a bourbon, "and we'd all do it over again the next night."

Everybody, that is, except the players. Or at least most of them. They enjoyed the on-court fun but not so much the after-parties. Their New York City experience consisted of a walk to the bus, a ride to the arena, a return to the hotel, and repeat, the bubble of their team hotel supplying everything they needed. Frequently fans figured out where their favorite team set up for the week, gathering in the hotel lobby in the hopes of catching a glimpse of their heroes, but access to the team floors was off-limits.

Villanova's Ed Pinckney grew up in New York. Coming back to the city was a welcome homecoming, competing in the Garden an unbelievable treat—and a great big nuisance. Satisfying ticket requests for extended family and friends proved down-right impossible, and those same friends and family members frequently didn't quite understand that he wasn't in town for va-cation. His buddies would pop into the hotel lobby postgame and call up to his room to see if they could visit, or they'd invite him out for a celebration. "They'd be like, 'Hey we're meeting over at 76th Street, can you come?'" Pinckney says. "I'm like, 'I have a game to play, are you kidding me? I can't.'" Carnesecca, wise to the allure of the city, parked his team in Glen Cove, New York, a good forty-five-minute bus ride away. "We played in our arena, and we were a road team," says St. John's star Chris Mullin. "Coach knew the deal. Nobody knows the city better than Coach."

Only Syracuse, it seems, had any fun, at least in the early years. In the 1980s, Boeheim didn't impose a curfew on his team, instead telling his players he expected them to be responsible for themselves. The Big East Tournament typically coincided with spring break, and freed from schoolwork and greeted by the comparatively balmy temperatures of the city, the players enjoyed their freedom. "We had a nice time, let's put it that way," says former player Sherman Douglas. If the schedule broke favorably and the Orange were slated for an evening tip-off, the players visited the city's restaurants and even the occasional club. It didn't seem to affect them much. In the first ten years that the tournament was played in the Garden, Syracuse either won or played for the championship seven times.

Sequestered or not, the players didn't need to be reminded of the importance of that tournament, and it wasn't just because of the NCAA Tournament bid on the line. The tournament served as the ultimate test for conference superiority, the entire season boiled down into a winner-take-all for bragging rights. The tournament made the regular season look like a middle school pickup game. It was there, after all, that Boeheim lost his mind after Michael Graham threw a punch at Andre Hawkins, and Ewing went after Pearl Washington with a haymaker, and Walter Berry denied the Pearl a shot at glory. It's also where Ray Allen battled Allen Iverson, and McNamara took Syracuse on an improbable run of four wins in four nights, only to be outdone five years later when Kemba Walker led UConn to five wins in five nights. And it was there that UConn and Syracuse played a six-overtime marathon.

Heroes and legends were born there.

The first year set the stage for all of that magic, the Big East Tournament of 1983 serving as the perfect crescendo to a great season in an already great league. On the heels of Georgetown's run to the 1982 title game, the league that year opened with three teams in the top twenty-five, including two in the top five—Georgetown debuting at number two and Villanova at number five. Those two schools, along with St. John's, would remain in the rankings for the entirety of the season, joined within a month by Syracuse and in February by Boston College.

Though respected nationally, teams still saw games against out-of-conference foes as potential proving grounds—they were determined to showcase their might beyond the Big East boundaries. Perhaps no day signified the conference's national arrival better than December 11, 1982. That afternoon both Syracuse and Georgetown played in a featured national broadcast, Syracuse hosting Houston, broadcast by CBS, and Georgetown meeting Virginia, aired on Turner.

Later that year Houston and its Phi Slama Jama collection of Hakeem Olajuwon, Clyde Drexler, and Michael Young would suffer a stunning upset at the hands of Jim Valvano and N.C. State in the national title game, but that December they arrived at the Carrier Dome with the same 5–0 record as Syracuse but a great deal more fanfare. A Syracuse team manager assigned to help the Cougars the night before the big game reported back that the players waltzed through their workout, head coach Guy Lewis barely directing his team as they fooled around, dunking. With a huge size advantage—at 6'8", Rautins ranked as the biggest starter on the Syracuse roster—and gifted at forcing turnovers with its press, Houston clearly expected an easy game.

Instead Syracuse beat the Cougars at their own game, forcing the Cougars into 19 turnovers and pushing the tempo for a 92–87 win. Rautins, who inbounded the ball against the press, remembers that the Orange broke through Houston's pressure so easily, he barely crossed half-court before his team scored.

In ordinary times, that might have ranked as the game of the day. Instead it served as just the appetizer for the "Game of the Decade," Virginia and Ralph Sampson versus Georgetown and Ewing. So big was the December game, to be played in front of a split house at the Capital Centre in Landover, Maryland, that

Georgetown AD Frank Rienzo wisely offered tickets only as part of a season-ticket package to fans, and sold the TV rights to Turner, earning Georgetown an estimated $600,000 off the one game. Newspaper reporters wrote breathlessly in the lead-up to the game, interviewing other coaches for their predictions and pulling out all the hyperbole. "Custer Versus Sitting Bull," offered a columnist in *The Washington Times*. The national broadcast included a pregame Countdown to the Showdown, and Turner positioned a camera at Charley's, a local bar in Charlottesville.

The hype really belonged more to the matchup between Sampson, the senior and elder statesman of the big men, and Ewing, the up-and-coming sophomore. As these things so often go, the game couldn't quite match the buildup. Virginia got the better of Georgetown, winning the game, 68–63, and Sampson got the better of Ewing, outscoring (23 to 16), out-rebounding (16 to 8), and out-shot-blocking (7 to 5) the younger player. The two connected for some one-on-one battles, but in the end Georgetown's youth couldn't handle Virginia's experience. It would be a harbinger of what was to come that season, the young Hoyas finishing 22–10, knocked out by Syracuse in the Big East quarterfinals and Memphis State in the second round of the NCAA Tournament—the only time that Georgetown failed to play in an NCAA title game in Ewing's four seasons.

As the early-season attention swirled around Georgetown, up Interstate 95, St. John's opened its season with considerably less fanfare. The year before, the Red Storm had lost to Alabama in the second round of the NCAA Tournament, squandering two chances to win when they were down just 1 point with the ball and 15 seconds to play. Carnesecca liked his team but worried about their toughness, growing so frustrated at one point during the preseason that he tossed his team from practice. They responded by knocking off none other than the defending national champions in the opening game, beating North Carolina in overtime. The Red Storm only got better as the season progressed, winning 14 consecutive games and losing just 4 regular-season games, including two to Boston College. Along the way Carnesecca loosened the reins a little bit, and his players, in return, tightened their control. They arrived for the first official Garden party at 24–4, riding the jet stream of hot-shooting Mullin, a beloved Brooklyn kid embraced like royalty by the New York crowd.

The honor of playing the first official New York Big East Tournament game went to Providence and Seton Hall, the two squaring off in the game between the eighth and ninth seeds, a basement-dwelling spot they'd hold for years. "I remember at one point there was discussion, like do we need this game, since it doesn't matter to anybody," says Carlesimo, who arrived at Seton Hall in the same season that the Garden debuted as tourney host. "I was like, 'Wait a minute, dammit. I was in that goddamned thing. You're not in the tournament if you don't go.'" Seton Hall prevailed, only to be summarily trounced by Boston College in the next game, the Pirates so in need of an assist that their mascot generated a technical foul and extra free throw after dancing too far over the end line during a BC free throw, hoping to be a distraction.

BC then beat Syracuse to advance to its first league final, while on the other side of the bracket, St. John's first topped Pittsburgh and then overcame a horrific first half to beat Villanova and advance to its first final as well. That the Eagles twice toppled St. John's in the regular season made for an easy story line, the Red Storm both times unable to overcome Boston College's pressing defense or contain tiny, whip-fast guard Michael Adams. But good teams tend to learn from their mistakes, and St. John's did, not committing so much as a single turnover in the first half and making it nearly impossible for Adams to get in the lane. He finished with just 5 points as St. John's claimed the tournament title.

Cynics and critics barked that moving the tournament to New York would give St. John's too much of a home court advantage, and some thought the league title proved them right. But among the Big East hierarchy, you'd be hard-pressed to find a complaint about a winning St. John's team. "St. John's won with Louie," Tranghese says. "That gave us instant credibility with New Yorkers and New York."

After the horn sounded, several players hoisted their diminutive coach atop their shoulders, parading around the man who had sat wide-eyed at the Garden in 1942. It was St. John's first title of any kind since 1965, when Carnesecca served as an assistant on Joe Lapchick's NIT-winning team. "Tonight we walk with kings," the coach said after winning the championship, parroting the line his former boss had used following that NIT title eighteen years earlier.

The crown wouldn't fit for long, however.

In Washington, D.C., another team awaited its coronation.

CHAPTER 5

JOHN THOMPSON, PATRIARCH OF HOYA PARANOIA

"He wanted people to hate him so they wouldn't hate his kids"

Tranghese's phone jingled on an October day in 1992. George-town athletic director Frank Rienzo was on the line, asking—or, more accurately, summoning—Tranghese to D.C. Just three years into his tenure as Gavitt's replacement, the new commissioner explained that he was in Miami, there to watch the Hurricanes take on Florida State in what had become an annual epic football showdown. Just a year earlier, Miami, along with West Virginia, Temple, and Virginia Tech, had joined the Big East, part of the league's new football division. The Hurricanes officially were Tranghese's responsibility.

Undeterred, the Georgetown athletic director asked his new leader to hop a flight the next day to D.C. His coach, Rienzo said, wanted to meet with Tranghese.

In March of that year, the Big East endured one of its most disappointing postseasons, failing to put a single team in the Sweet Sixteen for the first time since 1986. Tranghese aired his frustrations in the newspapers, saying, "The coaches and administrators need to do some soul-searching, and figure out a way to get better." The public airing didn't sit too kindly with John Thompson, Jr. He told Rienzo as much, and the AD relayed the message to Tranghese, suggesting he call Thompson. But Tranghese didn't see the point. He stood by his comments; besides, if Thompson wanted him, he knew where to find him.

The two didn't speak for the next seven months.

Which wasn't that unusual.

For thirteen years he and Thompson had worked side by side, Tranghese part of every major Big East decision since its inception. But his personal interactions with the Georgetown coach were sporadic. With a history going all the way back to his playing days at Providence, Thompson trusted Gavitt. If he needed anything, he went to Gavitt, and if there was a problem, Gavitt handled it. Now, though, Gavitt was gone, having moved on to the Boston Celtics as the organization's CEO, and Thompson wasn't quite sure what to make of his new boss.

But with the season nearing, Thompson decided it was time for a heart-to-heart.

Tranghese agreed to make a detour on his way home after the football game, and when he exited the airport in Washington, D.C., he found his ride waiting, Thompson behind the wheel. He whisked his league leader off to a restaurant, a nondescript diner in a part of town Tranghese says most folks wouldn't venture to visit, and where fewer still would bother the famous coach. For nearly thirty years, Tranghese didn't reveal the conversation to anyone. Now, though, as he sits inside a hotel conference room in Providence, Rhode Island, he feels compelled to share it, not just to explain Thompson's commitment to the Big East but to better illustrate who the man was.

The two talked for hours, initially chatting idly until Thompson got down to business. First he asked just who was making the decisions these days, worried that Tranghese might become more puppet leader than real leader. Tranghese assured him that wasn't the case, that he operated just as Gavitt did and would be his own man, not governed by groupthink. Appeased, Thompson asked, "Where do you see this league right now?" Tranghese pulled no punches, telling him he had real concerns, chief among them that people had gotten lazy, that they assumed being in the Big East made their programs good and had stopped doing the work to keep it that way. The two discussed at length what made the conference special, and what needed to be done to ensure it would stay special.

Happy with his commissioner's answers, and satisfied that Tranghese had the best interest of the Big East at heart, Thompson drove him back to the airport. "If you need anything," he said as he dropped Tranghese off, "you just ask."

Three years later, as his coaches and administrators balked at his idea to move the Big East Tournament final from Sunday afternoon to Saturday night, Tranghese asked. He called Thompson with his argument for the switch, explaining the business advantages of moving off Selection Sunday and owning the TV market, as well as the simple appeal of a championship played during prime time on Saturday night in New York. "Next thing I know, every coach and AD is supporting me," Tranghese says. "That was the influence John had. He is one of the most fascinating people I know. If John didn't know you or trust you, he'd test you. But if you passed your test, he would help you for life."

In Big East history, no player, coach, administrator, or official ranks as a more commanding, demanding, or polarizing figure than Thompson, and no team ranks as more commanding, demanding, or polarizing than Georgetown. Together, coach and program made for a formidable tandem, stalwarts of their conference who also figured in much of its turmoil. "We were not a feel-good piece," says guard Gene Smith, who came to Georgetown in 1980. By all rights, they should have been a feel-good story. Their tale included all of the ingredients—the out-of-nowhere, humble beginnings, riding gumption and grit to the pinnacle of their sport. But their edges cut hard in a world that preferred its stories wrapped in soft, pretty bows. The Hoyas, like their coach, didn't pander. They were outwardly hostile, proudly complicated, and sometimes contradictory, America's Black team run by a coach frequently accused of inverse racism. Intimidating, imposing, difficult—that's how people described Thompson, and thereby that was the persona his Hoyas adopted. Perhaps no program in NCAA history aligned more directly with its coach than Georgetown. "John had a certain philosophy," Lou Carnesecca says. "Whether you agreed with that philosophy or not, that was neither here nor there. He made sure it got out. I often felt like John was trying to get a message across."

Ultimately the message he delivered was one of unquestionable success. During Thompson's tenure, Georgetown rose from college basketball afterthought to national champion and nothing less than a cultural flash point. Its gear ranked among the most popular in the country, rappers turning Hoya jerseys urban cool, and the gray T-shirt Ewing wore under his game jersey becoming the go-to style for hoopsters of all ages.

All of this from a team that a year before Thompson arrived finished 3–23 and whose entire postseason history fit on an index card: 1943 NCAA runner-up, 1953 and 1970 NIT first-round loser. So lousy were the Hoyas that the 3–23 finish not only cost the head coach, Jack Magee, his job, but athletic director Bob Sigholtz stepped down as well, the school deciding that its athletic mission was flawed—or, maybe more accurately, didn't exist. The university tapped Rienzo, its well-regarded track coach, as its athletic director; in turn, he insisted that athletics at Georgetown was as relevant to the university's success as any academic department.

A month into his position, in February 1972, Rienzo hired Thompson as his basketball coach. Thompson grew up in a segregated Washington, D.C., the youngest of four. His father, who never learned to read, worked in a factory. His mother should have been a teacher, but the schools wouldn't honor her two-year certificate. Instead she worked as a maid. His mother pushed education, setting her son straight when he struggled as an elementary schooler at a Catholic school. He grew quickly, reaching his full 6'10" by high school, making him a natural for basketball. Archbishop Carroll recruited him to play, and Thompson became a star, leading his high school to two city championships and 55 consecutive wins. Plenty of coaches recruited him, including a diminutive assistant who came to a tournament in Newport, Rhode Island, to try to convince Thompson to consider St. John's. "Hell, Louie recruited me," Thompson said. "Louie came to the hotel we were staying in, sitting on the side of the bed, talking a mile a minute. Louie touched you a lot when he talked."

Thompson chose Providence largely because his mother felt an affinity with the Dominican priests who ran the place. But, shy by nature and guarded, Thompson struggled to fit in. He found a lifelong friend (and future assistant) in Bill Stein, a walk-on, and a safe haven and mentor in Gavitt, who refused to let his talented big man sulk, talking him out of his urge to transfer. Drafted by the Celtics out of college, Thompson spent two years backing up his idol, Bill Russell, but when he wound up in the expansion draft, he decided his playing career was over. Thompson returned to Washington, D.C., earned a master's degree in counseling, and took over at St. Anthony's High School as its head coach. In six years, St. Anthony's won 122 games and lost but 28, drawing the attention of a man looking for a coach.

Rienzo considered Morgan Wooten, who'd built DeMatha High School into a power (and Thompson's rival at St. Anthony's), and Jack Ramsay, who'd just been let go by the 76ers. Instead he opted for Thompson, hiring the twenty-nine-year-old only two years after Will Robinson became the first Black coach in Division I basketball. At the time, Washington, D.C., simmered with racial tension, the 1968 riots following the assassination of Martin Luther King, Jr., still fresh. Perched on a hilltop, Georgetown looked down upon its city literally as well as figuratively, boasting an air of elitism as a highbrow institution. The school first admitted women only in 1969, and years later would acknowledge that the public sale of 272 slaves helped pay off the school's debts in 1838.

Needless to say, it was not an easy place for a Black man to fit in. Just three years into his tenure, Thompson would learn exactly how difficult. After a 5–2 start skidded into a six-game losing streak, fans unfurled a banner from the McDonough Gym rafters: "Thompson the Nigger Flop Must Go." Race would serve as the subtext to everything Thompson did, from the players he recruited to their style of play and his own place in the coaching hierarchy. He fought against racial injustices, defiantly protesting two games to convince the NCAA to rescind a potential eligibility rule that would bench players with substandard SAT scores, and taught his players as much about their place in the world as Black men as he did about the X's and O's of a game plan.

Accustomed to the average performance of previous teams, the school president asked Thompson to make a few NITs, but Thompson did not do mediocrity. He championed Georgetown into becoming a winner much as he had done with Archbishop

Carroll, Providence, and St. Anthony's—by force of his own will. Thompson trusted his gut in recruiting, looking for players much like himself—talented, yes, but above all else, kids pushed by an almost insatiable hunger. He could teach skills; he could not coerce effort. He found big man Ed Spriggs, the former truck driver, at a pickup game. Gene Smith's only other offer came from Morgan State, at the time a Division II school. Sleepy Floyd grew up in the shadow of his Gastonia, North Carolina, buddy James Worthy, meriting a few eyeballs but no big-name offers. Thompson spent ten minutes watching him in a rec center pickup game, leaving so quickly Floyd thought, "I must have sucked." Instead the coach had seen all he needed; he met Floyd outside after the game ended, offering him an official visit. In Michael Graham, he saw a player who knew only one way to play—hard—and welcomed his physicality.

Even the great players he brought to campus created a stir. Ewing carried with him the sting of those special academic requests. Before graduating from high school, Allen Iverson spent eight months awaiting trial over an altercation at a bowling alley; he was convicted of a felony, but after serving four months of his sentence he was granted clemency by the governor, and his conviction was eventually overturned by an appeals court.

People barked at Thompson's unconventional recruiting choices, with their urban ties and, if we're being candid, Black skin. Critics crowed that Georgetown sold out its academic reputation for basketball, and opposing coaches groused that Thompson won because he operated under far lower admission standards than their schools allowed. The irony is Thompson dedicated more resources to academics than most of his peers. He used one of his assistant coaching positions to hire Mary Fenlon, a former nun, to oversee the Hoyas' academics, long before academic advisors became regular staff positions. He instilled a simple rule: cut a class, sit a game. Graham would help lead the Hoyas to their first national title in 1984, but Thompson bounced him from the school that same summer for failing to live up to his academic standards. "I made a mess of everything," Graham says. "Immaturity."

Floyd's knowledge of Big East hoops began and ended with the handful of games he could watch on Channel 5, provided he positioned the rabbit-ear antenna just right on his TV. He used his last visit to come to Georgetown only because his older sister studied at nearby Howard University and he thought he could see her. But Thompson put together a pitch unlike any other he'd heard, spending more time talking about the expected academic commitment than the athletic one. Floyd, convinced this was a man who would shepherd him into adulthood, committed on the spot.

For the entirety of his career, Thompson would keep a deflated basketball on his desk, a constant reminder that the ball one day would stop bouncing. It still sits in the Georgetown office, three coaches removed from his tenure. Thompson knew what his young players would come to learn: that they had no room for error. Critics waited for them to make a misstep, to embarrass the school or prove they didn't belong. The only way to combat that was to not make mistakes. Outsiders called them thugs, so the Hoyas wore suits and ties everywhere they went. Naysayers questioned their intelligence, so Thompson made sure they graduated. He educated his players both on the boundless possibilities of the world and on the boundaries that hemmed them in. The Hoyas grew accustomed to Thompson's "mental practices," where the coach would discuss current events. "He could hit you with things that you would talk about on the street corner, and then some academic shit. The dynamics, man, they were so rich for us," Smith says. "He made a point to let you know where you are in society, that you're a Black man in society. Be aware of that."

Ewing remembers days when Thompson simply stopped practice, grabbed a chair, and circled the players around him. The topics varied depending on what was happening in the world, but the message always stayed the same—be aware. "He'd just start lecturing us about life," Ewing says. "What life is going to be like."

He protected his players fiercely, limiting their access to the media and virtually sequestering them from the outside. "He wanted people to hate him," says Michael Wilbon, the *Post* reporter, "so they wouldn't hate his kids." It backfired to a certain extent, people growing irritated and frustrated with "Georgetown," the entity, largely due to the Georgetown coach's actions. He didn't relent, mostly because he never cared about the opinions of others. In a profession almost preoccupied with image and perception, Thompson lived comfortably as a lightning rod.

Some of it, certainly, included a little gamesmanship. He went to laughable lengths to keep his players away from prying eyes, craving the privacy but also enjoying the mystique it created. "I didn't like being the Evil Empire, but I marketed it," he said. "I used to tell kids, 'You know what? If you had an empty room and you told everybody don't go in, it immediately gives the room value.' So when we started to say that we're not going to do this or do that—hell, nobody was writing about us before that." Thompson's eyes twinkled as he recalled watching out the bus window as reporters followed the team to their hotel at the 1982 Final Four in New Orleans. Most gave up, eventually, not interested in chugging the ninety miles to Biloxi, Mississippi, where Thompson chose to sequester his team. "We came in to play the game, oh my gosh, we had no idea what was going on," Floyd says of discovering the excitement and the intrigue the Hoyas had created in New Orleans.

When the Big East played its tournament in Hartford, the Hoyas stayed in Snow Hill, a town thirty-five minutes away tucked in the Nipmuck State Forest. When it was in Providence, they opted for Goat Island, plopped in the middle of Narragansett Bay. "They were like a paramilitary operation at times," says Dick "Hoops" Weiss, who covered the Big East for the *Philadelphia Daily News* and New York *Daily News*. "Who knew where they stayed? It was an undisclosed bunker somewhere in the city."

Thompson knew he couldn't shield his players from everything, but he felt like he could protect them from some things. And if the real world crept in anyway, he met it head-on for them. Late one evening in 1989, Thompson called Wilbon at home. By then the two had built a foundation of trust, Wilbon learning firsthand how the coach operated. The *Post* reporter had spent his first year on the beat unable to talk to the head coach, Thompson declining any and all interviews he requested. Though frustrated, the young reporter refused to cave, mastering the art of the end around by talking to everyone about Thompson instead. That was the exact response Thompson had wanted; he'd been testing Wilbon to see if he had the stomach to really do the job, and Wilbon passed. Thompson eventually agreed to interviews, the relationship between the two growing so tight that Wilbon counts Thompson as one of the three most influential men in his life, alongside his own father and his first sports editor.

By '89, Wilbon had moved on to a columnist position, less involved in the day-to-day with Georgetown, but when Thompson called and began the conversation by saying, "Hey, motherfucker, you want to sleep or you want a scoop?" Wilbon knew better than to ignore him. At Thompson's behest, Wilbon met the coach at the basketball offices the next day, still unsure why he was there. The two piled into Thompson's big sedan and started driving, Thompson finally explaining his mission: He was searching for Rayful Edmond III, a Georgetown fan, a play-

ground hoops legend, and the city's most notorious and danger-
ous drug kingpin.

Edmond had been seen with two of Thompson's players:
John Turner, who knew Edmond via high school friends, and
Alonzo Mourning. Though the two weren't implicated in any
wrongdoing, the death of Maryland star Len Bias just three years
earlier from a cocaine overdose was fresh on Thompson's mind,
and he also was well aware how any affiliation with Edmond
might reflect on his program. He didn't want his players anywhere near Edmond. "I'm like, 'John, I have a *notebook,* what if
we find him?'" Wilbon says.

They frequented a few possible spots, Thompson leaving a
message behind at each place that Edmond should contact him.
"He didn't leave a number," Wilbon says. "Total badass."

Edmond did, in fact, show up at Thompson's office, the
coach revealed later on ABC's *Nightline,* explaining that he did
not interrogate Edmond but simply told him he wanted nothing
to be going on between him and his players. Months later, Edmond was sentenced to life in prison without parole, prosecu-
tors laying out a case that showed him as the mastermind of an
organization that brought 1,700 pounds of cocaine per month
into D.C. and was responsible for as many as thirty murders,
though Edmond was never convicted of the homicides. "People
went nuts" about Thompson's attitude and protectionism, Wilbon says. "But after a while, John was proven right on so many
big issues."

It all added to the aura of John Thompson, Jr., a man who
knew the influence he wielded and the image he projected. "I
was afraid of him the first time I met him," says Lisa Zanecchia,
the former assistant to the Big East commissioner. Before they
joined the Big East, Gary Williams and Rick Barnes, who would
become the Boston College and Providence coaches, respectively, used to sit in the nosebleed seats and watch Thompson

coach. They observed how he schooled his players, and how he worked the officials, using his height to full advantage to peer down at them when he questioned a call. When each got into the league and encountered Thompson on the opposite bench, they admit it took some getting used to.

Thompson actually missed his first chance to go head-to-head against Barnes at Providence. It was 1989, and Thompson was at the peak of his profession, with a national title and three Final Fours in his pocket. That year he used his stature to protest Prop 42, the NCAA ruling that would deny scholarships for freshmen who failed to qualify academically. He purposely walked out of a game against Boston College in protest and later, against Providence, he chose to not show up. Instead, his trademark white towel was left on his seat in his place.

With that as the backdrop, Barnes felt understandably nervous when he traveled to D.C. for his first real encounter with Thompson. He hemmed and hawed over approaching Thompson for the traditional pregame handshake, finally opting not to after Thompson nodded at him. After the game ended, a 76–74 win for the Hoyas but one in which the upstart Friars had a chance to win at the buzzer, Barnes started off the court, presuming Thompson wouldn't want to chat. Instead, Thompson grabbed him in a bear hug. "And I mean a bear hug," Barnes says. "He's got his left hand around my back, and I'm looking straight up at him. He said, 'You're a helluva coach.' I just said, 'Thank you.' I mean, here's this guy I've been looking up to for seven years."

Over time, those who got to know Thompson well would learn that the tough shell hid a man who loved to prank his friends, poke fun at himself, and help anyone who needed it. "It was a veneer," Carnesecca says. "He was a pussycat." Ewing recalls pregame locker rooms, the players listening to music to fuel them, the place filled with pent-up energy and nerves. Thompson would walk in and sashay a little two-step, busting up his players with his out-of-date moves. "I'd say, 'Coach, that dance is back in the day,'" Ewing says. "But he was doing that to loosen us up, take the air out of the room, to make sure we knew it was serious, but also to have fun."

After he retired, Thompson hosted a radio show on Westwood One, and people were shocked at the man they heard on the airwaves. "They didn't think I laughed," he said. During his coaching career, he used to suffer torment at the hands of Dennis Brogan, who played the part of Syracuse's unofficial mascot, the Dome Ranger. Brogan took great pleasure in needling the rival school's boss. Yet when Brogan hung up the cowboy boots for good in 1990, in a game against Georgetown, Thompson walked over before the game and presented him with one of his famous white towels, thanking him for the memories. "I thought he was an ogre, the biggest, baddest man in the world," Brogan says. "He was the cuddliest bear in the world."

The same man who infuriated the media to the point that *Washington Post* reporter Mark Asher coined the phrase "Hoya Paranoia" patrolled outside of Asher's hospital room as the reporter awaited surgery, kindly threatening the nurses and staff that there would be hell to pay if they didn't take care of his "brother." On the day that his father died, Wilbon flew home to Chicago, arriving to find his mother, Cleo, on the phone, refusing to end the conversation even though her son stood before her. When she finally hung up, she explained she'd been talking to "Coach Thompson." To this day, Wilbon doesn't know how he got the number or what the two discussed, only that at the funeral there were two huge wreaths—one from Georgetown athletics, and one from John Thompson and the Hoyas.

That's why Wilbon and others balk when asked if Thompson practiced his own racism, making his program available only to young Black athletes or shutting out white supporters. They point to the people he surrounded himself with and counted among his closest confidants—Stein, Fenlon, Rienzo, Auerbach, Gavitt, all of whom were white—and the praise he heaped on reporters he trusted, such as Weiss, Asher, Tom Boswell, and John Feinstein.

The issue, if it even can be considered an issue, is that Thompson didn't fit neatly in a box. He could be combustible and kind, infuriating and inspiring. He was an impossible riddle to solve—because he didn't want to be solved.

When it came to coaching his players, he was far easier to understand. "You should probably include a chapter entitled 'Motherfucker,'" Smith says. "That was our name." Thompson liked to remind his players, "You don't have to like me. And I don't have to like you. But we have to respect each other." Floyd chuckles at that one, recalling the very first game Floyd's mother attended. Thompson grew so incensed at what he perceived as a bad shot from Floyd, he stormed to half-court to berate the freshman, hurling his glasses onto the court and shattering them. Floyd sheepishly picked up the glasses, hoping it would lessen his time on the bench. "We definitely didn't like each other all of the time," he says. Thompson demanded commitment and excellence, having neither the time nor the patience for anything less.

On the first day of practice each season, the Hoyas ran a mile, the time standard determined by their position. Floyd set a record time. Yet Thompson, stopwatch in hand, announced that everyone had hit their time but Floyd. He offered the speedster a few minutes to catch his breath and run again. Full of indignation, Floyd refused the break and ran again, breaking his own record time, convinced he'd showed his coach up. It took him years to understand what really had happened. "He saw something in me that he could push me more," Floyd says. "And he was right."

Thompson poured all of his personality, knowledge, and ferocity into his team, crafting the Hoyas in his image. Georgetown antagonized and disrupted, unapologetically playing with such physicality that they practically dared officials to blow their whistles. Some did, but plenty didn't, opposing coaches figuring out what they were in for once they learned who was officiating. "John had this great tactic if he got pissed," Calhoun says. "He'd stand up and take that damn towel and flip it over his shoulder. I'd say to my assistants, 'We're fucked now.' I'd yell, 'You want me to flip my fucking towel?' It wouldn't have mattered if I did." Critics called it dirty. Fans called it smart.

Whatever it was, it worked. Georgetown teams were talented, deep, and the best sort of mean. In his freshman year, Chris Mullin dove for a loose ball at the same time as Spriggs. "He grabbed the ball and my head and squeezed it," Mullin says.

"People talk about Patrick, but let me tell you, Billy Martin was no picnic," Pinckney says. "You'd prepare for them, and go seven or eight deep in the scouting report. You never, never had to go that deep on other teams." During Thompson's tenure, the Hoyas would win 71 percent of their games, and after his first two years they failed to make the postseason just once—in 1998–99, when he resigned midseason.

Never, however, were the Hoyas more dominant than through the patch of the early 1980s, when Georgetown made the national championship game three out of four years. Heartbroken after being beaten in 1982 by Jordan and Carolina, and bounced the next year by Memphis State in the second round, the Hoyas coalesced into a force the following year, losing but three games in the entire 1983–84 season, not merely beating opponents but downright demolishing them. In the regular season, Georgetown won its games by an average of 15.7 points per game. Naturally, two of its three losses came against its Big East foes.

Villanova knocked off Georgetown in February, Massimino offering a peek into the game-planning mastery that would serve him well in due time by essentially collapsing his entire defense around Ewing. The big man would finish with just 2 points in the final 23 minutes, and was held without a shot in the last 13. Afterward, Massimino happily puffed on an oversized cigar while discussing the win as Thompson faced a barrage of questions from people wondering if his defensive-minded team lacked the proper offense to really succeed. Thompson dismissed the questions as idiocy, and when Georgetown proceeded to roll to 10 consecutive wins, plenty agreed.

Nearly invincible by late February, the Hoyas hosted St. John's, a team they'd beaten a month earlier by 22 points (a game that, notably, St. John's big man, Bill Wennington, missed with an ankle injury). No one expected much. Instead, Mullin put together a game for the ages, nearly shredding the vaunted press single-handedly, swishing and dishing the Red Storm to a 17-point first-half lead, and ultimately to a 75–71 win. St. John's would shoot an eye-popping 63 percent for the game, and Mullin finished with 33 points (this was before the 3-point shot), 5 assists, 4 rebounds, and 3 steals. At one point during the evisceration, Thompson lumbered to half-court and shouted, "Damn!" as Mullin drained yet another shot. Carnesecca turned and shouted, "What are you talking about, all those shooters you got over there?"

The punch in the snout turned out to be exactly what the Hoyas needed. They closed out the regular season with wins against Boston College, Pittsburgh, and Syracuse, and then rolled through the early round of the league tournament, dismissing Providence by 20 before exacting revenge against St. John's in the semis, winning that one by 11. That set up an epic Big East final against now fevered rival Syracuse. "It started with Coach Thompson, when he said what he said about Manley. He had a way to swim in their pain," Smith says. "But we picked it up. We hated them, the players, the fans, that fucking horse [the Dome Ranger, Syracuse's unofficial mascot]. I even hated that fucking horse." Adds Rautins: "There was no friendly banter at all. If Gene Smith bumps into me, you got four guys around you, all of them talking shit, ready to fight. That was the way it was with us. We hated them. They hated us."

In other words, the tournament championship didn't need manufactured tension. In a reversal of fortunes from that Manley game, Georgetown ranked second in the nation this time, while Syracuse couldn't quite match their rivals on the court. The Hoyas won the two regular-season games handily. Yet with four minutes to play in the championship final, Syracuse led, 57–54, when all hell broke loose.

Trying to rally back, the Hoyas worked the offensive glass, corralling three offensive rebounds on one possession, but were unable to score. Graham made a last failed attempt on a reverse scoop, and Syracuse's Andre Hawkins grabbed the rebound. Graham is the first to say that his style of play was not subtle. "I couldn't make a free throw, couldn't throw a rock in the ocean," he says. "I played toward my strengths, that's what I knew." He also knew Georgetown needed what he brought—a fierce power forward sidekick for Ewing. As Hawkins grabbed for that rebound, Graham fought for the ball, trying to dislodge Hawkins with a forearm. As the Syracuse big man fell to the floor, it looked as if Graham took a swing at him. "I wasn't swinging at him," Graham insists. "I figured I might get a tech, but not get tossed." The trailing official, Dick Paparo, ran into the play appearing to give an ejection hook to Graham. As the crowd reacted, equal parts jeering and cheering, Paparo huddled with the other officials, Larry Lembo and Jody Sylvester. After a lengthy consultation, they reduced Graham's infraction to an intentional—not technical—foul, allowing Graham to stay in the game. "They didn't throw him out," says Boeheim, still mystified all these years later. "Michael gets up and throws a haymaker at Andre, and they didn't throw him out." Instead, two minutes later, Hawkins drew his fifth foul, and Georgetown rallied and won in overtime.

Still fuming afterward, an incensed Boeheim ranted in the postgame press conference, tossing a chair in fury as he exited. Art Hyland, the supervisor of officials, wisely decided to wait a while before reaching out to Boeheim, but Tranghese, sitting in for Gavitt, who was in Kansas City for his NCAA Tournament Selection Committee duties, went to the locker room. "I felt so bad for Jimmy. His team played so hard, but he was out of his mind," Tranghese says. Flailing and gesticulating, Boeheim unintentionally headbutted his associate commissioner. Weeks later during the NCAA Tournament, Boeheim pulled Tranghese aside, asking why he told Gavitt Boeheim had headbutted him. "Because you did!" Tranghese says. Boeheim still insists he didn't, and Tranghese continues to swear he did.

To this day, Syracuse fans still believe they were robbed. But Georgetown? Smith lets out a nearly maniacal laugh when he recalls Boeheim's fury. "Oh, I got the biggest kick out of Boeheim throwing that chair," he says, before mimicking Boeheim's "the best team did not win today" statement with an exaggerated whine. "Oh, I love that."

The tournament title catapulted the Hoyas into the NCAA Tournament. After eking out a 37–36 win against an SMU team that intentionally tried to make the game a slog, the Hoyas got back to full throttle, easily disposing of UNLV and Dayton to advance to the Final Four at the Seattle Kingdome.

The first item on everyone's list, naturally, was finding Georgetown. Turns out, the Hoyas were hiding in plain sight. "We got off the plane, walked across the street, and went to the hotel," says Thompson, who sported a "Georgetown, Where

Are You?" button for much of the weekend. "They were writing like we were in Canada." Whether people could find the Hoyas or not, this time no one doubted they belonged. The 1982 final, coupled with the 1983–84 reign of dominance, proved that Georgetown deserved its spot among the game's elite. Or at least nouveau elite—the Hoyas were not quite perceived as being among the true bluebloods, unlike their national semifinal opponent, Kentucky.

By 1984, Kentucky already owned five national titles. The entire commonwealth treated the sport as its religion and the Wildcats as their gods. Anchored by its own seven-footer in Sam Bowie, Kentucky was coached by the much-beloved Joe B. Hall, Kentucky-born and University of Kentucky–educated. The Wildcats, team and fans, did not do upstarts, nor did they wilt, never dipping below sixth in the country all year, and hovering most of the time in the top three.

The Hoyas looked doomed early, digging a 12-point hole in the first half, and down 7 at the half, with Ewing benched with three fouls. But in an effort few will forget and Smith still never tires of talking about, the senior rallied his team with a magnificent effort no one saw coming. Overcrowding at the guard position rendered Smith a backup, and yet, plugged in for defensive energy, he suffocated the Kentucky backcourt, helping Georgetown claw back into the game. "We were playing eight, nine people, and you never knew who would be that intangible," Smith says. "I was like, 'Hey, you guys forgot about me.'" The Hoyas rattled off 12 unanswered points while Kentucky failed to score for nearly the first 10 minutes of the second half.

An exasperated Hall, unaccustomed to seeing his team so befuddled, threw his rolled-up program over his shoulder as the 53–40 Georgetown win neared. The Wildcats would connect on just 3 of 33 shots in the second half, Bowie and Kentucky's other big man, Melvin Turpin, going 0 for 12 in the second half. "They still tell the story about how Joe B. Hall sent a manager over to measure the basket afterward," says Weiss, the New York *Daily News* reporter. "He couldn't believe one of his teams got shut down that badly."

That set up an epic title game between the last two college basketball bridesmaids: Georgetown, 1982 losers after Jordan's bucket and Brown's errant pass, versus Houston, hearts crushed by N.C. State in 1983 when Lorenzo Charles stuffed Dereck Whittenburg's airball for a most improbable championship. It also pitted the game's two best big men in decades against each other, with Olajuwon and Ewing drawing comparisons to the 1968 national semifinal matchup between UCLA's Lew Alcindor and Houston's Elvin Hayes.

As these things often go, the predicted story line failed to play out. Olajuwon and Ewing entertained, but it was the supporting actors who starred. Five Georgetown players finished in double figures, led by freshman Reggie Williams (19), David Wingate (16), Graham (14), Michael Jackson (11), and finally Ewing (10), and the defense did the rest. With the vise closed on the Cougars, the Hoyas won the game, 84–75, and set an NCAA season record, limiting opponents to just 39.5 percent shooting.

The win made Thompson the first Black coach to win a national title, an accolade he bristled at his entire life, believing it implied others weren't capable of winning it all. He was first, he argued, simply because he had had the opportunity others did not. A first he did enjoy? Being the first East Coast school since La Salle in 1954 to win a championship, ousting the perceived elites in the process. "You were all so busy thinking about me being Black, you forgot that I beat those boys, too," Thompson said. "We had a pride in that."

It was that—what the championship meant for Eastern basketball and his nascent league—that occupied Thompson's mind as the clock wound down. He'd already removed his starters, allowing them to get a jump on their celebration, and decided to do the same. He eased back onto the scorer's table, where Gavitt sat perched behind him. The commissioner smiled from ear to ear. It had been just five years earlier that Gavitt huddled with Thompson, selling the coach on the idea of an East Coast–based league; just five years since the Big East had been born.

Now the conference sat atop the college basketball world, its legitimacy secured. Thompson leaned back and smiled the Cheshire cat grin of a man armed with a great one-liner. "How about the Big East now?" he said to Gavitt.

Turns out, the 1984 championship was only the warm-up act. The conference was about to stake its claim on the sport like no league had done before, or since.

CHAPTER 6

ST. JOHN'S, A TEAM EVEN NEW YORKERS COULD LOVE

"Eh, that's Louie being Louie"

Walking out of his high school gym at Power Memorial Academy in 1978, Chris Mullin spied Lou Carnesecca's very small but familiar figure off to the side. Mullin already had a reputation, cultivated from the Catholic Youth Organization courts at St. Thomas Aquinas, and cultivated by the mythmaking of New York. But he was just a freshman, years away from the nationwide frenzy his recruitment would set off. "You're going to play for me one day," Carnesecca said to the teenager. Mullin smiled. He'd been going to Carnesecca's summer camps for years and enjoyed the coach immensely, in a way only a New York kid could love a New York coach. That is to say, they understood each other.

Carnesecca's prophetic words would lead to a lifelong bond between player and coach—and, equally important, to one of the most critical partnerships in the Big East. The league may have had its offices in Providence and stretched its reach up and down the East Coast, but its epicenter was New York. Both of them brash, bold, and forceful, the city and the conference played off each other beautifully, the league taking its energy from the city, and the city breathing legitimacy into the league. The five boroughs produced many of the Big East's biggest stars—coaches who cut their teeth at the high schools, and players who honed their games on the playgrounds.

The partnership would have worked anywhere, but it soared in New York because the hometown team played some of its best basketball just as the Big East launched. Led by Carnesecca, St. John's won or played for two of the first seven league tournament titles, and earned NCAA Tournament bids in twelve of the first fourteen years, including four Sweet Sixteens, three Elite Eights, and a Final Four.

The city fell hard for its sharpshooting star and quick-talking coach. Looie, two *o*'s, no *u*—that's how New Yorkers referred to their coach. He was one of them, a by-the-bootstraps son of Italian immigrants who never saw a need to stray too far from home, the city offering everything he could possibly need. He grew up on East 62nd Street, where his father owned and ran the deli beneath the family apartment. Carnesecca helped with the business when he wasn't dashing from the basketball playgrounds to the baseball sandlots, or running numbers for the neighbor.

At Our Lady of Perpetual Help grammar school, a nun by the name of Sister Mary Joella planted the seed of a career in sports in her young student's head when she regaled the class with tales of famed Notre Dame football coach Knute Rockne. Wise to his size and his skills, or lack thereof, Carnesecca realized he would not cut it as a professional athlete, and declared his intentions to pursue a career in coaching. "I would have made three times the money cutting salami," he cracks. "I made a good sandwich." His parents preferred he become a doctor, and Carnesecca tried. After three years of medical service with the Coast Guard during World War II, he enrolled as a premed student at Fordham. It didn't take. He immediately transferred to St. John's, where he played baseball.

St. Ann's, his high school alma mater, offered him his first job, and his first chance to coach at the Garden. As a warm-up to a Knicks game in 1950, Carnesecca's St. Ann's squad took on St. Nicholas Tolentine, coached by Rocco Valvano, whose son, Jim, would lead N.C. State to a national title. Carnesecca was constantly thinking about, talking about, and tinkering with the sport. He used brooms to force his players to work on the arc of their shots, and he visited clinics on his endless quest for basketball knowledge. After an initial 11-loss season, St. Ann's lost just 23 games over the next six seasons. In 1958, the high school team finished 32–0. That same year, AD Joe Lapchick named Carnesecca to his staff at St. John's. The school then was a commuter school with just a small collection of varsity sports. Carnesecca's duties were numerous. Along with helping Lapchick, he was an associate professor of physical education, in charge of the intramurals, and the freshman baseball coach. His heart and his energy, though, were in basketball.

Jack Kaiser, the future St. John's athletic director, served as the varsity baseball coach in those days, and remembers coming in from the field during one of his varsity games, maybe about the third inning. Carnesecca should have been down on St. Nicholas Field, hosting a freshman team scrimmage/tryout against Queens College. Instead Kaiser glanced over toward a short fence behind the bench and spied Carnesecca and a player nearly twice his size towering over the fence. "It's Lew Alcindor," Kaiser says. "He's recruiting Lew Alcindor during baseball tryouts."

As Kaiser retells the story, a sheepish Carnesecca laughs and interrupts, going into full Carnesecca tale-telling mode. He spins a yarn that sounds downright impossible, if not improbable, but is vintage Looie. "You're not at the best part! Then I had to go down to the scrimmage." Still starry-eyed at the hope of getting the big man to stay home and play college ball, Carnesecca returned to his tryouts, spying a collection of shoddy-looking athletes. "Terrible-looking, glasses, socks on," Carnesecca says. "I said, 'You're all cut. I don't want these schmucks. You can't play.'" Upon hearing Carnesecca's declaration, Queens College coach Robert Tierney looked up and screamed, "What the hell are you doing? That's my team."

Carnesecca lost the recruit. At the time, St. John's had a mandatory retirement age of sixty-five, and when Lapchick reached it, the school forced him out. So Alcindor instead opted for UCLA, where he'd lead the Bruins to three national titles, later change his name to Kareem Abdul-Jabbar, and become one of the game's biggest legends. Louie was hired as Lapchick's replacement and the head basketball coach in 1965. He carried the torch well, taking the team to the postseason in each of his first four seasons. But when the pro ranks came courting, Carnesecca couldn't say no. In an absurd plot twist, Carnesecca agreed to take over the New York Nets of the ABA, but he postponed his arrival one year in order to honor the final year of his St. John's contract—and in that, his lame-duck year, the Red Storm went all the way to the 1970 NIT title game, losing to Al McGuire and Marquette.

Carnesecca dismisses his three-year foray into the pro ranks now with a wave of his hand. "There's something about it I didn't care for," he says. "It wasn't for me." The final year was dismal, the team losing and Carnesecca unhappy. Head coaching in the pros was too much about being a manager and boss rather than a coach. He admits now he got lucky and realized his mistake before it was too late; he shudders to imagine what might have happened had he stayed on in the pro ranks. His replacement, Frank Mulzoff, had done well, going 19–6 that year, but he wanted a three-year renewal contract. The university refused to offer more than two, and Mulzoff resigned. With St. John's out of a coach and Carnesecca out of a job, Kaiser, by then the athletic director, did the logical thing. He made a call.

The two met at a restaurant, and then finalized the deal in Kaiser's car while parked just outside the St. John's arena, agreeing over a handshake to the $22,000 contract. "Lou and I have spoken many times about how fortunate we were to have St. John's as our home," Kaiser says. To which Carnesecca adds, "It was home." Like the prodigal son, he returned in 1973 and never really left, a regular at games long past retirement and well into his nineties.

Sold in Italy on Gavitt's Big East dream, Carnesecca became one of the league's most popular and liveliest caricatures. Arms flailing, mouth agape, he stomped and stormed and shimmied his way down the sidelines, often venturing nearly to the other team's bench. Opposing coaches, angry that Carnesecca encroached on their real estate, grew even more irate as officials merely shooed him back to his territory rather than hit Carnesecca with a technical foul for trespassing. Boston College's Gary Williams, in fact, once grew so incensed with Carnesecca's creeping that he told his cat-quick guard Michael Adams to purposely brush Carnesecca if the coach got too far onto the court. "Sure enough, Louie is on the floor, and doesn't see Michael coming," Williams says. "The ref blows the whistle, but gives the ball to Michael. No technical. 'Eh, that's Louie being Louie,' the ref says."

Carnesecca spoke like a nonsensical poet, an eloquent Yogi Berra who turned the malaprop into an art form, and added to it a perfect Noo Yawk accent. On occasion he was conveniently hard of hearing, somehow losing his hearing aids at the most opportune times. During a contentious vote in a league meeting,

Providence coach Rick Barnes discovered the St. John's coach crawling on the floor in search of his hearing aid. "He had no idea what we were even talking about," Barnes says.

He and Massimino, two paisans, crafted an especially close friendship. They'd call each other names in Italian, and Massimino loved to tease Carnesecca, mouthing words so Carnesecca thought he was missing something. The two were so tight that Fox sports analyst Bill Raftery remembers being stunned when he looked up during a game to find them arguing at half-court. It turned out that after a lousy call had gone in Villanova's favor earlier in the game, Massimino had actually apologized to Carnesecca, but Carnesecca couldn't hear what he said. Instead he'd turned to his assistant, the man-to-man defense guru Al LoBalbo, for clarification. "I guess LoBalbo decided Rollie hadn't kissed the ring appropriately," Raftery says. "Al says to Louie, 'He called you a hot dog.' And that's what they were arguing about."

Not all of the fights were good-natured, and Carnesecca's sweetness would never be confused with being a pushover. Chris Plonsky, a former associate Big East commissioner, is the daughter of a western Pennsylvania football star, and a college athlete herself. She had the chops to do the job, and the thick skin to handle the crowd. Still, in 1986, when Plonsky walked into her first league meeting in Ponte Vedra Beach, she was greeted by a roomful of skeptics, the men worried they couldn't speak freely—and cuss regularly—with a woman in their midst. Gavitt assured his staff she could more than handle herself. "P.J. dropped the first *F*-bomb, and we were fine," Plonsky says.

But toward the end of the meeting, Carnesecca politely asked her to leave the room. "Oh, Louie, always the perfect, sweet gentleman," Plonsky says of the coach. The perfect, sweet gentleman had no sooner shut the door than he turned on his fellow coaches and roared, "All right, I want to know who the fuck said I was dying of cancer?"—addressing a recruiting rumor making the rounds that got so bad Gavitt ultimately would call a summit and read his coaches the riot act. "Do I know what happened?" former Villanova assistant Steve Lappas says. "No, but I was in the office when Louie called Rollie about it. I know Louie believed it happened."

It especially unnerved people that it was Carnesecca being targeted. The truth is, if you lined up almost everyone who ever had anything to do with the Big East, you'd be hard-pressed to find anyone who'd say anything bad about Carnesecca. Respected as much as anybody, he also charmed everyone he met. "Oh man, he's just the most genuine, honest, and really funny— one of the funniest people, actually—that I know," Mullin says. "He never forgot where he came from."

Raised in the same sort of neighborhoods as the kids he was trying to recruit, Carnesecca worked his background to his advantage. New York City teemed with great players, the playgrounds serving as proving grounds. Coaches across the nation had long plucked ballplayers from the Bronx to Harlem and all the blacktops in between to lead their teams. The formation of the Big East gave those players a reason to stay home. They could be heroes in their own backyards, play in a league every bit as respected as the ACC, and enjoy the fame that the conference's TV contract offered. Everyone in the conference benefited. Massimino got Pinckney from the same Bronx high school where Thompson found point guard Fred Brown, and Syracuse wooed the Pearl from Brooklyn. No one worked the city limits quite like St. John's and Carnesecca. "We never went out of town," Carnesecca says. "Maybe Jersey, that's the farthest we'd go."

He'd approach a high school player, New Yorker to New Yorker, with a simple pitch: Why leave? Plenty didn't argue. "I realized I had everything I needed at home," Mullin says. Ewing's decision to play in the Big East served national notice that the league merited attention. And Mullin's decision to stay home sounded an equally loud and important bell, convincing others that there was no need to go elsewhere.

By the time he committed in April 1981, Mullin had known Carnesecca for years, going all the way back to those early summer camps he attended. But the kid from Flatbush Avenue was now a star. The son of a hardworking former ballplayer and one of four kids, including three boys, Mullin crafted a game born of the curriculum of hard elbows and mercilessness that only brothers can dish out. Given the keys to the gym at St. Thomas Aquinas, he turned it into a nearly twenty-four-hour basketball classroom. Not naturally athletic, Mullin worked ferociously on fundamentals—jab steps and pull-ups, perfecting a left-handed shot that ended with a flick of the wrist, as if he were casting a magic spell, directing the ball where it needed to go. Early skeptics who scoffed at the doughy white kid's ability soon were silenced, Mullin unafraid to take his talents to the playgrounds, where his technical game matched up just fine with the pickup freelancers. "How you performed, that was your reputation," he says. "That's all you had."

Rarely did the ball have the audacity to disobey his instruction. Mullin led Power Memorial, former home to Lew Alcindor, to a freshman and JV championship. Early in his junior year, he transferred from Memorial to Xaverian, a Catholic school, looking to play for a coach who wouldn't limit his offensive capacity. After sitting out a year, as required by the city rules, Mullin appeared in his first game in 1981, against city power Christ the King. Mullin scored 13 of Xaverian's first 17 points, and finished with 33 in front of 1,000 fans. A legend was born. Typically an afterthought in hoops, Xaverian won the state title that year. The college coaches came calling from everywhere, Carnesecca at the front of the line. The coach promised he wouldn't hound Mullin, which the player appreciated, but when Duke, Virginia, and North Carolina came knocking at Mullin's front door, Carnesecca called again. "Can I just come in one more time for a visit?" he asked.

Mullin visited the other schools and enjoyed each immensely. "Never seen so much grass," he says. But the pretty campuses with wide-open spaces had nothing on the comforts of home and the coach he knew best. In April, Mullin committed to St. John's.

He laughs now at everything St. John's didn't have. When Carnesecca wanted to push his players to work harder, he'd yell, "This isn't a country club." "A country club?" Mullin says. "Uh, yeah, we know it's not." Even by the most utilitarian standards, St. John's was pretty bare-bones. Pre-practice training mostly consisted of running a few miles outside on the concrete, banging out a few sit-ups and push-ups, and getting on the court. The school didn't even have a weight room to offer.

But Mullin was never one for bells and whistles. He just wanted to play, and in Carnesecca he found a coach who spoke his language—and not just the fuhgeddaboudit dialect of native New Yorkers. The coach loved basketball the way his player did, loved to study it, rarely happier than when he was breaking down film. Carnesecca saw the gym the way a good teacher saw the classroom, a thing to be studied and taught. He invited other coaches in to teach specialties he himself hadn't yet mastered— Temple coach Don Casey explained to the Red Storm the essence of his 2-3 zone, for example—and he constantly credited the people he borrowed from.

Carnesecca's practices included so much dissection into the roots of a play—whom he'd borrowed it from, why he liked it, how it would work best—that his players often returned to the gym despite four-hour marathon practices just so they could shoot. "You'd go two hours and not get a shot up," Mullin says.

As much as Mullin loved fundamentals, not even he could match Carnesecca's attention to detail. Carnesecca would stop a drill to move a player over a mere two inches, convinced it made all the difference, and preached perfecting screening angles, insistent that the proper cut could be the critical element that resulted in a made bucket instead of a miss, a win instead of a loss.

The partnership between gym rat and perfectionist worked like a charm for St. John's, Mullin elevating the program to the national stage just as Ewing did down the interstate at Georgetown. The two players would tango for four years, inciting arguments around watering holes and watercoolers about which player was more critical to his program and which team was the best. Mullin versus Ewing played in the headlines as regularly as St. John's versus Georgetown, the league benefiting from the unbelievable bounty of having two transcendent players enrolled at the same time.

The Big East suited Mullin perfectly, its rough edges and sharp elbows the same as the ones dished out by his three brothers, its rugged atmosphere feeling like home. "Some of the gyms, it was like high school," he says. "You're taking the ball out of bounds and people are kicking you in the Achilles." Fans derisively chanted, "Chris-sy," thinking the average-looking kid couldn't possibly be anything more than a gunner whose weaknesses were about to be exposed.

Instead he exposed his opponents'.

Much as Thompson did at Georgetown, Carnesecca eased his star into things. Mullin faced just as much pressure locally as Ewing did nationally, the hometown hero expected to launch St. John's into national prominence. Despite his knack for scoring, Mullin could coast for his first two years, surrounded by veteran leaders in Billy Goodwin, David Russell, and Kevin Williams. That crew finished 21–9 in 1982, Mullin's freshman season, and won their first Garden party—the Big East Tournament title—

the following year. But after the vets moved on, St. John's needed to rediscover itself, and Mullin had to adapt to his new role. It was no longer enough to just be the point-maker; he had to lead.

After waltzing to an 11–1 start in 1983–84, losing just to number one North Carolina and challenged only by conference foes Providence and UConn, St. John's lost six of its next seven league games. It was a nightmarish stretch for everyone, but especially Mullin. Though he faced double teams and junk defenses, he also had to deal with the lofty expectations the city heaped on his shoulders. New Yorkers wanted more. They expected more. Carnesecca understood the albatross hanging around his player's neck and knew better than to add to it. During the losing skid, he didn't lecture or punish, but rather took a philosophical approach, shrugging and telling his young players they simply had to get back to the gym. The Red Storm responded with a five-game winning streak, including a 75–71 upset of number two Georgetown, a game in which Mullin not only scored 33 points but picked up 4 rebounds, 4 assists, and 3 steals.

St. John's, however, could not keep its steam, losing to the Hoyas in the Big East Tournament and to Temple in the first round of the NCAA Tournament. The Red Storm finished 18–12 during Mullin's junior year. Hardly a disaster, but not up to their standards, either.

That summer, Mullin joined a collection of collegiate all-stars in what would become an historic Olympic run. The 1984 version of Team USA would be the last group of amateurs to win the gold, the Americans running through the Soviet-boycotted field behind three future Hall of Famers in Mullin, Ewing, and Michael Jordan. Despite being together for months and playing on the same team, Ewing and Mullin didn't leave Los Angeles close friends, well aware they still had another year of college ball to go head-to-head.

That both returned to the league with gold medals dangling around their necks only ratcheted up the excitement around the 1984–85 season. St. John's returned a slew of veterans and an equally promising rookie class. Walter Berry, a native New Yorker, arrived from San Jacinto junior college as a big-bodied complement to Mullin's sweet stroke, and suddenly St. John's went from disappointment to the top of the charts to start the season. Before the season tipped off, reporters crowed that this would be Carnesecca's best team ever, and his best shot at what had been to that point an elusive Final Four trip. Carnesecca had gotten close before, losing to Penn in 1979 and to Georgia in 1983, when a 28–4 squad most thought good enough to make it to the title game was upset in the second round.

No stranger to hype, Carnesecca dismissed the expectations in vintage Looie-ese. "Last year we were fighting with water pistols," he said at the time. "This year we'll be fighting with guns—but some of the teams we'll face have cannons." Despite Carnesecca's fretting, St. John's steamrolled to a 24–1 start during which the Red Storm beat UCLA, N.C. State, Syracuse, and, most impressively, number one Georgetown. With Mullin's 20 and Berry's 14 in that one, the Red Storm held on for the 66–65 win in D.C., catapulting St. John's to its first number one ranking since 1951.

The Red Storm kept cruising, winning nine more. Georgetown did the same, regrouping after a loss to Syracuse for six consecutive wins, putting the two teams and two players on a regular-season collision course.

It came on February 27, 1985, with the nation's two best players playing on the nation's two best teams, squaring off in the nation's most famous arena, Madison Square Garden, which was hosting its first number one versus number two game in fifty years. The setup could not have been more sublime, a moment tailor-made for New York and featuring two coaches tailor-made for the tabloids. The sports pages were filled with stories, the head-to-head between Mullin and Ewing detailed much like a boxing match between two heavyweights. ESPN pushed the tip-off back to 9 p.m., wisely recognizing the appeal that the game held nationally, and scalpers were asking—and getting—as much as $1,200 for $12 tickets. "You could cut the pressure with a knife," says Georgetown president Jack DeGioia, who then served as the school's dean of students. "I don't ever remember intensity before a game like that in my life. Not in a tournament, nothing."

By then the Big East didn't need any more legitimizing. Rather, the game served as a celebration of the conference's dominance. Fans crowded in bars and living rooms across the country to watch—confirmed days later when ESPN announced the game had earned an 8.0 rating, the highest regular-season game in history to that point.

Charged with serving as the play-by-play man, Len Berman remembered advice Gavitt had given him years before, back when the league was just beginning: "Don't sell." The commissioner didn't want schtick, and didn't think viewers needed to be hoodwinked into recognizing the quality of what they were seeing. He'd believed that way back in 1979, and certainly believed it now. Berman told his producer he would low-key the intro. He wouldn't yell or hype, just set it up. "It's the city game," he began. "And the city is New York." Though Berman couldn't help injecting a little hyperbole: "ESPN, the total sports network, presents the game of the year," he added.

St. John's bused in from campus, fighting the traffic clogged around the arena for the big game. Even the hard-to-impress New Yorkers were stunned at the scene. "It was crazy," Mullin says. "The city was crazy."

Earlier that year, at a game inside a frigid Pittsburgh arena, Carnesecca, already battling a touch of the flu, had tossed on a sweater given to him by a friend. The Red Storm won the game, and Carnesecca decided the merino wool had something to do with it. Every game after, he donned the garish garment, the impossible color combination of turquoise, red, and brown becoming nearly as popular as Yankee pinstripes in the city. Everyone from high school coaches to then governor Mario Cuomo snapped up replicas, the student bookstore and area sporting goods retailers selling T-shirt versions to fans anxious for their own ugly sweater. It became a near national sensation. "I'm watching television, and Louie is wearing a sweater, and all of a sudden it's a lucky sweater," Thompson said. "This is the biggest bunch of bullshit."

Thompson had been and would continue to be on the receiving end of plenty of good-natured ribbing during the course of his career. Once at a game at Syracuse, the majority of the student body walked out with towels over their shoulders. In 1994, after postponing a game at Providence, claiming his team couldn't get in due to a snowstorm, the coach took the floor only to be greeted by a student dressed entirely in black, holding an umbrella over his head. "He didn't say nothing," Thompson recalled. "Just taunting me, holding that umbrella."

Though he hid it from outsiders, Thompson had plenty of imp in him as well. He loved to needle his friends and even his players. Telling no one his plan, Thompson sent one of his minions on a mission to the St. John's campus bookstore. After putting on his suit and dress shirt, Thompson shimmied into a Carnesecca sweater replica tee, the V-shaped pattern stretched across his barrel chest. He covered it up with his suit jacket, making sure to keep the buttons secure and holding it tight for good measure as he walked onto the Garden floor.

As the two teams took the court, the building buzzing with anticipation, Thompson waited until Carnesecca took his seat before walking toward him and opening his jacket like a trench-coat-wearing flasher, revealing the shirt for all to see. The court-side photographers started snapping away, while everyone—Carnesecca included—chuckled. "Complete surprise," Carnesecca says. "He dazzled me with that." The Sweater Game instantly entered into the lexicon and the league lore, the moment remembered now not just for its prankish good humor but also for defusing some of the tension in the building. Thompson smiled for years afterward at the misnomer assigned to the game, pointing out that it wasn't a sweater but a T-shirt. "Nobody realized that," he says. Including Carnesecca. Told some thirty-plus years later that his coaching foe only went for a cotton copy, Carnesecca balked. "He's so low-class! I mean, he had the money. He could've bought a sweater. Go for the extra buck."

Along with stealing Carnesecca's signature look, Thompson swiped the coach's mojo, too. St. John's 19-game win streak and its sweater karma ended with a thud, the Hoyas humbling the Red Storm, 85–69. "I didn't mind him winning the battle of the sweaters, but he beat me," Carnesecca says. "That hurt. That I took home." Thompson's copycat shirt didn't win the game any more than Carnesecca's original caused the 19 victories for St. John's, but Mullin remembers everyone turning around to look at Thompson, their attention on the importance of the game at hand momentarily diverted. "I didn't think it was too funny," he says. "I was too worried about beating Georgetown."

No one expected that to be the last meeting between the two teams that season, not with a Big East Tournament to be played. And ten days later they met in the Garden again, this time for the Big East Tournament championship. In between, Carnesecca plotted his revenge on Thompson. "He had to come up with a rebuttal," Kaiser says. The coach corralled his managers before the game, instructing them to tie a collection of white towels together. When the diminutive Carnesecca took the court, he slung one towel over his shoulder and the rest trailed behind him, the managers holding them aloft as if he were a bride with a train headed down the aisle. Thompson spent the first few minutes of the game coaching with a smile on his face.

Carnesecca's good humor didn't last quite so long. The white towels soon doubled as white flags of surrender, Georgetown rolling over St. John's again to claim the Big East title, leaving many—including Carnesecca—to believe the Hoyas that year were simply invincible. "The only team that could beat Georgetown," Carnesecca said after his team's 92–80 humbling, "is Georgetown."

He was almost right. Almost.

CHAPTER 7
PASTA, FAMILY, AND MASSIMINO
"Who the hell is this little Italian dude?"

The clock read two in the morning when Jay Wright decided to leave the gathering at his boss's house and go home. A young assistant on the Villanova staff, Wright had to prepare the scouting report for the next game, a *Big Monday* affair. Since Saturday night already had become Sunday morning, Wright decided it was time to get home and get to work. He quietly slipped out the door and returned to his apartment, where he watched film until his exhaustion got the better of him somewhere around four in the morning. His roommate, Bob Salmi, an equally hardworking video scout for the 76ers, came home from a road trip around dawn, checked the answering machine for messages, and immediately roused Wright from his slumber. Wright hit the playback button and heard Massimino, his head coach, fuming on the tape, telling his young assistant he was fired—the coach was angry that Wright had left so early.

If Georgetown ranked as the Evil Empire and St. John's as

the City's Team, Villanova was La Famiglia. Just as Nonna expected her brood for Sunday spaghetti, Daddy Mass demanded his family's presence around his table. "When you worked for Rollie," former assistant Mitch Buonaguro says, "it was twenty-four hours." Practices turned into all-day marathons, and road games included big dinners, but it was the post-home-game gatherings that topped them all. With his wife, Mary Jane, boiling up the water and cooking the pasta, Massimino held court at the head of his kitchen table, his staff and assorted hangers-on squished in elbow to elbow and knee to knee. Massimino didn't so much befriend people as absorb them, the limits of every table he headed stretched beyond capacity and the collection of people logical only in the context of Massimino. A young assistant might pass the bread to a co-worker or to Perry Como if the crooner happened to be in town. Mario Andretti was as apt to question a ref's call as Massimino himself, and Dodgers manager Tommy Lasorda popped in more than once.

Like all family dinners, the meals were occasionally contentious and especially loud, each play, decision, and call rehashed and dissected. The dinners ended only when Massimino said so, and they often dragged on until dawn, the visitors straggling home, their bellies blissfully full, but their heads swimming from all of the wine.

So Wright's decision to bolt early—even to work on basketball—did not go over well. Bleary-eyed and petrified his career was over, he arrived at his office at 6:30 the next morning. An hour later, Massimino walked in, strolling right by Wright's office without saying a word about the answering machine message. "I don't even know if he remembered the message, but he never said a word about it," Wright says with a laugh. "But that was him. I've never seen a person enjoy confrontation like he did. Most people avoid it. He thrived on it."

Full of bluster and short on temper, hair askew and shirttails flying, the son of an immigrant who made a living as a shoe-maker stomped his way to the top, yanking Villanova along for the ride. He was everything that the school, parked in a leafy Main Line suburb of Philadelphia and run by Augustinian priests, was not. "Rollie was chasing . . . who knows what he was chasing," star forward Ed Pinckney says. "But every game was so much, like he had something to prove."

Raised in a family much like the one he cultivated with his staff and players, Massimino grew up in Newark, New Jersey, and started on the lowest rung of the coaching ladder after grad-uating from the University of Vermont. He first worked as a junior varsity coach at Cranford High School, making $3,600. But he had a mind for the game, and a knack for creating great defensive schemes. "He loved to sit in an office and X and O," his former assistant Steve Lappas says. "He wanted to figure out new defenses so he could fool the other team. I can sum up Rollie in a nutshell: He wanted you to think he was doing this when he was really doing that."

The world moved slower in the late 1950s, the ladder of suc-cess not so quickly ascended and people in less of a race to get to the top. Massimino spent thirteen years at the high school level before taking his first step onto a college court, finally land-ing at Stony Brook on Long Island. After two years there, he joined Chuck Daly on the staff at the University of Pennsylvania, beginning a lifelong friendship that extended to the golf courses of Florida, where the two spent their semiretirement.

Massimino and his family were packing for a trip to Italy, where Massimino intended to interview for a job with the pro team based in Bologna, when he got the call that Villanova wanted to hire him to replace Jack Kraft. It was not exactly an upwardly mobile move. Penn at the time had won four consecu-tive Ivy League titles and ranked as one of the most consistent programs on the East Coast. After a national runner-up finish in

1971, the Wildcats fell to 11–14, the roster nearly depleted of good players by the time Massimino arrived in 1973. Thirty-seven years old and thrilled to get a job, Massimino was undeterred. He slapped a "Pass the Word: The Cats Are Back" bumper sticker on his car and gobbled up the miles in search of recruits. Despite the sticker's optimism, success did not happen quickly, with Massimino forced to rebuild his roster with nine freshmen in the first two years. But by year three, his defensive schemes installed, Villanova finally put together a winning record and a year later finished third in the NIT.

By then the Wildcats had joined the Eastern Eight, a collection of schools (including Pittsburgh, Duquesne, West Virginia, George Washington, Massachusetts, Rutgers, and St. Bonaventure) that had essentially seceded from the ECAC to craft their own TV contract. But Villanova owned the league, winning 29 of 37 games, the program's dominance catching the eye of Gavitt, Kaiser, and Rienzo as they eyed a Philadelphia footprint for their new league. The Villanova–Big East marriage proved an instant success, the Big East offering Villanova a bigger showcase for its program, the Wildcats bringing more talent and, notably, more personality to the conference.

Full of piss and vinegar, Massimino was a cartoon character ready-made for the big stage, anxious to tilt at windmills, pick a fight, and wash it all down with a nice glass of Chianti. He did not create his act for the Big East, but the league amplified it perfectly. Massimino's chronic quest for validation and respect crafted Villanova into the ultimate underdog, even if the description was oversimplified.

Ultimately his emotions would be his undoing. Massimino exited Villanova in 1992 in a huff, angry that the school wouldn't create a succession plan that would allow him to become athletic director, and ticked that the city of Philadelphia blamed him for the demise of its beloved city series, the Big 5. Massimino carried the anger around like an anvil for decades, not even speaking to Lappas, his former assistant, because he had the temerity to succeed Massimino. "To me it was a no-brainer to take the job," Lappas says. "It was a dream for me to be there as an assistant, and to get a chance to be a head coach in the Big East? No-brainer. Did it make everybody happy? No. But that's the way it was." Not until Wright took over as head coach and mended fences did Massimino reunite with Lappas and return to Villanova.

But before it forced him out of the program he helped establish, Massimino's personality added the perfect spice to the Big East dish. Here was the antithesis to the stoic Thompson and the lovable Carnesecca, an instigator like Carlesimo, but one who lacked the Seton Hall coach's subtlety. Massimino complained about officials as relentlessly as Boeheim did, but instead of posing like a plaintive whiner, he stomped the court like a whirling dervish. The tales of Massimino's outbursts rank as some of the best among the Big East tall tales, his fervor and feistiness turning everything into a fight.

At a game at Boston's Roberts Center, BC coach Gary Williams watched as Massimino mercilessly rode the officials for the first half, his Villanova team in a tussle with an undermanned BC squad. When the break came, Massimino chased after the refs, following them out of the tunnel. In only his second year at Boston College and worried his more seasoned opposing coach might get an edge, Williams gave pursuit after Massimino, opting to follow the Villanova coach rather than join his own team in the locker room. "I knew you'd pull something like this, you little son of a bitch," Williams railed at Massimino. Irate, Massimino responded, "Get back to your own locker room." Williams almost turned but then realized where he was. "This is my fucking gym," he shot back, the two sparring for a few minutes more before finally parting ways. Villanova wound up winning the game by 12.

Buonaguro, who insists he got the job because his last name ends with an *o*, remembers two separate trips to New York, one to Rochester and the other to St. Bonaventure. At the first, in a tournament final against Syracuse, an incensed Massimino, convinced the officials were giving the home-state team a better whistle, wound up behind the bench. To this day, Buonaguro isn't sure if Massimino fell over the bench or walked there. But the coach still gave a tournament official an earful about the referees.

At St. Bonaventure, a disconsolate Massimino, sure the officials had screwed his team into a loss, refused to get on the bus, hoofing it back to the hotel in his $400 Italian loafers. Upon arrival, he called his assistants, asking them to meet him at the hotel bar. Buonaguro walked in and saw Larry Weise, the former St. Bonaventure head coach and then athletic director, in a confab with the game officials. "We had to get him out of the restaurant," Buonaguro says of Massimino. "He wanted to fight them."

But Massimino celebrated as boldly as he blustered, creating a circle of friends that stretched from coast to coast and included a posse befitting Italian royalty. Staff members grew accustomed to breaking bread with celebrities, including Andretti, Como, and WWF champion Bruno Sammartino. Lasorda, a regular visitor, once helicoptered from downtown Philadelphia to suburban Norristown in order to keep a lunch date with the Villanova coaches but not risk getting stuck in traffic before first pitch against the Phillies. When Wright mentioned how fun it would be to see a performance by Como, who was playing a holiday concert at the nearby Valley Forge Music Fair, the singer left prime tickets not only for the coach but also for Wright and his then girlfriend (now wife), Patty. "How was it? It was a Perry Como Christmas concert!" Wright says. "It was awesome."

In return for their friendship, the glitterati were rewarded with seats on the bench, Massimino finding ushers at home and even road games who would create a second row for his famous friends. Before a game at the old Philadelphia Spectrum, Thompson confronted the coach about his bench who's who. The locker rooms in the old arena were next to each other, and both head coaches exited simultaneously, Thompson screaming that he "better not see that fucking guinea Lasorda on the bench." Unmoved, Massimino screeched back, "Fuck you. He's there tonight, and he's going to put the Italian curse on you." That was Wright's first game against Georgetown, and the then twenty-five-year-old was certain he'd have to separate the two from fighting. "It's *F*-bombs and ethnic slurs," he says. "And then they go hug each other and start laughing. Unbelievable." Eventually the NCAA established rules that limited both how many people could be on a bench during a game and who could be included. "It was the Rollie Massimino rule," Wright says.

His team was not necessarily built in his likeness. The Wildcats didn't shy away from confrontation, but they weren't exactly Georgetown, either. They did, however, adopt his little-man complex, even when it didn't exactly hold water. The truth is, Villanova was every bit its Big East peers' equal, and proved it immediately. In their first Big East Tournament, the 1981 version played at the Carrier Dome, the Wildcats faced Syracuse for the title in what still ranks as one of the best games in league history, a three-overtime thriller that ended only after Rautins scored on a tip-in with three seconds to play. "There's not a person I run into that wasn't at that game," Rautins says, chuckling at the embellishments.

But Massimino goaded his team into believing that they had to prove their worthiness. On the office wall behind his desk hung a sign that became his mantra: "Disposition to dominate." It wasn't good enough to be good enough; the Wildcats strove to be the best. Before the NCAA put limits on such things, the

Wildcats practiced as long as the coach saw fit, weekend double sessions the norm rather than the exception. "It was awful. There is absolutely nothing good I can tell you about practice," says John Pinone, a three-time All–Big East player who starred at Villanova from 1979 to 1983. "Between classes, he'd have you come in and get 100 shots up. Do it again after your next class. Practice at three, and if the cafeteria closed at six, hope you'd be done by five so you could sprint in before it closed." The players learned which day was cheesesteak day, sending a runner over ahead of the pack to hold as many sandwiches for his teammates as possible.

Possessed by a near mania to play the right way, Massimino simply could not abide laziness or foolishness. He employed a favorite tactic for practices he thought were less than exemplary, halting the Wildcats mid-drill and insisting they start over. "I mean like get on the floor and stretch, start over from the beginning," Pinckney says. Or he'd yell to his managers, "Get the buckets," and line his players up for punishing seventeens, a drill in which the players had to complete seventeen sprints across the width of the court in under ninety seconds. Players regularly vomited afterward—hence the buckets. After bad road trips, the Wildcats would head into the annex, a rubber-floored metal shed addition to the fieldhouse that felt like a sauna thanks to an uncontrollable thermostat.

Long before film sessions became part of regular practice sessions, truly committed Wildcats would set up a reel-to-reel projector in the locker room and watch games, looking for an edge. No detail was to be overlooked, no extra step not taken.

He worked his staff equally hard. The assistant assigned to scout was expected not just to be able to break down every single offensive play but also to lay out how the opponent might play against every conceivable defense. Massimino prided himself on taking teams out of their comfort zones and taking away their options, manipulating and maneuvering his defensive schemes until he landed on the perfect wrinkle to disrupt an opponent's plan. "He'd show [an opponent] one defense as a zone, but, knowing what they were going to do, he'd switch to a man-to-man," Lappas says. "So all of a sudden a team is running a zone offense against a man-to-man defense." In today's era, where nearly every game is televised and the Internet offers services exclusively built for scouting, finding such nuances isn't terribly hard. At that time, though, it meant hitching up a 35 mm projector and watching whatever game film an assistant could find. Unable to edit, the staff played entire game films for the players, stretching practice another ninety minutes or more, just so the Wildcats entered each game armed with as much information as the assistants could gather.

Yet as demanding as he was, Massimino wanted a democracy, not a dictatorship. Assistants were expected to voice their opinions and come up with solutions to problems, not merely exist as robots at the head coach's disposal. "In practice, if you didn't say something for five minutes, he'd kill you," says Buonaguro, who joined the Villanova staff as a twenty-three-year-old in 1977. Like Wright, he enjoyed an immediate baptism into the twenty-four-hour-a-day world of working for Massimino, the days bleeding into nights. But he also realized that in the course of those endless duties, he learned every trick of the coaching trade. "I remember him telling me, 'Look, if you're going to get anywhere in coaching, you've got to be a good all-around coach.'" So along with designing defenses, building offenses, and recruiting players, Massimino taught his young assistant how to schmooze alumni, deal with the media, work with the administration, and communicate with players.

If that had been the end of it, it would have been enough, but Massimino brought as much dedication to his socializing as he did to his work. Sunday practices morphed into Eagles watch parties at the head coach's house, players and staff invited over in the days when televisions weren't standard in dorm rooms. In part it fueled Massimino's insatiable need to be around people, but it also fostered the notion of the team as family, a hokey concept that morphed into a team chemistry that, when developed properly, evolved into an almost kinetic connection.

This was all part of the pitch Massimino made when he walked into recruits' living rooms, wooing parents and players with the promise of togetherness and pasta and sealing the deal with the allure of the Big East. He struck the perfect note, selling the chance to play among the conference's titans but as an underdog, finding players who were as hungry as he was to prove something.

Before summer league basketball exploded into a big business, the best of the best gathered at Howard Garfinkel's Five-Star Basketball Camp in the Pocono Mountains in northeast Pennsylvania. The summer of '79, the roster read like a future who's who—Ewing, Mullin, Charles Barkley, Karl Malone, Michael Jordan, all targeted for college two years later, all on the top of every college coach's priority list. Slightly down that list sat a collection of players who bonded over their B-list status—Dwayne McClain, Gary McLain, and Pinckney.

Buonaguro recruited McClain and McLain to Villanova, and asked the two to help make the pitch to Pinckney, a scrawny kid out of the Bronx known as "EZ Ed" who Buonaguro thought could be a star. Pinckney's world was small, his knowledge of basketball limited to St. John's, the Louie and Bouie Show in Syracuse, and the collection of brand-name teams featured on television, most from the ACC. He thought he was good enough to play for any of them. The schools, though, didn't seem to agree. "I'm playing on these AAU teams in New York City and I have this buddy, Mullin, and I can't get recruited to the schools he's going to," Pinckney says. "He'd say, 'You going there?' And

I'm like, 'Man, they're not even looking at me. I got Providence and this other school, Villanova.'" Which, of course, made Pinckney the perfect target for Massimino.

The head coach and Buonaguro rolled up to 1817 Story Avenue in the Bronx in a big Cadillac, Massimino overruling Buonaguro's worries that the ostentatious car might not fit in the neighborhood ("Rollie was not subtle about anything," Buonaguro says), and took the elevator to the fifth floor. "Our whole neighborhood, the apartment building is looking out the windows like, 'Who the hell is this little Italian dude getting out of the car with the Jersey license plates? What the hell is going on?'" Pinckney remembers. The youngest of seven and something of a mama's boy, Pinckney was tailor-made for Massimino's pitch. His mother, a nurse, knew little and cared less about her son's future basketball career, interested only in a place that would nurture him and see to it that he graduated. In Massimino she saw a man with a plan that suited her. "Honestly, my family was thinking, 'Hey, go play in the Big East, that's good, but you're going to get an education and come back and go to work,'" Pinckney says.

Instead he and his Five-Star B-list buddies formed the nucleus of a team that delivered to Villanova, the Big East, and college basketball one of its most unforgettable moments. Even without the Wildcats and their upset victory, the 1985 Final Four would rank as a transcendent moment for the conference. From nothing, the Big East had birthed two teams that owned college basketball. In the seventeen-week season that year, either Georgetown or St. John's held the number one ranking, the Hoyas ceding the top spot after losing to the Red Storm in January, and regaining it following the epic Sweater Game a month later.

That the two steamrolled to Lexington, Kentucky, and the Final Four surprised no one, and their successes alone would have shown the Big East's might. Party-crashing Villanova took things to another level. Billed forever as the ultimate Cinderella champion, the truth is the Wildcats actually were underachievers in the 1984–85 season. By their senior seasons, Pinckney and company had 67 wins and twice had been to the Elite Eight, losing as freshmen to Houston and to North Carolina as juniors. They entered their senior season with big but what they believed to be reasonable dreams. Accustomed to the demands of their coach and one another, the Wildcats easily mastered the family connection Massimino preached. They genuinely liked and trusted one another, but for reasons that all these years later no one can quite determine, it didn't manifest itself right away on the court.

A 13–3 start masked the Wildcats' warts, but a 30-point night by Maryland's Len Bias began the exposure, the loss to the Terrapins sending Villanova into a tailspin. The Cats lost five of their next seven games, including a humiliating and nationally televised 85–62 loss to Pittsburgh in the regular-season finale, a game in which the starters played so poorly, the coach yanked them early in the second half and made them watch as the gap between the two teams grew wider. Massimino was exasperated. Here was a team that had everything he strove for—experience, camaraderie, defense—and yet ended the regular season a very pedestrian 18–9.

The Wildcats avenged the loss to Pitt, beating the Panthers in the Big East Tournament, but after a loss to St. John's, they barely snuck onto the newly expanded NCAA bracket, making it as the eighth seed. Still, they viewed the tournament as a new season and believed that despite their lackluster regular season, their coaching staff had armed them with a secret weapon for March. "Give us a handful of days to prepare for someone— there was just a quiet confidence," says Harold Jensen.

Massimino packed a playbook that included no fewer than

fifty-five defensive schemes for his team's tourney journey, intent on using the absence of a shot clock, which had been used experimentally during the Big East regular season that year, to his team's advantage. Villanova would average a record-low 55.2 points per game during its six-game run to the title, turning the clock into a sixth defender. Befitting a team coming from a low seed, the Wildcats did not exactly storm their way to the Final Four. They needed a last-second defensive stop to beat Dayton (at Dayton), had to overcome an eight-minute scoreless drought against top-seeded Michigan, and then get by Maryland, the team that had started their tailspin months earlier, to reach an Elite Eight date with North Carolina.

Despite the power of his own league, Massimino considered the Tar Heels the standard-bearer and their coach, Dean Smith, the sport's epitome of class and success. Which may be partly why the first half of that game ate at Massimino so much. Villanova played horribly, missing 20 of 26 shots in the first half, saved only by a McClain and-one play at the halftime buzzer that made it 22–17. Smith opined later that, considering how poorly his team shot, Massimino had to feel good at the half. He did not. His aggravation at the boiling point, Massimino stormed into the locker room and gave the most absurd speech in the history of rallying cries, a talk known fondly as The Pasta Speech. "Do you think I want to be doing this?" Massimino screamed to his team. "Do you think I want to be screaming at you? Do you fuckers really think I want to go to the Final Four? Listen, there's so much more to life than that. Do you know what I'd really rather be doing now more than anything? Than being here in this room? I'll tell you. I'd rather be at home, sitting behind a big, steaming, heaping plate of spags. Yeah, that's right. Macaroni! Linguine with clam sauce. I'd rather be doing that than losing this damn game! Now get out there and do what got you here in the first place."

"It definitely cut the air in the room," Jensen says. "I will say this. He became a different coach in the tournament, and what I mean by that is he came down a notch. He really tried to simplify and kind of almost mellow the situation: 'This is a basketball game. This is what you do. Don't get caught up in the fact that the lights are brighter.'"

Galvanized by the garlic and roused by the ragù, the Wildcats connected on 16 of 21 shots in the second half, outscoring the Tar Heels by 17 in the final 20 minutes. At game's end, with the Wildcats running out the clock using the four corners offense Smith had invented, Smith called his starters to the bench, allowing Massimino to enjoy his moment. Pinckney jumped on the scorer's table, arms spread, while Massimino celebrated with his son and assistant coach, R.C., before his players hoisted him onto their shoulders.

Villanova's win silenced any lingering Big East critics, the nascent league doing what no conference had done prior or since: sending three teams to the national semifinals. Were it not for Memphis State, which beat Boston College in the Elite Eight on an Andre Turner bucket with 1 second remaining, the conference would have gone four for four. "Dave was like a Christmas tree that whole weekend," says Pierce, the Boston reporter, of Gavitt. "He was the happiest human being in the whole world."

While Villanova fought its way through the bracket to the title game, St. John's and Georgetown barreled their way to Rupp Arena, St. John's challenged just once, by Arkansas in the second round, and Georgetown hardly breaking a sweat. They all converged on Lexington, Kentucky, in a hoop-mad commonwealth fevered to host the Final Four. Georgetown towered as the obvious favorite, and Villanova was the lovable underdog, the Wildcats' hotel lobby constantly stuffed with fans giddy that their upstart team had made it so far.

Media and pundits understandably saw the national semifinal between St. John's and Georgetown as the bigger game, disappointed that the bracket didn't put the two teams opposite each other for the championship. Befitting their status as a warm-up act, Villanova and Memphis State tipped off first. The Tigers had size via Keith Lee and William Bedford, but they also had skill with Turner at the guard spot, and had been averaging 72 points per game. But Massimino's defenses befuddled Dana Kirk's squad into a pretzel, Memphis State managing just 45 points to Villanova's 52. Afterward the Wildcats sat in the stands to watch the headliners, while the coaching staff found seats at the press table. Buonaguro had the Georgetown scout, but he didn't need a lot of information; he'd prepped the Wildcats for the Hoyas during the regular season and knew the team well.

Secretly, the staff and players hoped the Hoyas would win. Had the coaches said that aloud, folks probably would have checked their temperatures. No one wanted to play Georgetown, the Hoyas by then working like a wrecking ball. "We were high-fiving each other out of sight when Georgetown won," Jensen says. "It's crazy to think. I mean, people were like, 'You really want Patrick Ewing on Monday night?' 'Yeah, we do.'" The Wildcats understood they matched up better against the Hoyas, having played them close in each of their games that season, while a 15-point Big East Tournament loss to St. John's still lingered in the back of their minds. "Bad matchup for us," Pinckney says of the Red Storm. "Just bad."

Georgetown had the same hold over St. John's, the Hoyas winning both the Sweater Game and the Big East Tournament title in the run-up to the Final Four. Though he didn't filibuster quite as much as Massimino did in the Pasta Speech, Carnesecca did his best to similarly take the pressure off of his team. After the disappointing Big East tourney loss, he told the bus driver to pull over to Dante's, the team's favorite Italian haunt just off campus. The Red Storm shuffled in, and their coach encouraged them to open the menu and order what they wanted. "I remember it like it was yesterday," Mullin says. "He said, 'I'm with you after wins and losses.' He always knew what button to push."

But there was no magic button to fix St. John's problems against Georgetown. In the national semifinal, the Hoyas continued their dominance over their rival. Suffocating Mullin and allowing him to take just one shot in the entire second half, Georgetown won easily, 77–59. In the final game of his collegiate career, Mullin scored just 8 points, ending a 101-game streak of double figures. Carnesecca entered the disconsolate locker room and did his best to strike a positive note, reminding his players of all they had to be proud of, all they had accomplished, but at the time no one could see it. "Not only do you lose the chance to win a championship, but your career is over," Mullin says. "It's just, I don't know. It's just, wow. That's it. It's all over in one night. You're done. I think I was more tired and worn-out by the finality of it all than anything."

Heartbroken, Mullin went home to New York. He didn't even turn on the national championship game, and has only seen it in snippets since.

The dominant win only added to Georgetown's lore. Reporters casually tossed around the word *dynasty*, the national title game against Villanova viewed as a mere formality en route to Georgetown's coronation. The Wildcats knew no one thought they had a chance, but Massimino and his staff game-planned endlessly. He pressed managers into service, dishing out yellow pinnies so that when his team practiced their offense, they'd face an eight-man defensive squad. He boiled down the playbook to a handful of sets, but planned it so that the Wildcats would switch defenses frequently, starting with a zone but switching to a matchup or man-to-man in the hope of confusing the Hoyas. They'd double-team Ewing, a wrinkle they hadn't used in the regular season, and above all else, they'd be patient. During its NCAA Tournament run, Villanova made the lack of a shot clock its ally, and the Wildcats would rely on that strategy even more against Georgetown, working the ball for the best shot so as not to squander possessions.

On the morning of the championship, the team gathered for its regular pregame meal at the hotel—pasta, of course. Massimino wasn't one for early-morning speeches, but he made an exception that day. Rather than fire and brimstone, he spoke quietly, telling his team to envision winning. "Rollie really thought we were going to win," Buonaguro says. "He conveyed that. People ask me what the key was to the whole thing, and, well, I thought Rollie's take on the whole thing was winning. There was never any ounce of being afraid or the moment was too big." Coaches all say that, but Massimino had reason to believe it.

The Big East had not only elevated his program to national heights but demystified Georgetown. Others across the country saw the Hoya Paranoia, the formidable Thompson, and the imposing Ewing and wilted at the mere thought of handling it all. But to the Wildcats, the Hoyas were just another conference opponent. "That Georgetown team inspired fear all over the country, but not in us," Lappas says. Backed by a crowd that was as much anti-Georgetown as it was pro-Villanova, the Wildcats put together a game that still mesmerizes to this day, a taut contest that went down to the wire and, with the magic that only March can bring, turned everyday players into stars.

Unlike so many of his peers, Jensen grew up at the knee of the Big East. Raised in Connecticut, he frequented UConn and Providence games as a kid, where he'd watch Georgetown's Floyd in awe. Talented but scrawny, he was tickled when his hero coaches came calling to recruit him. Massimino showed up to his house wearing a pink suede jacket, Buonaguro lugging a projector into the living room. His parents scrambled in the attic to find a screen, and after a few technical difficulties, everyone settled in to watch a video the staff had put together about Villanova. Jensen liked the pitch, but he liked even more the way the Wildcats played. He thought he could see himself in their lineup.

But he didn't quite fit in as seamlessly as he hoped, averaging just 2.7 points as a freshman and 4.5 in his sophomore year. He spent hours in Massimino's office, often in tears, frustrated that he couldn't realize his own expectations. Yet Massimino never waffled in his support, not just saying what Jensen needed to hear but allowing his actions to speak to his confidence in his player. He kept putting Jensen in, big moments in big games, convinced the kid would find his stride.

In the title game, Massimino called his number again, sending the sophomore in from the bench for Dwight Wilbur five minutes into the game. Nearly four decades later, Jensen weeps at the memory, overcome that his coach and his teammates believed in him. "They had my back. They wanted me to shoot the ball," he says through his tears. "They looked at me just as they did everybody else. I can't tell you how that felt, to be out there like that. It was just, 'Do your thing, man. We're here for you.' It just—I can't even tell you now how that felt." Jensen would become the poster child for Villanova's Cinderella run, the inconsistent guard draining all five of his shots and four of his free throws for a box score of perfection: 14 points.

Three times in the close game, his second-half buckets put Villanova back in the lead, and his last two free throws, made with 1:10 left to play, gave the Wildcats a 61–56 lead and officially put Georgetown into desperation mode. At game's end, he was named to the all-tournament team. "It's making me cry right now, it truly is," Jensen says. "It was such a combination of feelings, of accomplishment, of relief, of belief in yourself and in a team, jubilation, an incredible roller coaster of emotions. It's very hard to describe. It's like a shock. You did it. You did. You did what you came to do, and you made your dreams come true."

History says that the Wildcats played the perfect game, and to an extent that's true. A slew of things did magically come together for Villanova that day. They shot flawlessly, connecting on 22 of their 28 shots, and deftly controlled the tempo to keep Georgetown at bay, winning the game, 66–64. Despite playing with the flu, Pinckney outdueled Ewing, scoring 16 points and 6 rebounds to Ewing's 14 and 5. But theirs was not a game won on a fluke shot or last-minute heroics; it was a forty-minute exercise in discipline, executed flawlessly. "People say it was the greatest upset of all time," Lappas says. "It's nice people say that, but we didn't think so."

The loss stung bitterly for Georgetown, but the players remained on the court to applaud their conference foes as the Wildcats received their trophy, and Thompson graciously commended Villanova for its victory. After the game Rienzo marched down the hallway, searching for Massimino. When the Georgetown athletic director found him in the locker room, he pulled a cigar from his pocket and presented it to the victorious coach. "There was still such incredible camaraderie," Tranghese says. No one then could appreciate how the game would resonate for decades, but they did understand how much it meant for the Big East. Villanova added more than just another championship trophy to the case; it proved that the league didn't merely inherit good teams but created them.

The Wildcats returned to a packed hotel, the crowd stuffing the lobby so tightly the players couldn't move more than fifty feet in an hour. The grown-ups headed up to Massimino's suite, the celebration spilling into the hallways, while the players jumped from room to room or burned up the hotel phone lines, calling friends back home. When Villanova returned to Philadelphia, the city hosted a parade for its champions, an estimated 75,000 along the parade route and another 30,000 gathering at JFK Plaza to celebrate the victors. For days and weeks after, people mailed trinkets and cards to Jensen, Villanova's win resonating across the country as a victory for the little guy.

The title amplified the Big East in ways that not even the forward-thinking Gavitt could have imagined. But the league also was headed for a major transition. The Big East rose to incredible heights largely on the backs of an incredible recruiting class. The end of the 1985 season also closed the book on the college careers of Ewing, Mullin, and Pinckney. Having reached the apex, the league now faced perhaps its greatest challenge since inception: maintaining its high bar of excellence.

CHAPTER 8
PITINO AND THE 3-POINT REVOLUTION
"Best coaching job I've ever witnessed"

Slicing and dicing through a defense that no one sliced and diced their way through, Pearl Washington finally arrived at the last Georgetown defender between him and the basket, the seven-foot wall of Patrick Ewing. Most people—or at least most ordinary people—paused here. Washington did not pause. Instead he went up and over the man who turned shot blocking into an art form, gently laying the ball in over Ewing's head. CBS announcer Billy Packer, apoplectic at Washington's audacity, turned to Boeheim and mouthed, "What's he doing?" Boeheim responded with one of his standard-issue shrugs. "That's just Pearl," he said.

As the Big East segued out of arguably its greatest generation of players, it fittingly turned to a man whose game couldn't be stopped as the bridge to the conference's future. "He was a dazzler," Lou Carnesecca says of Washington. "He was here, there, and everywhere." With a game born on the playgrounds, Washington shake-and-baked to the rim with flair, leading a second wave of players that proved just as critical to the league's development as the first. If the dominance of the more established teams helped solidify the Big East's foundation, the emergence of new blood in the mid- to late 1980s, taking the baton from upstart Villanova, cemented the conference's power. By the time the conference celebrated its tenth anniversary, six of its nine members had competed in a Final Four, spreading its wealth in a way not seen in any other conference in the country. By comparison, the ACC, long the standard-bearer in college basketball, had sent just five of its members to the Final Four by 1989—and the league was twenty-six years older than the Big East.

But before the new blood could have their day, Washington enjoyed his. A year behind Ewing and Mullin, Washington did not want for attention. In 1984, in just his fifteenth collegiate game, he took the kick-out on a missed free throw and pushed the ball just beyond the half-court line, where he launched a nearly two-handed push shot from midcourt, swishing the bucket to give Syracuse a buzzer-beating win over Boston College. As the Carrier Dome screamed in dizzying euphoria, Boeheim walked over to shake Gary Williams's hand. "He's already standing next to me, like he knew it was going in," Williams says. "Get the hell out of here."

In due time, folks would come to expect such heroics from the kid from Brooklyn, whose style separated him from the crowd. But in some ways, Washington was a hoops Everyman. He didn't jump particularly high, play particularly fast, or shoot particularly well, but he crafted a game built on such elusiveness and street smarts, it seemed otherworldly. "Someone asked me who was the most difficult player to guard, and I said Pearl Washington," John Thompson, Jr., said. "We were known for defense, and if we pressured Pearl, he went by us, and if we came to him, he still went by us."

Before all that, before the national audience raved at his razzle-dazzle, the oldheads in the Brownsville section of Brooklyn weren't terribly amused. They nicknamed the whippersnapper Dwayne Washington "Pearl," more out of derision than compliment. Angry that the kid kept blowing by them on the court, they sneered, "Who do you think you are, the Pearl?"— referencing Earl "the Pearl" Monroe, the phenom of a decade earlier. In fact, he did, and soon everyone else agreed, the legend of the Pearl growing like whispers down the lane in New York.

Boeheim remembers the first time he went to see Washington play at Boys and Girls High School, pulling up to the gym to find the line to get in wrapped around the building. Such was the allure of Washington. Hyped by the New York City tabloids, he grew into a living legend, his exploits covered with sensational headlines—the time he scored 39 to upset Camden High School, the top team in the nation, or the game where he dropped 82. "I saw him play in high school," Ed Pinckney says. "You talk about going and watching a great actor on Broadway. It was the same with him."

Widely considered the best guard to come out of New York City in decades, he kept a stack of his recruiting mail, the letters promising the sun and the moon in return for his commitment. But Washington didn't want to stray too far from home and kept his list of potential colleges short, winnowing it to Syracuse, St. John's, and Villanova. Carnesecca opted for Mark Jackson, and the Wildcats took Jensen. Washington preferred Boeheim's up-tempo offense anyway, and Boeheim wisely didn't try to over-think things once Washington came to town. "You couldn't get the ball from him, so I basically took a spread offense and put four guys on the baseline and said to Pearl, 'Go,'" Boeheim says. "Our guys would run up to screen, and he'd wave them away. He'd just beat the guy."

It was a perfect marriage—a basketball showman given the

Action gets under way during the final game at Manley Field House in Syracuse, New York, on February 12, 1980. Georgetown spoiled Syracuse's party by breaking its 57-game home court winning streak, and John Thompson Jr.'s postgame declaration—"Manley Field House is officially closed"—served as the birth of a contentious rivalry between the Hoyas and the Orange that would define the Big East for decades.

The driving force behind the conference, Dave Gavitt, after one of his patented huddles in New York with the coaches who helped the Big East achieve national prominence. Pictured are (left to right) Jim Boeheim, Jim O'Brien, John Thompson Jr., P.J. Carlesimo, Rollie Massimino, Lou Carnesecca, Paul Evans, Dave Gavitt, Jim Calhoun, and Rick Barnes. Gavitt convinced them to move the Big East Tournament to Madison Square Garden, which made the Big East synonymous with the Big Apple's basketball mecca.

Patrick Ewing was one of the most sought-after recruits in college basketball history. His decision, announced at a press conference on February 12, 1981, to attend Georgetown and partner with John Thompson Jr. was a turning point for the upstart conference. It catapulted the league to new heights, turned Georgetown into a national power, and sent Ewing on the road to eventual NBA stardom after a storied career as a Hoya.

The only coach/player pairing in the conference's initial years that could come anywhere near rivaling John Thompson and Patrick Ewing was Syracuse's Jim Boeheim and Dwayne "Pearl" Washington. Pearl's electric style of play helped Syracuse consistently fill the 30,000-seat Carrier Dome, while he played for the school, from the 1983–84 season through the 1985–86 season. While Boeheim and Syracuse wouldn't capture a national championship until 2003, the drive to that title undoubtedly began with Pearl's commitment.

Boston College's Gary Williams shouts instructions to his team's guard Michael Adams—possibly regarding boxing St. John's coach Lou Carnesecca out of the action should he encroach onto the court of play, as was Carnesecca's habit—during the 1983 Big East Tournament final against St. John's at Madison Square Garden.

Chris Mullin and Kevin Williams of the hometown favorite St. John's celebrate their victory over Boston College in the 1983 Big East Tournament championship game—the first time the event was held at New York City's iconic Madison Square Garden—by carrying Lou Carnesecca off the court.

Two of the league's legends—Lou Carnesecca and John Thompson Jr.—share a light-hearted moment on February 27, 1985, after what became known as the Sweater Game. In the first matchup of the number one and number two ranked teams in the Garden's history, Georgetown sought to avenge a loss to St. John's earlier in the season that ended the Hoyas' 29-game win streak. In the midst of pre-game warm-ups, Thompson opened his jacket to reveal his playful tribute to Carnesecca's lucky sweater. Thompson's levity helped his team play loose and win that night, but even Carnesecca had to laugh.

The final seconds tick off the clock during Villanova's mammoth upset of defending national champion Georgetown on April 1, 1985, during the national title game in Lexington's Rupp Arena. The 1985 tournament was a crowning achievement for the Big East that saw the conference place an unprecedented three teams—St. John's, Villanova, and Georgetown—in the Final Four and cemented its stature as a basketball powerhouse.

In the 1986–87 season, Providence's brash upstart of a coach, Rick Pitino, and his hard-charging guard Billy Donovan took the league by storm by embracing a new, chaotic style of basketball that relied on the 3-point shot. Providence rode the strategy to a surprise berth in the Final Four, where they lost in the national semifinal to conference rival Syracuse. Pitino and Donovan are seen here during their Southeast Regional final victory over Georgetown, in which the Friars avenged a Big East Tournament semifinal loss to the Hoyas a few weeks earlier.

Jerome Lane's thunderous destruction of the backboard on January 25, 1988, inspired Bill Raftery's iconic call "Send it in, Jerome!" on ESPN's broadcasts. Gavitt's decision to partner with the upstart network when launching the conference proved prescient, as the Big East's *Big Monday* package turned the league into a national powerhouse just as television rights for sporting events exploded.

P.J. Carlesimo chats with former Seton Hall coach Bill Raftery during the Pirates' dream 1989 season, which featured a Cinderella-style March run to the national title game and proved that the Big East was a crucible that could help elevate any of its members to the Final Four.

Georgetown coach John Thompson Jr. was ahead of his time when it came to advocating for social justice and supporting his players both on and off the court. His unwavering support for Allen Iverson helped propel the undersized guard with unlimited heart to stardom and a series of epic clashes with UConn's Ray Allen. Thompson and Iverson are seen here during the 1995 Big East tournament at the Garden.

(left) UConn's Jim Calhoun cuts down the net after defeating Duke to win the 1999 national championship. The victory was the culmination of the scrappy Calhoun's remarkable rebuilding job at Connecticut, which transformed the Huskies from the "Northwestern of the Big East" to a national power and helped the conference enter a new era.

As the late hours of March 12 became the early morning hours of March 13 during the 2009 Big East tournament, everyone at the Garden knew they were witnessing a special game that at times didn't seem like it would ever end. An epic chapter in the relationship between the conference and the Garden, the six-overtime clash between Syracuse and UConn was an instant classic that helped send Gavitt's successor, Mike Tranghese, into retirement in style and positioned the conference for a new era.

The Big East's past, present, and future unite as former Villanova coach Rollie Massimino (right) celebrates Villanova's 2016 national championship with Jay Wright. Villanova's title triumphs in 2016 and 2018 proved that the reconstituted Big East could still compete—and win—on the national stage.

biggest stage in the sport. Washington's play electrified fans to the farthest reaches of the Carrier Dome, his presence making the folly of a 30,000-seat basketball arena suddenly seem sensible. Before he arrived, Syracuse's best single-game attendance mark had been 20,401; by his junior year, the Orange averaged more than 26,000. "He's the only person who could fill the place overnight like that," Boeheim says.

Syracuse vaulted into the top twenty-five after that court-storming, game-winning shot against Boston College, and remained there until Washington declared for the NBA following his junior season. In between lived enough highlights to stuff a room's worth of reels. "The '84 game in New York [against Georgetown], he made a crossover move, pulled up, and hit a jump shot," Tranghese says. "It's the loudest I ever heard the Garden." A local store that year printed T-shirts that read "On the Eighth Day, God Created Pearl." Few would argue, so beloved was the player, so amazing his skills.

Washington earned Rookie of the Year and All-American honors, and added flair to a league that by the time he arrived was becoming well known for its fisticuffs. "It was not an easy league to officiate in," says Art Hyland, the longtime supervisor of officials. "Where the kids were coming from, they were tough city kids. They didn't mind playing physical, using a forearm." The Big East eventually would become so volatile, its star players running into so much foul trouble, that the league would experiment with six fouls, desperate to keep guys from fouling out. Though every team was guilty of injecting some physicality into the game, no team did it better than Georgetown, and no player burnished his reputation on it more than Ewing.

Naturally, a year after the 1984 tournament final melee between Michael Graham and Andre Hawkins, Georgetown and Syracuse reunited at the Garden for the Big East semifinals in yet another must-see event. The crowd felt like a who's who,

Tom Brokaw and Dan Rather among the people there to take in the rematch. By then, everyone loved the Pearl Washington Show. No one, save Georgetown fans, loved Ewing. He was too big, too menacing, and frankly, too good. But just because Washington played pretty didn't mean he played soft. Early in the game, he shoved Ewing out of position from under the basket, and for good measure, added a hard elbow to Ewing's gut. The officials missed the extracurriculars, but it's clear on replay, Ewing even doubling over after the gut punch. What no one missed, though, was Ewing's response—"a haymaker from Bayonne," Pierce, the reporter, calls it.

By miracle and mercy, it didn't connect. Dennis Brogan, the Dome Ranger, was sitting within inches of the play. "When Patrick Ewing swung, I ducked," he says. "I told Pearl later, 'He didn't touch you. He touched your aura.' If he had hit him, it would have taken his head off." While Washington danced away and Ewing lay on the floor, the TV replays showed Washington's uncalled jabs, but no one in the Garden—including the officials— saw what had happened. "When that happened, we had to make a decision, and hopefully make the right one," says Tim Higgins, who was on the call with Larry Lembo and Jody Sylvester. "Posterity shows maybe we didn't." Instead Washington was whistled for only a personal foul, while Ewing was assessed a technical, to the delight of the jeering fans, who thought the whole thing fit with who Ewing was. "He shoved me, and I just hit him in the ribs," Washington admitted after the game. "It was just reaction."

Ewing got the final word, his 15 points and 12 rebounds solidifying the Hoyas' win, but Washington's willingness to go toe-to-toe with the biggest, baddest star in college basketball only burnished his reputation. That year, 1984–85, while three of its Big East peers made history by reaching the Final Four together, Syracuse lost to Georgia Tech in the second round of the NCAA Tournament.

But the following year, with Mullin and Ewing in the pros, Washington took center stage.

During the 1985–86 season, Syracuse floated in the top ten for all but two weeks of what would be Washington's final year, never dipping below twelfth. In New York in the annual tournament, Washington gifted fans and the conference with yet another unforgettable night in Madison Square Garden, and proved that the Big East still had just as much draw and appeal as it had in the Ewing and Mullin heyday. In an epic final against St. John's, the Red Storm clawed back from 13 down, pulling ahead when Ron Rowan hit an off-balance floater. But 8 seconds still remained on the clock, and Washington remained on the court. He had 20 points and 14 assists already, and plenty of onlookers figured he was also packing another miracle in his arsenal.

Washington raced downcourt, but as he released his shot at the buzzer, Walter Berry chased him down. The two had grown up friends and rivals in the city, meeting for a memorable summer tournament at King Towers in Harlem, fans claiming rooftops, tree limbs, or any other perch available to see the showdown. Washington, ever the showman, arrived on a motorcycle and dropped 50 to Berry's 46.

This time, though, Washington couldn't best his buddy, Berry blocking Washington's shot from behind and securing the win for St. John's. Berry ultimately would go on to win Big East Player of the Year honors, as well as the Wooden Award as the nation's best player, but on that night in New York, he took a backseat to his rival.

In Syracuse's three-day tournament run, Washington scored 68 points and handed out 29 assists. And though his team failed to win the title, he nonetheless was voted the tournament's Most Valuable Player, the first time a player from a losing team was so honored. Washington had already left the court by the time the awards were announced and was back in the locker room, devastated, while St. John's celebrated. It was left to Tranghese to coax Washington back onto the court, the league administrator apologizing profusely that the heartbroken player had to come back out. "Walter Berry, Mark Jackson, all of those St. John's kids—they did not have one iota of envy," Tranghese says. "They all ran out and embraced Pearl. I've never seen another player captivate the Garden like Pearl did. It was an iconic moment."

With Pearl connecting the league to its next chapter, the Big East continued on with its unbelievable story. In a year's time, after Pearl had moved on to the pro ranks, Syracuse would finally reach its first Final Four—and it would be joined by an upstart that no one saw coming save its whip-smart and brash young coach.

Arriving straight from a spot as a Knicks assistant to the head-coaching gig at Providence, Rick Pitino bullied his way into the league in March 1985, cocksure and unabashedly arrogant. At his first league meeting that summer, Pitino made sure everyone knew he wasn't going to be pushed around. By 1985, with their stars on the rise and their programs reaching new heights, the coaches were starting to feel and enjoy their power. Gavitt had to work twice as hard to make sure they all followed his strict mandate of supporting one another and the league at all costs.

He used getaway weekends, which doubled as annual league meetings, to keep the peace. From Bermuda to Puerto Rico to California to Florida, he annually invited his staff, the coaches, and their spouses to mingle, golf, and dine, expecting the coaches to air their grievances behind closed doors and keep their mouths shut thereafter. Even privately, the cast stuck to their public personas, the more fiery coaches caterwauling and pointing fingers, while Carnesecca tried to make nice, Boeheim complained, Raftery cracked jokes, and Thompson, on the rare occasion he chose to attend ("I don't golf," he said by way of explaining his absence), puffed on a cigar in the corner.

The schedule was simple—meetings, dinners, golf, rinse and repeat—but Gavitt crafted them as if he were staging treaties between hostile nations. "He and my mom would literally do the [dinner] seating arrangements themselves," Gavitt's son, Dan, says. "In their minds, they were creating camaraderies and relationships, even if they were uncomfortable ones." And plenty were uncomfortable. The meetings lasted hours, beginning at eight in the morning and sometimes stretching until late in the afternoon, following the whims of those present, rather than any formal agenda. Coaches hurled accusations across the table, calling out dirty recruiting tactics, months-old complaints about bad calls, favoritism, and anything in between.

Each year Gavitt invited Hyland, his supervisor of officials, to make a quick presentation, but any attempts at civil discourse quickly devolved into screaming matches, the coaches recalling every bad whistle from the previous season. The Big East counted some of the best officials in the nation among its crews—Jim Burr worked sixteen Final Fours in his career, John Cahill and Higgins ten apiece, Paparo seven, and Lembo four—and they handled the personalities and pugnaciousness of the Big East with aplomb. They gave coaches as much leeway as they could, and tried to let the players play. "You have to understand, these guys were all type A," says Higgins. "And they were not used to losing."

At the meetings, Hyland sat placidly and let the coaches spew their venom. At Carnesecca's behest, he even crafted a picture

book so that the coach, known for an especially sharp tongue—
"He used words I never even heard of," Higgins says—could
more easily identify the official he wanted to complain about.
"We'd spend four hours cursing, throwing every ref in the league
out," Boeheim says. "At the end of one meeting, we were supposed to rate the top ten refs. We wanted them all blackballed.
And Dave would step in. 'OK. We're keeping all of them.'"

Whatever differences couldn't be settled in the meetings or
over dinner would be pushed to the golf course. Gavitt made
the pairings with intent, sending feuding coaches off on the carts
together. At Saratoga, Gavitt sent Raftery and Massimino, who'd
spent the entire meeting screaming at each other over a subject
long since forgotten, out for a round. "They came back, they
were drinking, laughing, and hugging," Tranghese says.

But in 1985, not even Gavitt could ease the tensions. Bucky
Waters, a former broadcaster and coach, presented an offer to
the coaches that year. Wilson, the ball company, was willing to
pay a total of $67,500 if all the coaches would agree to use their
basketballs the following season. This was long before coaches
made millions off of contracts and millions more off of shoe
deals. A ball deal was a big deal.

But Massimino argued that Villanova, Georgetown, Syracuse, and St. John's, each already a national champion or Final
Four participant, ought to get $12,500 apiece, with a $3,500
share for Seton Hall, Boston College, UConn, Providence, and
Pittsburgh. Pitino, new to the league but hardly afraid, politely
raised his hand. "If we're all in this together, I think we should
all get $7,500," he said.

Pitino says now that he was egged on by Carlesimo, who
convinced him that Massimino would listen because of his NBA
background, and Tranghese backs Pitino up on this. Carlesimo
pleads innocence regarding such a setup. But no one disputes
the outcome. After maybe a beat of silence, Massimino erupted:

"You fucking young whippersnapper, who do you think you are?" Figuring he had to stand his ground, Pitino went right back at the more established coach, the two nearly coming to blows. Gavitt suggested they table the conversation, and naturally paired the duo for golf. It didn't work. "Ninety-five degrees, unbelievable humidity," Pitino says. "I walked all eighteen holes."

Not until the fall did they figure out the ball deal. Carnesecca, who missed the summer fireworks, listened as Massimino made his pitch again before the season. "Let me ask you a question," Carnesecca said in response. "If the eight of you come to my mother's house, and she serves apple pie for dessert, am I going to cut you four big slices and four small, or eight of equal size? When you move out of a house, you don't take the chandeliers. You leave the chandeliers. Let's leave the chandeliers." The coaches agreed to equal shares of $7,500 apiece, Pitino earning what he thought was an important piece of respect as he tried to make something out of Providence.

The great irony of the Big East did not go unnoticed by Gavitt. The league he created took off with even more success than he could imagine, but his own school—Providence College—languished in the basement. The Friars failed to win more than five league games in the conference's first six seasons, Pitino inheriting a squad that finished 11–20 overall and 3–13 in the conference.

Pitino knocked the entire program on its ear and shook it for good measure. When two players showed up thirty minutes late for their first meeting with their new coach, he made them run five miles a day for six days (five times six equals thirty) at five in the morning. He created a round-the-clock program that essentially boiled down to three practice sessions per day. The Friars would work out individually in the morning before class, as a team in the afternoon, and double back after study hall concluded at 10 p.m., for either scouting report work or shooting drills. "It was shell shock for a lot of guys," says Providence guard Billy Donovan, who would go on to be an NBA coach and a two-time national championship–winning coach at Florida. "If you weren't a basketball junkie, it could be really hard."

Fortunately, Donovan was a gym rat, though initially he wasn't quite sure if he should stick around the Providence gym. A Long Island kid who came out of high school the same year as Washington, Mark Jackson, and Kenny Smith, Donovan was thrilled when Pitino's predecessor, Joe Mullaney, invited him for a visit to Providence. He was less thrilled when he spent most of his first two years as a spectator, stuck on the bench watching the Ewing, Mullin, and Pearl Show. He thought maybe he ought to transfer, but found few schools interested.

When Pitino came in, Donovan liked the new coach's up-tempo brand of basketball, and liked even more that Pitino had a plan for him. Pitino told the guard if he got his mind straight and his body right, he could have an amazing career. Donovan lost 20 pounds and logged hour after hour in the gym, blossoming from a 3-points-a-game scorer to 15 points a game, tripling his playing time, and helping the Friars jump to 17 wins and into the NIT semifinals. It was a stunning reversal of fortunes for both player and team, and Pitino had reason to believe Providence would be even better the following year.

Delray Brooks, a onetime high school basketball player of the year and Mr. Indiana, had left Indiana, frustrated over a lack of playing time under Bob Knight, and transferred to Providence. He'd be eligible in December, the 6'4" guard adding some much-needed size to what Pitino called his "Smurf backcourt," with the 5'11" Donovan and 5'11" Carlton Screen.

Pitino also thought his team might have a secret weapon. Before the 1986–87 season began, a man by the name of Ed Steitz, a studious and deliberate former athletic director, up-ended college basketball. The secretary-editor of the NCAA rules committee, he convinced his group of twelve to vote in favor of adding a 3-point shot to the college game. The ACC had experimented with the long-distance shot years earlier, but tabled it after coaches complained bitterly that it took away from the essence of the sport. Steitz, though, studied the shot for years. As early as the 1970s, he put some markings on his driveway and told his son, Bob, to start launching, inviting neighborhood boys to defend him. Years later Steitz attended clinics, tournaments, and games, creating shot charts to better understand how the game was being played.

By the early 1980s, college basketball had become a scrum, the big men creating a mess of bodies in the post while guard play had all but been eliminated. Steitz thought it was time to add the 3-pointer. Not many agreed, a preseason National Association of Basketball Coaches poll revealing that 65 percent of the coaches were against the new shot. Massimino convinced his Big 5 peers in Philadelphia to begin a letter-writing campaign against it, and Duke head coach Mike Krzyzewski loudly denigrated the shot. Knight said he hoped Steitz would be proven to be as useful as Ford's failed Edsel.

While his peers complained, Pitino saw opportunity. "It's not what I saw in the 3-point shot so much as what I saw in our team—overweight players who couldn't play," Pitino says. "We needed to find a gimmick, and we found two. The full-court press was good to us, and the 3-point shot. Once Billy went from Billy the Pear to Billy the Kid, we became a very good team." Before the Friars' first practice that year, Pitino had a manager put a piece of tape on the floor, where the 3-point line would sit. He pulled Donovan, Brooks, and Pop Lewis onto the court and showed them the tape. "I don't want you shooting anywhere but beyond this line," he told them. "The worst shot you can take is on the line." From that first practice, Providence worked on taking threes and defending threes, Pitino determined to be the best at taking the nouveau shot and the best at stopping it.

He thought if the Friars took around 16 or 17 threes a game, and made 5 or 6, they'd have an advantage. An exhibition game against the Russian national team proved his calculations were off, with the Russians taking 32 three-pointers to the Friars' 24. Pitino revised his math, telling his players they needed to take around 22 and make 7. "It was incredible how we changed," Donovan says. "All your life you're taught defensively to run all the way back to the paint, build out, and guard the ball. His whole thing was, 'We're not going to run back. We're going to get to the 3-point line.' He was so far ahead of the curve." As Pitino thought it could, the three became the great equalizer for Providence, turning a mediocre team into a competitor.

The same team that won but three Big East games three years earlier started 6–2 in the league, beating Villanova, eleventh-ranked Georgetown, and number fifteen St. John's in that run. As Pitino predicted, his opponents were ill-prepared for the newfangled shot, and the Friars did indeed win by making threes and stopping them. In a 96–78 rout of Villanova, Brooks alone sank 8 of 9, while the Wildcats were 0 for 6.

As his team began to assert itself, Pitino continued to do the same. Just as he did in that '85 meeting, he continued to stand toe-to-toe with the legends in his league, recognizing that he had to show his Friars the sort of fight he expected them to play with. In the game against Georgetown, senior Jacek Duda, a big body not known for much production, met the Hoya freshman Mark Tillmon, a McDonald's All-American, at the rim as Tillmon went for a breakaway layup. Duda not only fouled Tillmon but unintentionally pinned his finger against the backboard. An irate Thompson stormed down the sideline screaming, "Is that the way you teach your players to play?" Kneeling in front of his bench, Pitino had no idea why Thompson was yelling until one of his assistants explained that the fury was directed at him. For good measure, Thompson added "punk" to his verbal assaults. Incensed that Thompson was screaming at him, Pitino also was slightly amused at the irony that the Georgetown coach, known for his physical, brawling style of play, was labeling his team dirty. "We had an altar-boy-type team," he says. "If a fight breaks out, maybe one or two of our guys fight. The rest start praying."

Pitino went right back at Thompson, at one point suggesting the coach "grow up." The two met at midcourt, still jawing. "I'm standing there, basically screaming at his navel," says Pitino, referencing the massive height difference between the two. They eventually retreated to their corners, each assessed a technical foul. Providence won the game, 82–79. Years later, Thompson confessed with a chuckle, "I knew our team didn't have it that night. I was just trying to get them going." A month later, Georgetown would exact resounding revenge, thumping the Friars, 90–79, in D.C.

But Pitino's grand plan worked. Providence did, in fact, lead the nation in made 3-point field goals per game (8.24), riding the wave to a stunning turnaround, finishing fourth in the Big East with a 10–6 record. Few expected much more. But, having dared to dream, the Friars dreamed bigger, thinking they could even win the Big East Tournament. Instead they were rolled once again by Georgetown in the semifinals, the 84–66 loss demoralizing the previously giddy team. "I tell the team, 'One of the few teams in the nation that has our number is Georgetown,'" Pitino says. "'We're not going to see them again. Don't worry about it.' I made this big speech."

The next morning, Selection Sunday, after a brief meeting, the team headed back to Rhode Island. The bus had just crossed into Connecticut when a state police officer flagged down the driver, asking him to pull over into the parking lot of a rundown building. Pitino exited the bus with the officer and went to a pay phone, where the coach learned his six-month-old son, Daniel, who had had complications since birth, had died. Pitino never returned to the bus, leaving in the patrol car while the team trudged back to campus. "Such a difficult and emotional scene," Donovan says. "To sit there and watch it all happen, everybody just sitting there, it was just awful."

Later that night, the Friars gathered to watch the bracket reveal without their coach, the Friars' name popping up as sixth seed opposite Alabama-Birmingham. "Just no emotion," Donovan says, the team still numb from Daniel's death. After delaying its NCAA Tournament departure a day so the players could attend Daniel's funeral, the team met for their flight to Birmingham, site of their first weekend of games. Donovan remembers boarding the plane, terrified he'd have to sit next to his head coach. "What do you say?" he remembers thinking. Sure enough, the coach took the middle seat, Donovan flanking him on one side and Brooks on the other. Before the uncomfortable college kids could stumble on their words of condolence, Pitino put his players at ease. "I could tell they didn't know what to say or do," Pitino says. "I just told them, 'You can help all of us by focusing on winning. The longer this goes, the easier this will be for me. Basketball is a meaningful distraction.' And that's exactly what happened. You don't get over it, but you have to get through it, and they helped me do that."

Worried about his head coach, Gavitt instructed Tranghese to travel with Providence, and the assistant commissioner watched mesmerized as the fates conspired in the Friars' favor. They should have faced top-seeded Illinois in the second round. Instead, Austin Peay upset the Illini. They should have lost to Austin Peay, trailing by 10 with less than 6 minutes to play, but rallied to win in overtime. Alabama brought 28 wins, an SEC title, and a league MVP in Derrick McKey to the regional semi-final, but Donovan hit five 3-pointers and scored 26, and the

Friars limited McKey to just 11 points, well below his 18.9 average, in the 21-point rout. "We wanted so badly to be happy, and I remember waiting somewhere to get picked up and I looked at Rick and said, 'You OK?'" Tranghese recalls. "He says, 'I'm as good as I'll ever be.' Best coaching job I've ever witnessed."

Fate, of course, can be as fickle as it can be helpful. "Who do you think we have to play to get to the Final Four?" Pitino says. "Georgetown." Pitino offered a quick pivot on his previous speech, insisting that his team, in fact, was lucky to face the Hoyas—because Georgetown had twice pulverized Providence, there was no way the Hoyas would take the Friars seriously. For a little insurance, the coach used his one day off between games to essentially re-create the Friars' entire offensive approach. Knowing that the Hoyas would guard the 3-point line ferociously and deny Donovan, Brooks, and Lewis, Pitino put the game into his frontcourt players' hands. It seemed foolhardy at best. Only Dave Kipfer, a senior, averaged double digits; the rest were utility players. And the 3-point shot was the most reliable weapon in Providence's very slim arsenal.

And yet there went the Friars, executing their new offense to near perfection. Twenty of Providence's first 24 points came from inside the lane, little-used Steve Wright scoring 12 in the first half. Brooks and Donovan essentially served as decoys, the two taking a single 3-pointer apiece. With their defense caught off guard and their offense unable to handle the relentless press, the Hoyas barely challenged, the Friars rolling to the Final Four on the heels of an 88–73 rout. A teary-eyed Pitino watched as his players did most of the work of snipping down the net, with Pitino himself ascending to make the final cut.

On the other side of the bracket that year, a Syracuse team without a transcendent star put the finishing touches on its own magical season, led there by a player whose success was every bit as unexpected as Providence's. Sherman Douglas grew up in

D.C., switching from ACC obsession as a youth to being a Big East diehard in his teens. Georgetown, parked practically in his backyard, dominated the scene and turned basketball into an attitude. He loved it, loved the Big East brashness and all of these schools just a short drive away going at one another. And they were on TV, a big deal to a young kid.

But at just 6'0", Douglas also understood his literal shortcomings. He wasn't surprised that Thompson didn't come knocking at his door. Disappointed, sure, but not angry. And he went to Syracuse knowing full well what he was getting into—a lot of time on the bench, being a spectator for the Pearl Show. "I just wanted to be in that league," Douglas says. "People thought I was crazy, going with Pearl, but they didn't understand my expectations. I believed in myself." Besides, Douglas had seen what could happen up close. Michael Graham had gone to his high school, Spingarn, and had just won a national championship. There was always a chance.

He went to his first practice determined to show what he could do against Washington. It went as expected, which is to say not well. "He was a man-child, and I was just out of high school," Douglas says. He didn't back down, just worked harder, still certain he belonged—until his coach kept recruiting people at his guard position. While Douglas bided his time on the bench, Boeheim added Earl Duncan and Stevie Thompson to the roster, both hotshot recruits out of Los Angeles. That Boeheim could entice the two to the snowbanks of Syracuse spoke volumes about the Big East's expanding reach. Years earlier, if the coach went out west, people asked where Syracuse was. But with the conference buoyed by the expanding ESPN contract, now when he traveled through the airport, a baggage handler stopped Boeheim to ask him how the Pearl was doing.

Boeheim's gain, though, threatened to be Douglas's loss. Worried where he fit in the coach's plans, he spent many a night his freshman season wondering if he'd made a mistake. But then Washington left early for the NBA, and at Duncan's first practice, Douglas did to him what Pearl had done to him. "Sherman was the most competitive kid I'd seen. He'd fight you for a nickel," Boeheim says. "Earl came in thinking he'd get Pearl's job. Sherman mercilessly beat him every damned practice. Every play, he just killed him." Duncan wound up failing to qualify academically as a freshman and, unable to beat out Douglas the following year, transferred. "Sherman pretty much ran him out of town," Boeheim says.

Of course, fans didn't see what Boeheim saw in practice, and understandably no one expected much out of Douglas. They hoped he could be a good enough facilitator to manage a talented team that included Thompson, Rony Seikaly, Greg Monroe, and freshman Derrick Coleman. Instead Douglas, a 5-point, 2-assist player as a freshman, turned into a 17-point, 7-assist force of nature as a sophomore. "I could see something there, but I don't think anyone saw what happened," Boeheim says. "I didn't see it, and then all of a sudden, he's the best guard in the league. He was great right away." What Boeheim underestimated, what everyone underestimated, was Douglas's competitive fire. Boeheim now likens it to the same fire that burned inside the greats, Michael Jordan and Kobe Bryant—a need to beat the opposition every day. What Douglas lacked in skills, he overcame with desire, daily effort, and energy.

And while no one could match Washington's flair, Douglas brought his own verve to the game, teaming with Thompson to make the alley-oop an art form. Syracuse fans still talk about the time Douglas made like a football center and hiked the ball nearly the length of the court to Thompson in a regular-season game against Indiana.

But it's Syracuse's epic March run that solidified Douglas's place in the school's history and added even more cachet to the

Big East. During Washington's tenure, the Orange never managed to get out of the first weekend of the NCAA Tournament, losing to Virginia, Georgia Tech, and most frustratingly to David Robinson and Navy in a game played at the Carrier Dome. Yet along came Douglas, nicknamed "The General," leading a charge that barreled through North Carolina and all the way to within a buzzer-beater of a championship. "It started with Pearl. He was the godfather of modern Syracuse basketball," Douglas says. "He was the guy that put us on the map. It was just up to us to keep it there." By knocking off the Tar Heels in the Elite Eight, Syracuse legitimized its spot among the national powers and even added more credence to the might of its league. Two years after putting three teams in the Final Four, here came the Big East again, taking up half the national semifinals.

Boeheim had a genuine fondness for Pitino, dating back to the early years when he wooed him onto his staff on the day of his wedding. The two remained close after Pitino left Syracuse to become head coach at Boston University, Boeheim giggling to himself as the fiery coach bullied his way into the Big East coaches' meetings.

He respected the Providence team maybe more than most, impressed with how Pitino manipulated the 3-point line to his benefit. Boeheim says he still believes that had the Friars made the title game, they likely would have won it all, so ill-prepared were Indiana and UNLV to face the onslaught of shooters. But Boeheim, matched with Providence in the semifinals, wouldn't be caught sleeping. He'd seen the Friars up close and knew well that, no matter how small and unathletic they might appear, they weren't to be taken lightly. The Orange had beaten the Friars twice that season and understood how to handle them. They'd force Donovan to drive, deny him open looks, and use their considerable size advantage, courtesy of Seikaly and Coleman, to their advantage.

If he had any worries that his team might be overconfident, Boeheim put them to rest the morning of the semifinal game. He walked into the team meeting to find his players uncharacteristically agitated, everyone yelling and hollering, and strangely hyped. Turns out one of his walk-ons had gotten hold of a newspaper article in which Providence assistant coach Gordon Chiesa opined that the Friars were glad they were facing Syracuse in the semis. "I didn't have to say anything," Boeheim says. "I just said, 'Let's go play, guys.'"

The game between the two will not go down as a thing of beauty, Providence's pressure doing its best to muck up the rhythm of things (the Friars fouled Syracuse thirty-three times) and the Big East animosity leading to an actual fist-swinging fight. A shoving match between Douglas and Brooks spread to the frontcourt, where Coleman and Kipfer went at it, too. "Oh my God, punches thrown, three guys on the ground, technical fouls," Donovan says. "It looked like a hockey game." Officials assessed Douglas with a technical and the game went on, but the ugly didn't stop, at least not for Providence. The Friars shot just 5 of 19 from the arc, Donovan so much a non-factor he went 3 for 12 in shooting and hit but one 3-pointer. Syracuse ousted its league rival, 77–63, moving on to face Bob Knight and Indiana in the title game.

To this day, Boeheim considers the championship the one that got away. Syracuse led Indiana by eight early in the second half, and did essentially everything to position itself to win a national title—except make free throws. Lousy shooters at the line all season, the Orange missed 9 in the game and 2 in the final minutes, the most damning when Coleman clanked the front end of a one-and-one with 28 seconds to play and Syracuse up 73–72. Boeheim went to a box-and-one, Douglas ensuring that sharpshooting Steve Alford wouldn't get the last shot. That left junior college transfer Keith Smart with the ball and a decision to make, launching a shot over the fingertips of Howard Triche and into Indiana history. To this day, Indiana fans still simply call it The Shot.

While the Hoosiers celebrated their unexpected victory, the Orange quietly gathered in their locker room before returning, gutted, to their team hotel. "I just went to sleep," says Boeheim. To this day, Douglas says he's not over the loss, and when asked how long he carried it with him, Boeheim chuckles ruefully. "Until 2003," he says, referring to the year Syracuse finally won it all.

Even in defeat, Syracuse's appearance in the title game was powerful for the league. It marked the fourth time in the Big East's less-than-ten-year existence that at least one conference team contended for the championship, a run matched only by the much older and more established ACC. And not even that vaunted league could match the Big East for variety, with five Big East members making the Final Four by 1987 compared to just four for the ACC. "Our league empowered everybody," Boeheim says. "Most leagues, you had a couple of teams that were there all the time. In our league, you could go from the bottom to the top."

Indeed, maybe no team proved the power of the Big East better than the one that would come next: Seton Hall.

CHAPTER 9

OUT OF THE CELLAR AND INTO THE CHAMPIONSHIP FOR THE HALL

"It was like witnessing something that seemed impossible happening"

Upon the occasion of his first trip to a Big East coaches' meeting in the summer of 1988, Rick Barnes walked into the pro shop at the Ponte Vedra Beach resort. He'd just been named the Providence head coach, brought in after Pitino bolted for the Knicks and a one-year run by Gordie Chiesa ended in a near revolt by the players. Barnes arrived in the Big East from George Mason, where he'd spent part of a season watching John Thompson's mastery from those upper-deck seats. Understandably, the thirty-four-year-old, who still carried a slight southern drawl from his Hickory, North Carolina, roots, felt a bit nervous about the upgrade in the company he was keeping, not to mention the verbosity of his new Northeast peers.

As he browsed the pro shop, Barnes spied Seton Hall's P.J. Carlesimo piling up golf shirts and other trinkets at the sales counter. "Hey, Hickory," Carlesimo yelled. "Get yourself some shirts." Worried about the possible sticker shock, Barnes demurred. Recognizing Barnes's hesitancy, Carlesimo tried to ease his concerns: "Don't worry about it. We're charging it to Gavitt." Sure enough, a few weeks later, an irate Gavitt stormed into Tranghese's office, asking about the sizable bill from the golf shop. "I might have done that," Carlesimo says now with a chuckle.

Forgive Carlesimo his thievery, but Seton Hall probably needed the assist the most. Even compared to their fellow cellar-dwellers, the Pirates sat well below the standard, lacking in just about every way a program could lack—tradition, facilities, cash flow, appeal. You name it, Seton Hall didn't have it. The Pirates' high-water mark ran all the way back to the 1952–53 season with an NIT championship, a lone beacon of success in a string of otherwise lean years.

Along with unsuccessful, the program was almost neglected. The accommodations were so bad, the players schlepped down the street to a local gym to work out, and money was so tight it took years before the assistants even earned full-time salaries. As for the university itself, it didn't shake off its commuter roots for decades, its picturesque campus unable to overcome the blight of the nearby Newark neighborhood. When Andrew Gaze arrived for the first time from Australia, he remembers the coaching staff offering salient advice: "When you exit the campus, do not turn right unless you have a lot of company."

Only Gavitt could see anything that resembled potential. Another Catholic school tied exclusively to basketball, Seton Hall had the right geography and fit well with the other schools. He believed it would be buoyed by the company it kept. Eventually he'd be proven right, but "eventually" took some time. "Dave's vision was not Seton Hall's," says Bill Raftery, the former Hall coach turned analyst. As much as the league could raise up laggards, it could stomp on them, too, and Seton Hall took its lumps maybe more than any other team in the league's early history. The Pirates won a total of 14 league games in their first seven years as a conference member.

All of which made the realization of Gavitt's dreams all the sweeter. In 1989, he stood alongside Raftery in the hallway outside the Seton Hall locker room, minutes after the Pirates disposed of UNLV to reach the Final Four. The commissioner cried tears of joy. "Dave used to tell us, as a conference we're only as good as our weakest link," Chris Plonsky, his former associate commissioner, says. "That this league could lift Seton Hall, that's the real measure of it all."

If the entire existence and success of the Big East read like some sort of fairy tale, then no school fills Cinderella's slipper better than Seton Hall. That same year, 1989, when the Pirates reached the Final Four in Seattle, CBS sent a reporter to the streets of New Jersey to ask people where Seton Hall was located. Few could answer. Now the school boasts a national reputation and name recognition built almost entirely and exclusively on its relationship with the Big East.

In hindsight, it's easy to see why no one knew where Seton Hall was prior to its involvement with the conference. There was no reason. The Pirates were less than an afterthought. Not even Richie Regan, who starred on that '53 NIT team, could coax success out of his alma mater. He spent ten years as the Pirates' head coach. He won 112 games.

By 1969, Regan had moved into the AD's chair, naming Raftery, a former star player at La Salle and head coach at nearby Fairleigh Dickinson, as his successor. Regan, in his day, had shared office space with the Bayley-Seton League, a women's auxiliary group; Walsh Gym, a relic built in 1939, offered nearly nothing in the way of amenities. The school tried to give Raftery a boost, dressing up the locker rooms and fixing up his office some, though really anything would count as an upgrade. "That still didn't get us to first base with Syracuse," Raftery says of his slight upgrades. None of his assistants were full-timers. Hoddy Mahon doubled as a schoolteacher, and John Murphy worked as a lieutenant in charge of the Newark Police Youth Aid. Raftery raised the school's visibility some, using five regular-season games at the Garden to woo name-brand opponents to the area. Every once in a while they'd steal one—they beat Rutgers there in 1977—but never would the Pirates return the gesture and offer to play on the road, Raftery knowing all too well that losses awaited his team away from home.

As Raftery predicted and feared when his athletic director informed him of the school's move to the league years earlier, the Big East was a rather tall leap for the Pirates. In their first season, they won but one game, against Providence, losing the other five by an average of 21.4 points. It got so bad in a game against St. John's that Raftery summoned one of his managers, a kid by the name of Tommy Slattery, to deliver a note to Lou Carnesecca. "Dear Lou, I surrender. Love Bill," Raftery wrote. "PS: want to work against a 2-3 zone?" Kneeling in front of his bench, Raftery watched as Carnesecca put on his glasses, read the note, and nodded his head. Raftery went to the zone for the rest of the game.

Good-natured and self-deprecating to a fault, Raftery tried to play off his woebegone team. Charlie Pierce, the reporter, remembers sitting in a tiny office with maybe three desks for postgame interviews after Seton Hall got trounced yet again. Raftery poked his head in. "Don't suppose any of you want to talk to me?" he said.

There comes a point when losing is no longer a laughing matter, and Raftery reached his point during the 1980–81 season, putting his hand through a glass door in frustration after a 2-point loss to Georgetown. The Pirates would muster just four conference wins that season, and Raftery, with four kids at home, considered a career pivot. Years earlier, when he was still playing at La Salle, his coach had sent Raftery over to meet with Bob Wolff, tasking Raftery with feeding the broadcaster info about the Explorers. Wolff, who worked as the Knicks' announcer, knew a thing or two about talent, and he'd told Raftery he ought to consider a career in broadcasting one day. The idea had stuck with Raftery ever since.

Gavitt still served as the Big East's color analyst, and one night while the two were out to dinner, Raftery mentioned he might like to try out the gig one day. Gavitt said he planned to step back from the role that year, in 1981–82, and gave Raftery two days to make up his mind. Aware that he had to secure his kids' future, and not so sure about his own job security, Raftery jumped at the TV job, making the move official on October 28, 1981. It was too late in the game to launch a real search, so Mahon took over as the interim head coach. For his first TV assignment, Raftery called a game at Seton Hall against Princeton.

Raftery's best player, Dan Callandrillo, reluctantly remained with the Pirates after Raftery left, bawling at the press conference when the news was announced. Callandrillo wound up winning Big East Player of the Year honors that year, staking his claim early with a series of buzzer-beating winners—including in the game that was Raftery's TV debut. After he hit the game-winner, Callandrillo, who'd first met Raftery when the coach happened into a pub where he worked as a fifteen-year-old bartender, ran over and kissed his old coach right on the lips. "I said, 'Danny, in the mob, when they kiss you on the lips, it's over,'" Raftery says. Instead it was just the beginning, Raftery becoming one of the most beloved and respected broadcasters in college basketball, his colloquialisms ("Onions!") and memorable calls ("Send it in, Jerome!") becoming part of the sport's lexicon. Given a catbird seat, he witnessed some of the Big

East's most memorable moments, and the coach who struggled to win in the league became as much a part of the conference's legacy as anyone.

Regan cast a wide net after Mahon finished 11–16, considering the assistant among his choices but putting the heavy sell on Gary Williams, then the head coach at American. Williams ultimately opted for another Big East gig, taking the Boston College job, which is when Regan turned to Carlesimo. The Wagner coach fit the mold perfectly. His dad, Pete, commanded nearly as much respect in hoops circles as Gavitt, and the two were close friends. A former athletic director at Fordham and onetime football teammate of Vince Lombardi, Pete Carlesimo is credited with saving the NIT from extinction after the NCAA invoked a role prohibiting teams from choosing an NIT bid over an NCAA invite.

But Carlesimo was not one to ride his old man's coattails. He worked at Fordham, also his alma mater, and New Hampshire as an assistant before becoming a head coach at Wagner. When he took over at Seton Hall, agreeing to a three-year deal worth $35,000 annually, he was just thirty-three.

He, along with Williams, would add new flavor to the Big East mix, each charged with formidable tasks. Unlike Carlesimo, Williams had something to work with at Boston College. For years the Eagles had played second fiddle to Holy Cross, but when the Crusaders rejected Gavitt's overtures to join the Big East, the two schools reversed fortunes. Led by Dr. Tom Davis, Boston College overtook its rival, reaching the Elite Eight in 1982. But lured by the promise of a more lucrative salary, Davis headed out west, to Stanford. The school opted for Williams, just thirty-seven, a familiar face who'd served as Davis's assistant five years earlier. Williams was nearly giddy with the step up from his previous job. "When I was at American, we didn't even have a gym to play in," he says. "We went to Fort Myers military base in Arlington. I get Boston College and we have the Roberts Center. It's my own gym, an actual place to practice!"

Combustible, foul-mouthed, and prone to profuse perspiration, Williams earned and wore his "Whacko" moniker proudly. More of an imp, Carlesimo loved needling his more established coaching peers and pulling off pranks. He'd ride up on a golf cart before dinner as Lisa Zanccchia, Gavitt's assistant, was setting up, swipe a shrimp off a serving tray, and ride off, shouting, "There better be shrimp at dinner!" Both coaches, however, felt the enormous pressure of their new jobs when they headed to St. John in the Virgin Islands, site of the 1982 league meetings. "I knew all of those guys, and played against some of them, so they were friends," Carlesimo says. "But it was a little different sitting in that room the first time."

He also knew what he was up against. He took over Seton Hall just as Mullin and Ewing were reaching their peaks. Though he managed to convince the school to splurge on full-time positions for his staff, he played in a crummy old gym in desperate need of a renovation. His first ESPN game, he remembers, came at home against St. John's and Mullin; technicians were forced to run cables out through a propped-open door to get enough juice. And while Walsh Gym was finally undergoing some renovations in 1985, the Pirates split their home games between the Meadowlands and a West Orange arena that doubled as an ice hockey rink. "It's freezing cold, maybe three hundred people in there, and I'm thinking, 'This is the Big East?'" says former Seton Hall assistant Bruce Hamburger.

What Seton Hall lacked in amenities, Carlesimo made up for in affability. He charmed people—administrators, fellow coaches, Gavitt, and especially recruits. Seton Hall offered playing time and a coach who seemed like a nice guy.

At least he seemed that way until practice started, when the players were never quite sure which version of Carlesimo they might get. "Half the time you'd be thinking, 'Are you going to crack a joke or make us run?'" says Jerry Walker, who played for the Hall from 1989 to 1993. Carlesimo was a stickler for details, expecting his assistants to prepare detailed scouts and riding his best players harder than the stragglers. Players who shot worse than 80 percent at the free-throw line were given an extra dose of suicides to run, and they learned quickly that when the coach's face got a little red and his voice jumped an octave, they were in trouble. "I like to call it direct communication," says Gaze, his Australian accent adding special emphasis on the word *direct*. "Very direct communication."

To say Carlesimo's first years were lean ones would be kind. In his first four seasons, the Pirates won a combined seven Big East games. In 1985, while the conference celebrated its three-out-of-four Final Four, Seton Hall limped into the offseason with just one league victory, and it took the very last day of the regular season to get it.

Carlesimo still peddled hope and optimism. The graduation of Mullin and Ewing, he knew, offered at least an opening to move up in the standings, and he believed the Pirates could shimmy through. The Hall was never going to attract the top players in the area, but the riches of the Northeast recruiting beds offered plenty for everyone. And he liked the kids who were a little rougher around the edges, anyway. A place like Seton Hall needed players who were hungry. Besides, Carlesimo could sell the one thing the Pirates could offer more than anyone else: playing time. His pitch finally found receptive ears, and Carlesimo was able to sandwich two recruiting classes together and build what would be the foundation of the Hall's turn-around.

Some of those players came with big credentials—Mark Bryant, from Maplewood, New Jersey, ranked among the state's most coveted high schoolers, and Darryl Walker had earned

New York State Player of the Year honors—but Carlesimo also dug around for some diamonds in the rough. Ramon Ramos, a 6'8" kid who loved to play volleyball on the beaches of Puerto Rico, was such a raw recruit at sixteen that Boeheim dismissed him. Carlesimo stayed true, and eventually would reap the benefits. Ramos twice was named to the All–Big East first team.

But if Providence caught lightning in a bottle and shot its way into the top of the standings, Seton Hall was on the slow, slogging path. By the dawn of the 1987–88 season, the recruits expected to create something were juniors and seniors, but they had crafted very little. "They got their heads kicked in those first few years," Hamburger says. The Pirates went from one league win to three to four, and at that point Carlesimo faced the end of his contract. Plenty figured he faced the end of his tenure, too. The university's student senate went so far as to cast a vote demanding Carlesimo's resignation; eight out of twelve wanted the coach gone. "People were calling for his head," says Darryl Walker, who was part of the promised renaissance.

By then, Gavitt had issued something of a league decree, ordering the teams that played in tiny bandboxes to move to bigger arenas by the start of the 1987 season. Villanova moved out of the "Cat House" into the Pavilion, and Georgetown out of McDonough Gymnasium to the Capital Centre in nearby Landover. While Boston College built a new arena, it played its games at the Boston Garden, and Seton Hall left Walsh behind for good, busing over to the Meadowlands Arena, a 20,000-seat multipurpose building just off the New Jersey Turnpike.

It was a big ask for a lousy team, not just to fill so many more seats but to expect the student body to find their way to the place, a fifteen-mile ride from campus. "We hated playing there," Darryl Walker says. "We wanted to be on campus." The Pirates had played there sporadically before moving there permanently, but never successfully, going winless in the arena for four consecutive seasons. Even the big names failed to draw a crowd. Just 8,000 came to watch the Pearl and Syracuse drub the Pirates by 23 in 1986.

Needless to say, it all did not bode well for Carlesimo's future. "If we have a 'bad' year, then we have to figure the future of our program," Larry Keating, who succeeded Regan as AD in 1985, told the *Courier News* that year.

Nearing the end of its first decade of existence, the Big East certainly did not need Seton Hall to succeed in order to secure its reputation. Syracuse, Georgetown, Villanova, and St. John's offered more than enough might to carry the conference. But if its otherwise soft middle and lousy basement could become competitive, that would only bolster the Big East's command of the sport. It would also realize Gavitt's original dream of making every team in the conference nationally relevant. More than that, Gavitt genuinely liked and believed in Carlesimo, so much so that he went to South Orange to talk to Keating and university president Monsignor John Petillo. Eight years into the league, not a single coach had been fired. Gavitt wasn't about to let that change. "He talked them out of firing him," Tranghese says. "He said, 'You've got to give this guy a chance because they're going to be really good next year.'"

When the Pirates started the year 2–6 in the league, not even Gavitt's backing seemed enough to save Carlesimo. John Paquette, now the Big East associate commissioner, worked as the school's sports information director at the time, and recalls a New York reporter telling him, "I do not want to write this story," meaning the one in which Carlesimo loses his job.

In the way these things tend to happen, Seton Hall's turnaround did not come accompanied with trumpets or horns. It was in an ordinary game, in Storrs, Connecticut. Ramos tipped away a steal with 10 seconds left, allowing the Pirates to hold on for a comeback 61–59 win. Though it would have been a significant loss, it was not a big win; UConn was not much better than Seton Hall. But a team that for so long couldn't find a way to break through finally made a winning play. And that flipped a switch, as if the Pirates suddenly understood what it took. They would beat six of their final eight opponents, losing twice to Georgetown, but then upset the Hoyas in the Big East Tournament, en route to their own holy grail—an NCAA Tournament bid. Though Seton Hall lost to Arizona in the second round, Carlesimo earned a four-year extension.

The following season, 1988–89, the Pirates welcomed back the class that got the ball rolling—Ramos, Gerald Greene, Darryl Walker, and John Morton—for its senior year, and added an Australian player who turned few heads when he arrived that October.

Carlesimo had first spied Gaze during a 1986 exhibition game when the Aussie came over for a tour with his team, the Melbourne Tigers. He was not an entirely unfamiliar entity. Gaze's father, Lindsay, is a Hall of Famer considered the architect of Australian basketball, and a longtime friend of Gavitt and Pete Carlesimo. Lindsay Gaze helped set up the exhibition games, the Tigers barnstorming through eight of the nine Big East teams, finishing up with Seton Hall in the retrofitted ice rink.

Gaze dropped 44 on the Pirates that night, and afterward, as Gaze munched pizza and guzzled soda in a postgame dinner, Carlesimo and his assistant John Carroll put on the hard sell, trying to convince him to stick around and play in the States. But Gaze felt an affinity to his National Basketball League team and fostered just one dream—to play for his national team at the Seoul Olympics in 1988. He returned home to Victoria, flattered but not interested. Seton Hall, especially Carroll, refused to take no for an answer. The assistant coach called so often that Gaze's parents wondered about the international call charges the school was amassing. "He can talk to the bottom of the ocean with a mouthful of marbles," Gaze says. "That is, he can talk."

Carroll's persistence finally paid off. In 1988, the NBL fast-tracked its schedule to accommodate the Olympics, leaving an eight-month gap between seasons—a gap that just happened to fall in line with the American college basketball schedule. Hot off averaging 23 points in the Olympics, Gaze arrived in South Orange in October. Gaze would spend six months in the States, just long enough to squeeze in a college basketball season. Cynics viewed Gaze as little more than a mercenary—especially after his club team admitted it put $25,000 in a trust fund for him, in defiance of the NCAA's amateur status. The NCAA never charged Gaze or Seton Hall with a violation, though the innuendo never quite faded. "I don't hold it against people if they don't believe me. Very few do," Gaze says. "But I was well behind academically, and though there was an opportunity to fill a void in my schedule, there was also a chance to get some credits out of the way."

There is no arguing what Gaze brought to a rugged and experienced Seton Hall team—shooting. He had a beautiful stroke, and added just the dimension the Pirates needed. His new teammates welcomed him warmly, even if they struggled to understand one another despite all of them speaking English. "The first week or so, I needed a translator when Darryl spoke," Gaze says. "I could get every fourth word out of his mouth."

But they all spoke the language of basketball, and Gaze was impressed with the toughness of the team he'd just joined. Yet even with so much talent, the old Seton Hall stigma proved difficult to shake. The Pirates were picked seventh in the Big East preseason. Upon hearing that news after attending a few practices with his new mates, Gaze returned to his dorm stunned. He grew up watching Big East games on a projector, his father passing on game films he scored from the States. Gaze understood well the rigors of the league, but seventh? "I was like, if this is the seventh-best team, what the hell kind of league did I get myself into?" Gaze says.

The Pirates responded to the disrespect with a 13-game win streak to open the season, starting the year off by winning the Alaska Shootout. "It was like, 'OK, this is who we are now. This is where we're going,'" Darryl Walker says. "We saw ourselves as contenders in the Big East." Others remained skeptical, and understandably so. This was, after all, a team that had yet to sniff so much as a plus-.500 season in conference play.

By the luck of the league draw, the Pirates were gifted the ultimate show-me game to start Big East play—at home against fifth-ranked Georgetown. The Hoyas, loaded again with freshman Alonzo Mourning, remained the standard-bearer, Thompson rolling into New Jersey with an Olympic bronze medal earned that summer in Seoul. Keating hoped for a crowd of 10,000, at least enough to open the upper deck at the Meadowlands. Instead the game attracted more than 19,000, a legit sellout and the largest crowd to watch a college basketball game in the arena's seven-year history, including NCAA Tournament games.

It served as the perfect setup for Seton Hall's official arrival party, the Pirates roaring back from a 9-point second-half deficit and winning, 94–86. After so much hardship and struggle, Carlesimo found himself soaking in the moment. "There was a time in the game, for whatever reason I don't know, I looked around and thought, 'Wow, this is it,'" Carlesimo says. "Usually you don't have that chance, but I came out of a timeout, looked at the crowd, looked at the guys on the other team." The euphoria ended quickly, the Hall brought back to earth a mere four days later when second-ranked Syracuse handed the Pirates a 90–66 dusting. But the successes finally far outweighed the disappointments for Seton Hall, the Pirates rolling to a 24-win regular season. Though bounced again by Syracuse in the Big East Tournament semifinals, the same team that just a year earlier had celebrated merely getting an NCAA Tournament invite now eyed winning the whole thing.

Ranked eleventh in the nation and seeded third in the West Region, the Pirates were far from a long shot but still did not fit the bill as favorite. Georgetown and Syracuse, seeded one and two respectively, were considered far more likely Big East national championship contenders. Given 30-to-1 odds to actually win a title, Seton Hall zipped by Missouri State and Evansville in the first weekend, setting up a Sweet Sixteen matchup against Indiana and legendary coach Bob Knight. The two coaches had met decades earlier, back when Knight was the head coach at Army, giving clinics, and Carlesimo a teenage camp counselor. By the time the two tipped off in Denver for the Sweet Sixteen, Knight owned three national titles, and Carlesimo still had a losing record at Seton Hall. But the Pirate players didn't care about any of that. They'd spent years in the Big East going head-to-head with legends weekly. They didn't intimidate easily. "We knew we were good," Darryl Walker says.

Any lingering doubters soon came around after Seton Hall not only defeated Indiana but handed Knight his worst NCAA Tournament loss at the time, a 78–65 drubbing. That pushed the Pirates to the brink of the Final Four and a date with UNLV. Despite all the team had accomplished, despite a defense that suffocated opponents regularly and finished second only to Georgetown in the Big East, oddsmakers favored the Runnin' Rebels to make the national semifinals. UNLV head coach Jerry Tarkanian even admitted that he thought Arizona, his team's Sweet Sixteen opponent, was better than the Hall. Though confident, the Seton Hall staff feared the matchups, worried how the offensively gifted Gaze might handle UNLV's talented forward Stacey Augmon, who averaged more than 15 points per game.

Quite well, as it turned out. Augmon shot just 4 of 12, and Tarkanian ended up sucking on his ever-present towel for emotional support as the Pirates unraveled UNLV just as they had Indiana. The Rebels also suffered their worst postseason loss, an 84–61 shellacking, as Seton Hall, a team that hadn't even been able to muster five league wins two years earlier, punched their ticket to the Final Four. A grinning Carlesimo saluted his parents in the stands as the game ended, while Raftery, the old Hall coach, sat courtside with his entire family, overcome with emotion. "It was like witnessing something that seemed impossible happening," he says.

The win left the Pirates as the last team standing in the Big East. Georgetown lost to Duke in the East Region final, and Illinois eliminated Syracuse in the Midwest. Though he would have loved to see another three-out-of-four Final Four, Gavitt was overjoyed that the Pirates would represent his league in Seattle. Standing alongside Raftery in the hallway outside the Seton Hall locker room, Gavitt wept with joy, thrilled for Carlesimo but also at the true realization of his league vision.

By then the Pirates had been on the road for two weeks, going from Tucson directly to Denver. Carlesimo opted to extend their western swing, taking his team to California en route to Seattle. The team was gaining popularity, the national media finding its way to the little-engine-that-could story. Paquette remembers the hotel operator thanking him when he checked out of his hotel room, tired from fielding so many requests to speak to the man who arranged interviews. But it's not like the Pirates required the Georgetown treatment. In California, they stayed in scenic Marina del Rey, Carlesimo rewarding his players with two days off before reigniting practice at nearby Loyola Marymount. Gaze and some teammates rented a convertible during the break, tooling around to enjoy the sunshine in anonymity.

Back home, it was another story. While the team went on to

California, Hamburger, the assistant coach, returned to New Jersey. The Meadowlands played host to the East Region final, and since the assistant coach had the advance scout, he went back to watch the Elite Eight game between Duke and Georgetown, as the winner would be the Pirates' national semifinal opponent. Part of the Seton Hall ticket plan that year included tickets to the East Region final, and Hamburger soon found himself a minor celebrity, fans and alums thrilled to greet the assistant. When Carlesimo called that night, Hamburger filled in his boss about the frenzy. "We had no clue out there how big a thing we were back in Jersey," he says.

The Pirates were an equally big deal to the Big East. Gavitt rode his joy all the way to Seattle, site of the Final Four. He made up T-shirts and sweatshirts, declaring on the front his league as "Beast of the East," and on the back listing the six schools (Georgetown, St. John's, Villanova, Syracuse, Providence, and Seton Hall) that had reached the Final Four. Zanecchia sold them out of Gavitt's hotel room. "We didn't have a lot, so they went fast," she says. "Boy, did we have a good time."

The truth is, most folks figured that was how Seton Hall would approach their national semifinal appearance—with a casual "happy to be here" attitude, especially in comparison to their opponent. By 1989, Duke was making its third national semifinal appearance in four years, the Blue Devils en route to becoming the dominant program it would be for decades. But winning the title for the Blue Devils proved elusive. With the team anchored by senior All-American Danny Ferry and freshman Christian Laettner, who years later would make his own NCAA history, the stars appeared aligned for Duke. Duke needed only to get past upstart Seton Hall to have a shot at a national title against either third-seeded Michigan or top-seeded Illinois.

The Pirates were as new to the Final Four scene as the Blue

Devils were familiar with it. They went wide-eyed to press conferences, amazed at the number of media representatives present, and stood slightly in awe at center court inside the Kingdome, where 40,000 fans were on their feet screaming. The cocoon that had served them so well, keeping the hype and the excitement away, suddenly burst, and the Blue Devils jumped to an 18-point lead eight minutes into the game.

The Pirates failed to score on their first seven possessions, and with four minutes until the half, they had just one field goal but seven fouls, repeatedly sending the Blue Devils to the free-throw line. Fans and reporters started recalling other epically humiliating Final Four games—Penn's 33-point halftime hole against Michigan State and Magic Johnson in 1979, and the 11-point first half that stunned Joe B. Hall and Kentucky against Georgetown in 1984. "I'm wondering if we're going back on the red-eye at midnight to Newark," Paquette says.

But the Pirates, including Carlesimo, never lost their cool. As demanding and demonstrative as he was in the heat of things, the coach knew to keep his composure when things seemed especially out of hand. "It was more like, 'Keep fighting. Don't give up. It's still early,'" Darryl Walker says. "I didn't hear him yelling at all." No one did, really. Gaze remembers Greene, a tough kid out of Bedford-Stuyvesant, chiding his teammates, telling them to remember where they came from, that they were city kids and not about to roll over. Otherwise the huddles were composed and determined. "The Big East mentality, it really helped us," Hamburger says. "We'd been through some stuff, and the Big East, it was so good then, every game was a battle. So it was, 'OK, here we go. We've been down before against great teams and great coaches. Let's figure this out.'"

Back in New Jersey, another city kid watched the game on television. In the years to come, Jerry Walker would become a driving force in ensuring that Seton Hall's magical 1989 run was not just a onetime fling. But at the time he was just a senior at powerhouse St. Anthony's High School rooting for his future school, and taking grief from his high school teammate Bobby Hurley, who was headed to Duke. As the Blue Devils' lead grew, Hurley kept calling to taunt his friend.

But while Hurley was yapping, another Walker was working. Darryl Walker, no relation to Jerry, drew the task of containing Ferry. Early on, it didn't go well. The Duke star led that early Blue Devil charge and would finish with 21 first-half points while Walker struggled with foul trouble. But before the first-half buzzer sounded, Walker started to find his defensive rhythm, bodying Ferry with more authority. With the Pirates still trailing big, Walker forced a turnover that ignited an outburst no one saw coming. "I show my kids tape of that steal all the time," Walker says with a grin. By the time Seton Hall was through, the Pirates went from down 18 to up 18, the team that couldn't score to start the game amassing 75 points in just 25 minutes. Ferry, unstoppable early, mustered just 5 of 16 shooting in the second half.

"I started calling Bobby," Jerry Walker says. "'Hey, Bobby, heh heh heh heh.' He wouldn't answer the phone." Seton Hall, a team known for its defense all season, pinned 95 points on Duke and advanced to a national championship game against Michigan.

Darryl Walker is a grown man now, out of college for more than thirty years. He still has not watched a replay of the Pirates' title game against the Wolverines. He can't bring himself to do it. "Nope," he says. "I will not watch it." Gaze only watched it for the first time in 2014, on the twenty-fifth anniversary. He then proceeded to not sleep for two days. It is that kind of game, the kind that stays with a man forever, impossible to shake.

It was, in actuality, a great game—played at a high level, pushed to overtime, and with unbelievable performances from both teams. Glen Rice had 31 points and 11 rebounds for Michigan, and John Morton had 35 for the Pirates. As improbable as the Pirates' spot in the title game was, Michigan's might have been even more unlikely. Their head coach, Steve Fisher, was an interim coach tapped nearly on the eve of the NCAA Tournament after Bill Frieder incensed his athletic director, Bo Schembechler, by announcing he'd leave for Arizona State at season's end.

Yet the game is remembered by many—and by everyone who roots for Seton Hall—for a questionable call. With nine seconds left and Seton Hall up by 1, Michigan's Rumeal Robinson searched desperately for a shot, driving down the middle and toward the basket. Robinson had just passed the ball to Mark Hughes when John Clougherty blew his whistle, calling Greene for bumping Robinson on his drive. Three seconds remained on the clock. While fans howled, the Seton Hall bench barely reacted. Carlesimo folded his arms behind his head, as if he were about to rest on a pillow, and merely called out to Clougherty by his first name. He didn't cuss, just yelled, "No way, John. No way." The Pirates were opposite the play, without a clear view, and too engrossed in the moment. Hamburger remembers glancing down to see what kind of free-throw shooter Robinson was (not very good), trying to prep for the final three seconds.

But Robinson made the free throws, and though Walker got one last shot, his 3-pointer bounced high off the backboard as Michigan won the title. "That was it, the last shot of my career," Walker says.

In the immediate aftermath, the Pirates were more shell-shocked than angry, exiting the floor numb while Michigan celebrated. At the time, CBS typically interviewed the losing coach after the game. Carlesimo politely declined the interview, keeping his head down and walking to the locker room. The players beat their coach there, huddling up outside. "It doesn't matter," Greene told his teammates. "We know what we accomplished and it was pretty amazing." The Pirates carried that grace and dignity with them through the trying postgame press conferences, answering the questions without once blaming the officials. "That was P.J.'s message," Hamburger says. "After the game, he never once threw the ref under the bus. The message was that if we took care of things ourselves, it wouldn't have come down to that, and nothing should take away from what we accomplished anyway."

They hadn't seen the replays, not until later. Hamburger remembers going back to his hotel room after dinner, flipping on the TV around two in the morning, and finally watching the replay. "Man, yeah, then you're pissed," he says after seeing the phantom foul. Devastated, the Pirates flew back across the country the next day, boarding their commercial flight, connecting through Dallas. Paquette spoke to his assistant during the layover. She said there would be a lot of people to greet the Pirates when they returned. Considering they'd lost, Paquette thought maybe 100. There were closer to 1,000. The next week Carlesimo headed to Yankee Stadium, invited to throw out the first pitch. The coach, still a bachelor, brought Paquette with him. The two walked through the dining areas, greeted warmly by people who congratulated Carlesimo for a great year.

Suddenly everyone knew where Seton Hall was and who the Pirates were, and understood the might of the Big East. In its first ten years, five Big East teams played in a national championship. Two won the title; the other three each lost by a single point.

Soon it was time for one more to have a chance.

CHAPTER 10

FROM YUKON TO UCONN: THE HUSKIES' RISE FROM OBSCURITY

"What the hell kind of league did I get myself into?"

They arrived a bit starstruck, taking in the packed gym and the nearly 4,000 fans that filled it. Such was life on the take side of a guarantee game, and American International College was meant to be the proverbial lambs brought to be slaughtered—and paid for their troubles on the way out the door. The Aces held up their end of the bargain on that December day in 1964, trounced by host Connecticut, 98–67, as star player Tony Kimball dropped 30 points and added 28 rebounds.

But newspaper accounts from the game also laud the "outstanding hard worker" for AIC, a 6'5" forward by the name of Jim Calhoun. "I was fortunate. I had 27," says Calhoun, nailing his point total more than fifty years later. "But to me, a guy from a smaller school, the way they packed it in, with the band and all that stuff, that was big-time. That was the big time."

Not everyone agreed with Calhoun's assessment. Not, that is, until the Huskies' patsy opponent became their Hall of Fame leader, the once wide-eyed visitor crafting one of the Big East's most successful programs out of nearly thin air.

On the court, UConn did not have as steep a hill to summit as Seton Hall. The Huskies at least won a few games here and there, 15 combined in years two and three. But in 1986, they sank to the bottom of the league standings, done in when leading scorer Earl Kelley was declared academically ineligible. Privately people wondered if maybe this one time Gavitt had made a mistake. "The Northwestern of the Big East," people snickered about UConn, comparing the Huskies to the equally ill-suited Wildcats of the Big Ten. Head coach Dom Perno, though well liked by his peers and his players, resigned shortly after.

The problems ran much deeper than Perno. UConn was in such disarray that the university president commissioned a twenty-person task force to examine the athletic department. The findings, issued a month after Perno resigned, read like a sixty-six-page indictment, arguing that the department was isolated from the rest of the university and failed to properly allocate its resources. Athletic director John Toner, the man who had bravely and brazenly taken the Big East leap on behalf of his school, shouldered much of the blame, making his quest for Perno's successor that much more pressured. "This is the biggest challenge facing UConn athletics," Toner, who died in 2014, said at the time. "The Big East is the big leagues, and it has to be done right. This is the first time we're hiring a Big East coach."

Up the Mass Pike in Boston sat Calhoun, practically screaming, "Pick me! Pick me!" Wildly successful as the Northeastern head coach, he yearned for the big time.

Calhoun never learned the directions to Easy Street; his life had been one detour after another. As a teenager Calhoun lost his father to a sudden heart attack, learning the news during a baseball game when someone cruelly yelled that he needed to hustle home, his dad was dead. The oldest of six, Calhoun committed to caring for his family, and after just three months he abandoned a basketball scholarship at Lowell State to return home as a stonecutter, making grave markers and handing the money over to his mother to support the family. Only the insistence of his high school coach, Fred Herget, convinced Calhoun that a life as a laborer in Braintree, Massachusetts, would not serve the family nearly as well as a college education. Herget helped him secure a scholarship to American International in Springfield. Each year the Aces would play the Huskies—UConn once graciously coming to AIC's campus to open up the new gym—and each year they'd lose.

But Calhoun starred, earning Little All-American honors (given to non–Division I players) and helping his team to its first NCAA Tournament bid. In his senior year, the future UConn coach would take the floor as the future Big East commissioner called his name—Tranghese, a graduate student at the school at the time, worked as the school's public address announcer. "Small world," Tranghese says. "Such a small, small world."

Given the chance to resuscitate his own life, Calhoun then made a career out of resuscitating basketball programs. He led Dedham High to a 38–1 record in two years, using that success as a springboard to the college ranks. He was hired at Northeastern in 1972, and while Gavitt was putting the Big East together, Calhoun was navigating Northeastern into the Division I ranks. He handled it flawlessly, leading his squad to the NCAA Tournament in just their second year of eligibility, and in five of his six years there.

The Huskies played some of the big boys as part of the ECAC, and the fierce competitor in Calhoun wanted desperately to compete among them more regularly. He watched enviously as the Big East came together, seeing immediately the genius in Gavitt's plan. "At Northeastern, we're winning, we're starting to get players, we go to the tournament, but when you look at the

Big East, that was the place to be," he says. "Then they're on TV. It was just amazing."

Smart coaches were scared of taking on UConn, seeing the job for what it was—a likely losing proposition in such a formidable conference. To Calhoun, it was just another place in need of a second chance. At forty-four, he was young enough to want the challenge—and foolish enough to think he could handle it. When Calhoun signed a seven-year contract (worth $70,000 the first year), Jim Boeheim told him, "You'll need at least that." But then the Syracuse coach added the kicker: "But they need you more than you need them."

Boeheim was right. With Calhoun's success at Northeastern, another opportunity was sure to come his way eventually. But UConn couldn't afford a mistake. Its future on the precipice, it needed someone who would reshape the entire program, and by extension mold the entire athletic department.

Calhoun brought fresh energy and fresh ideas. He hosted a tailgate before football games, trying to use the crowds there to drum up support for his team, and he put together the school's first coach's show—*Calhoun's Court,* a weekly half-hour TV show that played on a local affiliate. He started a basketball camp on campus, and it served several purposes—a way to get himself more money, a means of adding to his profile, and a way to expand UConn's reach.

But there were some problems public relations couldn't overcome. The Huskies played in the "old leaky Field House," as Chris Plonsky referred to the team's thirty-year-old, 4,000-seat arena, the same one that had captivated Calhoun as a player. Strategically placed buckets caught the water before it hit the court, and on days that recruits were in town, the staff would hide the buckets during a very quick tour. "Everything was just old," says Rutgers head coach Steve Pikiell, who played on Calhoun's first team. The school stopped hosting Big East games at the Field House in 1986. Instead they played at either the Hartford Civic Center or New Haven Coliseum, both requiring students to find their way off campus to watch the team play. The university finally broke ground on Gampel Pavilion in 1987, but it wouldn't open its doors until 1990.

Worse, outside of the state, the Huskies struggled with an identity crisis. For a while, Calhoun had to offer spelling lessons by way of introduction. "People thought we were the Yukon Huskies," he says. "Like Alaska. I'd have to say, 'No, with a U, not a Y.'" Calhoun's first Big East meetings were held in Puerto Rico, and Calhoun remembers walking on the beach with his wife, Pat, after the first gathering with his fellow coaches. "Honey," he told her, "you're not going to see me for the next six months." Jay Wright, who came on as a Villanova assistant in Calhoun's second season, remembers how the others "all felt sorry for him," so difficult was the climb for the Huskies. In Calhoun's first year, UConn lost by 21 to St. John's, a chasm made all the wider as Lou Carnesecca refused to call off the press. Calhoun believed the old coach was trying to humiliate him and his team. Carnesecca, in fact, was trying to teach Calhoun a lesson. After the game, the older coach offered sage advice to his young and impatient peer. "Irish," Carnesecca said, using his favorite nickname for Calhoun, "you can only coach one team at a time."

UConn did have a few advantages. For starters, unlike its Big East brethren, it did not have to battle anyone else for attention. Other than the Hartford Whalers, there was no other big game in town. Consequently, the Huskies enjoyed near manic fan devotion. "We'd have a kid fly in from Arizona, a recruit, and people would see him in the airport and yell, 'UConn,' or they'd know his name," Calhoun says. "It's not like when you fly into Newark to get to Seton Hall. We could captivate a state." They also got incredible media coverage. "The Horde" was what folks called the huge media contingent on the UConn beat, every newspaper big and small devoting at least one reporter to UConn. Granted, such attention cut both ways. When the program struggled, the Huskies heard about it. At least people cared.

The Huskies' biggest advantage, though, was Calhoun, who ranks as one of the all-time worst losers in college basketball. (Years later, he would not be able to even muster up one good thing to say about the epic six-overtime loss to Syracuse because his team lost.) "Irish blood," Calhoun calls it. It boils quickly and constantly. He simply could not abide failure, and he hated being considered less than—less than any team, less than any coach, less than anyone. It suited his fan base perfectly.

As a state, Connecticut suffers an inferiority complex. Sandwiched between Boston and New York, it's treated more like an irritating highway to pass through than a place of its own. UConn fans loved the idea of a coach who would stand up for them and help give the state some swagger. Howie Dickenman, a Perno holdover who remained on Calhoun's staff, told his new boss that if he could get himself tossed from a game, the fan base would eat it up. It wasn't necessarily a big ask. *Irascible* is a word you'll hear a lot if you ask people to describe Calhoun. "Some of the things Jimmy Calhoun said? Woof," John Cahill, the longtime official, says. "To us, to his officials, to players, to anyone."

It smacks of armchair psychologist, but in Calhoun's case, the inner fire fueled by the sudden loss of his father carried him through his professional life. He knew how suddenly things could change, and he not only grabbed opportunity, he wrung all its possibilities out of it. To not work was to cheat a chance. "He taught me about having a sense of urgency," says Khalid El-Amin, who would help take Calhoun to his first national title. "He held all of us to a higher standard. For me, he was perfect because he challenged me to rise to the occasion. He wasn't for everybody, though."

As he promised his wife, Calhoun worked endlessly and tirelessly. He read newspapers from other Big East cities, intent on knowing what was going on elsewhere, and scoured the country for recruits. Like Carlesimo, Calhoun used the Big East as part of his marketing strategy. He'd ask players if they'd heard from Georgetown or St. John's, and when they invariably said they had not, he'd respond without pause, "Well, how'd you like to beat them?" Once they got to campus, players learned quickly that while Calhoun could tolerate mistakes, at least slightly, he could not tolerate a lack of effort. He'd signal for a timeout and use the entire break to scream at his team; he stalked the sidelines with such determination, the floors probably wanted to beg for mercy. As a pro, Scott Burrell played alongside Michael Jordan and, as explained in *The Last Dance* documentary on Jordan, was a frequent target of Jordan's disdain. Burrell laughs off Jordan's criticism. "Coach Calhoun was a hundred times harder than that," Burrell says. Rather than dole out uniforms on the first day of practice, players were handed ugly, faded gray T-shirts and shorts, the implication simple: They'd have to earn their way into a uniform. Nothing would be handed to them.

Two-mile runs ended with two-hour practices. A typical practice "was never typical," according to former Husky Chris Smith. "Oh, Coach was tough, but you gotta realize he was trying to establish himself as well. He worked us to the brink, but the way we played demanded that." Pikiell remembers calling home, moaning to his dad about Calhoun's demands. He did not find a receptive audience. "Do what he tells you," his father told him. Pikiell, one of nine kids, was on a full scholarship. "My dad wasn't paying my tuition."

Calhoun made roster reconfiguration his first priority, not just securing players but ensuring that their eligibility was handled properly. The disconnect between the athletics department and the university cited in that task force report manifested itself in the academic progress—or lack thereof—of the Huskies' roster. Cliff Robinson and Phil Gamble both attended summer school to recalibrate their academics, earning back their eligibility but with strict probationary limits. Calhoun essentially re-recruited two of Perno's players, convincing Tate George and Pikiell to come to UConn, and then searched far and wide for others.

He quickly learned the pecking order with recruiting, working hard to land a player only to lose out at the last minute to one of the more established Big East teams. Rather than settle for second-tier Northeast players who probably couldn't handle the rigors of the league, he went outside the league's footprint. He found Rod Sellers in South Carolina, John Gwynn in Maryland, and Nadav Henefeld all the way across the globe in Tel Aviv after taking a flyer on a piece of advice from the late Marv Kessler, an instructor Calhoun had known for years from the Five-Star Basketball Camp in Honesdale, Pennsylvania. "We didn't say no to anybody," Calhoun says. "We weren't going to get Derrick Coleman and Sleepy Floyd, but we could get guys who could grow into that."

He also got a little lucky. Calhoun eventually would coach thirty-one future NBA players and eight All-Americans. Yet asked to name the most important player in his program's history, the coach doesn't hesitate. "Chris Smith," he says. From nearby Bridgeport, Smith would lead his high school team to one state title and a runner-up finish, earning state Player of the Year honors along the way. He intended to go to Syracuse, where he'd join his good friend Billy Owens. "And then I told my mom," Smith says with a laugh. "She said, 'We'll never get to see you play.'" Instead Smith chose to stay home, arriving in Storrs in 1988 and opening the floodgates for the state university. Prior to that, virtually all of Connecticut's top players had left the state for college; even worse, a lot opted to go to other Big East teams. Charles Smith went to Pittsburgh from Bridgeport, earning Big East Player of the Year honors for the Panthers, not the Huskies. Michael Adams, from Hartford, took Boston College to the Sweet Sixteen and Elite Eight. John Pinone, also of Hartford, helped elevate Villanova, and Trumbull's Harold Jensen became the Wildcats' star in the 1985 title game.

Calhoun also knew intuitively that his great equalizer would be defense. It would be a while before his teams could go head-to-head with most of the Big East rosters offensively. They wouldn't come ready-made with the same kind of talent. But by playing hard and scrapping, the Huskies could be disruptive. Not only was it a style that suited the coach, but it was one he knew well. Years earlier the young coach had called in a few chips, getting a friend of a friend of a friend to set him up for a visit with the Wizard of Westwood. Over two-plus hours, first at Pauley Pavilion and later at his apartment, John Wooden laid out the basics of the 2-2-1 press that made his UCLA teams so strong. Calhoun carried the lessons back east, employing them with his Northeastern teams to great success. He knew the press could help close the gap at UConn, too.

He was right, Calhoun engineering a swift and—at least from the outside—stunning turnaround. In Calhoun's twenty-six seasons as head coach, he would have but one losing season, his first, but even in that year the progress was so evident that at the final game of the season, a win against Seton Hall, the fans sent UConn off with an ovation, convinced better things were on the horizon after the 9–19 finish.

Their faith was immediately rewarded, the Huskies improving to 20–13 overall the next year, and though they won but four Big East games that season, two of them—against number nine Syracuse and number fourteen Georgetown—showed the promise of what UConn might be. At the Carrier Dome, in front of 29,000 screaming fans, Robinson hit two free throws with two seconds left, UConn's defense dismantling a Syracuse team that averaged 95.5 points per game. The Orange hit the 50-point threshold with 2:39 left in the game . . . and never scored again, losing 51–50. It marked Syracuse's lowest scoring output since that memorable last game at Manley Field House, 250 games and seven years earlier.

Three weeks later, the Huskies struck again, beating Georgetown for the first time since the 1981–82 season. Though the Hoyas weren't ranked as high as Syracuse, the game in a lot of ways meant more. It was played at the Hartford Civic Center in front of 16,000 fans, an all-time record crowd for a New England college hoops game.

The Huskies couldn't carry the momentum from that victory—they lost five of their final six league games to finish in ninth place—but earned an NIT bid, the program's first postseason berth in five years.

They then proceeded to win the whole thing, beating Ohio State for the championship, the program's first national title of any kind. Fans stormed the Madison Square Garden court, Gamble leading a chant of "U-Conn, U-Conn" that ricocheted around the place and back on campus. Students who didn't make the game celebrated at the student union and at the neighborhood bars, honking horns and setting off firecrackers. "That elevated everything," Calhoun says. "All of a sudden, everywhere you went it was, 'Hey, UConn!' People were so excited."

Sports often don't follow neat, linear projections, and saddled with the new weight of expectations, UConn failed to continue its trajectory the following year. The Huskies weren't bad; they won 7 Big East games but only 18 overall in 1988–89. This time the NIT bid that had been so eagerly accepted a year earlier felt like a letdown. Even worse, this time they were bounced in the quarterfinals, losing to Alabama-Birmingham in the Field House swan song. Afterward, Calhoun lamented that he saw a team that reminded him of his fiery squad from a year earlier, only it wasn't the one wearing blue and white.

The disappointment didn't last, and rarely reared its head again during Calhoun's tenure. The following season, the Huskies, older and wiser, put together one of those magical seasons that by then the Big East was known for. A program that only a handful of years earlier had been left on the garbage heap finished the season ranked fourth in the nation, achieving 30 wins, coming home with a Big East Tournament title, and within an overtime buzzer-beater of the Final Four. The word *meteoric* doesn't do the climb justice; the ascension was so quick it left people struggling to wrap their minds around it. After beating Syracuse for the Big East Tournament crown, the dam broke on what felt like a statewide catharsis. As the public address announcer begged the spectators to keep order, fans flooded the court in celebration, hugging and crying. Smith, the tournament MVP, wound up covered in blue paint, courtesy of a bear hug from someone who'd smeared the school colors all over his chest.

Though there had been plenty of big moments and signature wins as the Huskies rose, this represented so much more. Ever since Calhoun had joined the league, the Big East had served as a measuring stick. His team and his own coaching acumen were only good insofar as they compared favorably to those of his league peers. Now he and the Huskies officially stood on top of the mountain. "Coach cracked an actual smile," Pikiell says with a laugh. "Maybe the second time I'd actually ever seen one."

In practical terms, the win meant even more. The Huskies, back in the NCAA Tournament for the first time since 1979, earned a number one seed in the East and two home games, playing the opening rounds in Hartford. To the delight of the very partisan crowds, they eased past Boston University for their first NCAA win since 1976, and took care of Cal in the second round. That set up an easy ride down the interstate to the Meadowlands, the New Jersey sports complex parked along the NJ Turnpike, and a Sweet Sixteen date with Clemson.

Followed joyfully by their fans, the Huskies built a 19-point lead with 12 minutes left, sending Husky nation into bedlam. It did not have the same effect on the Tigers, who'd spent much of March coming from behind, including from being down 19 in their previous game against La Salle. They mounted what can only be construed as a 30–10 all-out attack, coming all the way back to take a 70–69 lead on David Young's corner 3-pointer. Tate George's shot came up short for UConn, and the Huskies had to foul, sending Sean Tyson to the line for Clemson. Game announcers Dick Stockton and Hubie Brown deemed the game over, beginning to wax eloquent about Clemson's propensity to win ugly. Even after Tyson clanked the front end of the one-and-one off the front of the rim, they spoke as if the end result was a foregone conclusion—understandably, what with 94 feet to cover and one second to get there.

Huddled during a timeout, though, the UConn players and staff calmly discussed their next move. "Home run one," Calhoun says. "Everyone knew what we had to do." All season the Huskies practiced endgame scenarios—home runs one through five, the number indicative of the time on the clock. They knew the play. Burrell set up on the baseline. A freshman from Hamden, Connecticut, Burrell was a three-sport high school star, a good enough pitcher to be drafted by the Seattle Mariners and a starting quarterback for his high school team. He originally planned to go to Miami to play basketball and baseball, but Dickenman was relentless, leaving notes on Burrell's doorstep before he even awoke for school. Eventually Burrell would split his time, playing in the minors during his UConn summers before segueing into an eight-year NBA career. In that March moment, all of Burrell's athletic skills coalesced in a play so perfect it still earns him a hero's welcome at UConn.

With every inch of 6'11" Elden Campbell eclipsing the left side of the court, Burrell made like a QB throwing a corner pass, finding George, who created just enough space against Tyson at the other end of the floor. In one fluid move, George caught Burrell's pass with his back to the basket, turned, and hoisted a 17-foot shot over Tyson. The ball hung in the air as the buzzer sounded, and then swished through the net, securing the Huskies' win.

Calhoun ran around the court in disbelief, while his players mosh-pitted at midcourt in celebration. "I'm not sure it really hit us until after," Smith says. "You're playing these games, and you don't realize that millions and millions of people are watching. We didn't understand how big it was."

The Huskies did, however, understand that their journey wasn't over. On the doorstep of the Final Four, they were set to face their most formidable foe yet. By 1990, Duke had been to three of the last four Final Fours, a dynasty in the making. The Blue Devils knew everything that the Huskies didn't about playing in big games. But UConn's insouciance had been its calling card all season, the Huskies rolling like a boulder downhill, immune to this notion of what they should or should not be capable of. "We just felt like we couldn't lose," Pikiell says. "No matter who we played."

And so naturally, here they came at Duke, defending and scrapping and pushing the Blue Devils into overtime. It was, by all accounts, a magnificent game, taut and fierce, and again coming down to the final seconds. UConn led 78–77 with the ball and under a minute to play, but after trying to drain the clock, George was forced to take a bad three from the corner that fell well short of the basket, giving the Blue Devils a chance to win it. Bobby Hurley, the player who a year earlier had teased Jerry Walker, his high school teammate, during the Seton Hall game, pushed the ball downcourt as the game clock dipped below five seconds, and tried to pass to a teammate in front of his own bench. George jumped the passing route, timing the play perfectly, but as he neared the sideline he fought for his balance to stay in bounds, the ball dribbling off his fingertips and out of bounds. George doubled over at the waist during the dead ball, clutching his two hands in front of his face, as if wishing them to grab the ball. "He has great hands," Smith says. "That's not like Tate. But even then, we thought we'd win."

The Blue Devils had just 2.6 seconds left to pull off a miracle. Calhoun elected not to guard the inbounds pass, as Clemson had done to him, and Duke got a quick give-and-go with Laettner, who leaned in and dropped a floater at the buzzer. A game after experiencing the joy of buzzer-beating March Madness, the Huskies watched their season end. A stoic and grim-faced Calhoun embraced Mike Krzyzewski as UConn shuffled off the court.

Heartbroken for his players, Calhoun greeted them in the locker room and reminded them of all they had accomplished—and, more, what they had established. In their four years, the seniors had carried the Huskies from nowhere to the brink of the Final Four, giving a formerly anonymous university a national platform. "In a lot of ways, it wasn't like Coach, at least not after a loss," Smith says with a chuckle. "He was hugging everybody. He felt like we gave it our all." So, too, did the entire state of Connecticut. The Huskies returned defeated, but to a heroes' welcome, fans greeting the bus as it arrived on campus, the state legislature later inviting the team to the capitol to fete their success. "Jim Calhoun brought the program up from the bottom of the ocean," Charlie Pierce, the Boston-based reporter, says. "For Dave [Gavitt], that was it. That was the final triumph. Everyone had had their shot."

That game served as a beginning for UConn. "I tell my players all the time, 'Leave a legacy,'" says Burrell, now the head coach at Southern Connecticut. "We did that. We couldn't see it then, but we should have. We turned that program around." The Huskies became mainstays in the NCAA Tournament and a dominating force in the Big East.

What no one realized, though, was that the game also signaled the end of the Big East.

Two months after the Huskies' run ended, the Big East endured its first personnel change, and it was the biggest switch of them all: Gavitt left to become the Celtics' CEO. The Big East was Gavitt's baby, and to abandon it just eleven years in seemed incomprehensible. Yet at his core Gavitt was a native New Englander, and this was a chance to partner with his lifelong friend Red Auerbach and resuscitate the Celtics, New England's beloved franchise. The Celtics needed him. He couldn't pass it up. Gavitt also figured he was leaving the league in very good hands.

Though the nine athletic directors did a thorough job looking for Gavitt's replacement, they chose the obvious. Tranghese interviewed at a hotel at Boston's Logan Airport. Asked why he thought he could do the job, Tranghese gave a candid answer that sold the ADs on the hire: "Dave's my best friend in the world, but I'm not Dave. If you think you're getting Dave Gavitt 2.0, don't hire me."

Tranghese took over a league that by all outward appearances seemed dominant and secure. The new commissioner, though, knew better. The Big East sat on a college athletics fault line, and the tremors already were starting. As both Gavitt and Tranghese had predicted years earlier, football posed a serious threat to the basketball-centric league. Elsewhere in the nation, the pull of the pigskin already had undercut once-powerful conferences. The Southwest Conference, for example, lost Arkansas to the Southeastern Conference because of football, all but writing the death certificate for the old league. Tranghese knew that his league, with only three football-playing schools (Boston College, Syracuse, and Pittsburgh), was ripe for the picking. Just days on the job, Tranghese convened a meeting with his ADs, explaining why football was so important and what the league would stand to lose if it didn't act. "We couldn't lose Syracuse," Tranghese says. "It was that simple. The whole face of the league would change." The athletic directors grudgingly admitted that they needed to add more football schools, and after only two weeks as the boss, Tranghese flew to Miami to meet with athletic director Sam Jankovich. Dominant despite operating as an independent, the Hurricanes were enjoying the attentions of multiple suitors. Having just added Florida State, the ACC was now courting the Canes, as was the SEC.

For the Big East, Miami was not a natural fit. There is nothing East about South Florida, and Miami brought absolutely nothing to the basketball table. The school dropped the sport in 1971 and only restarted it in 1985, enjoying tepid results. But it would add immediate football legitimacy; more, it would bring security. In October 1990, the Hurricanes invited to join the Big East. By year's end, Tranghese brokered deals to add West Virginia, Virginia Tech, Rutgers, and Temple as affiliate football-only members. (Rutgers and West Virginia would become basketball members in 1995, and Virginia Tech in 2000.)

This was not Gavitt huddling with lifelong friends, building up allegiances for the betterment of the schools and the sport. This was pure preservation, schools added because they said yes, not because they fit a mission. No one argued that it had to be done, but that doesn't mean anyone liked it, either. "The first three years that I worked as commissioner, I'd like to have a dollar for every time I thought about just leaving this crap," Tranghese says. "People had basketball issues. People had football issues. It was just hard."

As if football expansion wasn't enough to make the league vulnerable, basketball entered its most difficult transitional period at the same time. In the span of two pivotal weeks in 1992, Rollie Massimino left Villanova in anger for UNLV and Carnesecca retired. No one could match the personalities of those two, and being the man to follow The Man was no easy act. "I grew up in the Bronx, a half-assed Division III player, son of a Greek immigrant, and here I am in this room with Thompson and Calhoun and Boeheim," says Steve Lappas, who took over at Villanova. "All I wanted was to be a D-I head coach my whole life, and I got this opportunity—but wow, what an opportunity."

By then, *Big Monday* games, featuring the Big East and Big 8, were TV staples, and schools annually pocketed more than $1 million from their TV contracts alone. From its inception through the 1991 season, the Big East failed to place a team in the top ten of the final Associated Press poll just once—in 1981.

At least the league's basketball reputation preceded it, so luring players to join its teams no longer required a leap of faith. They all wanted in. The league's brilliant and prescient partnership with ESPN served it well, the network expanding its reach and thereby that of the Big East. The broadcasts, led by colorful commentators and filled with splashy graphics, felt more like dramas. Kerry Kittles, who would become a 1996 consensus All-American at Villanova, sat in his New Orleans living room watching Big East games. It never occurred to him to stay home for college. Out in California in the late 1980s, Mike Hopkins pedaled home on his bike from school, determined not to miss a single second of *Big Monday* games, even though they tipped off at 4 p.m. West Coast time. "They'd do these halftime shows on Walter Berry growing up in Brooklyn, and I'd tape them all and watch them over and over again," says Hopkins, who would play at Syracuse and serve as Boeheim's longtime lieutenant before becoming head coach at Washington. "You'd watch local games on KTLA Channel 5, and it was like, there's no juice. Where's Dick Vitale? The Big East was the standard."

In some ways, the balance of power shifted. As the old-guard coaches moved on—Carlesimo would leave for the Portland Trail Blazers in 1994 and Thompson, Jr., would retire in 1999—the players became the focal point. From 1990 to 1999, the league produced thirty-three first-round NBA draft picks.

Two of those picks, Allen Iverson and Ray Allen, put on a perfectly timed only-in-the–Big East finish in 1996. Prior to that year and with Thompson's assist, Tranghese had practically bullied his coaches into moving the tournament final from Sunday afternoon to Saturday night. The decision, though wise, meant breaking off from CBS, which televised the semis and the final and was known as the home of the NCAA Tournament, and going all in with ESPN. "Honestly, I was a jerk about it," Tranghese says. "It was probably the biggest fight I ever had." But like his old friend Gavitt, Tranghese had the good fortune of good timing. "The first one, that was 1996, Allen versus Allen," Tranghese says. "Boom, there you go."

It is nearly impossible to quantify Allen Iverson—as person, as impact, as lightning rod. Dave Teel, the longtime columnist and basketball reporter at the *Daily Press* in Newport News, Virginia, remembers getting a call on his office phone one day, a friend imploring him to drive down to Wake Forest and watch the AAU Nationals being conducted there that July. That was the first time Teel saw Iverson play in person. He was gobsmacked, amazed by Iverson's combination of athleticism and fearlessness. For months after, Teel paid the favor forward, inviting friends to join him at Iverson's Bethel High School games in Hampton, Virginia, taking particular pleasure in bringing those who thought the diminutive guard could in no way live up to the hype.

"It was like taking folks to church," Teel says. "They were converted." As Iverson's legend grew, the crowds at those games swelled to the point they had to play at the nearby Hampton University arena, people flocking from all over to see the electrifying player who competed with such wild abandon.

As a junior, Iverson quarterbacked the football team to a state title and was in the middle of doing the same with the basketball squad when a fight broke out at Circle Lanes bowling alley on Valentine's Day 1993. Chairs were tossed and sides were taken, white high schoolers against Black. A woman was knocked unconscious and needed six stitches after being hit on the head with a chair, another woman broke her thumb, and a man broke his arm. Soon the authorities were coming for Iverson, charging him with three felony counts of maiming by mob—an offense put in the books, ironically, to prosecute lynchings. Three others, all friends of Iverson's, also were charged.

The fight and the fallout splintered the community, creating a division so bitter people claimed it was the most intense racial divide the region had felt since the Martin Luther King, Jr., assassination. In the midst of it all one day, Teel took another call in his office, the caller not even bothering to identify himself, just bellowing, "David, what in the hell is going on down there?" It was Thompson. The Georgetown coach wasn't calling so much for a report on a recruit as for a report on society, trying to understand how the fight had led to such serious charges. He figured Teel, a well-respected journalist in the area, would have the answers. The reporter did not.

An old-time lawyer convinced Iverson and his family that the seventeen-year-old would be better served by a bench trial than by a trial of his peers, and after months of haggling, Circuit Judge Nelson T. Overton convicted Iverson in July, sentencing him to five years in prison. "A jury of adults wouldn't have convicted that kid in a million years," Teel says. "Instead, he had an old-school no-nonsense judge who sends him away."

Iverson spent four months in prison until new lawyers took over the case and Governor Douglas Wilder, the first Black governor in Virginia, granted Iverson conditional clemency and ordered his release. Among the conditions were that the eighteen-year-old Iverson could not play sports and had to pursue his high school diploma. Two years later, the Virginia Supreme Court overturned his conviction.

For Iverson, the damage already was done. Critics who had been quick to label the kid from the rough side of town a thug believed their opinions to be vindicated, and the schools once desperate to add the high school All-American to their rosters backed off.

Worried about her son slipping through the cracks, Ann Iverson drove to visit the one coach she thought could save her son: Thompson. She thought he could provide the structure and discipline he needed, and nearly begged the coach to take a chance on him. Certainly there was some altruism at play. Thompson saw the unfairness in Iverson's treatment, and believed the kid deserved a chance. But Thompson needed Iverson, too. By the early 1990s, the Hoyas weren't nearly as dominant as they once had been. Thompson regularly attracted great big men to campus, including Dikembe Mutombo and Alonzo Mourning, but their guard play had dipped. After that loss to Duke in the 1989 Elite Eight, Georgetown failed to make it out of the first weekend of the NCAA Tournament for four years and was relegated to the NIT in a fifth. "I would be hypocritical if I didn't acknowledge the fact that this is someone who is exceptional at basketball, and I am a basketball coach," Thompson said at the time.

Thompson understood Iverson, maybe better than Iverson understood himself. The coach gave the player the discipline he needed, but also understood he couldn't rein him in on the basketball court. Iverson played on instinct, his game a masterful ad lib, and Thompson found the fine line between structure and letting Iverson be Iverson.

"If there was one guy that could stretch the envelope, it was Iverson," says Rich Chvotkin, the Hoyas' play-by-play man. He recalled a charter flight to a game during a snowstorm when Iverson kept kicking snow at teammate Jerry Nichols. Nichols came from Jackson, Mississippi, and Iverson kept needling him, asking if he'd ever seen snow before. It was silly and childish, and if it had been anyone else, it probably would have earned a rebuke from Thompson. "Allen's the only guy that could get away with that," Chvotkin says. "Of course, no one else would have done it, either."

Others were not so easily placated. Critics scoffed at the notion that a kid with such a checkered past could enroll at a prestigious school such as Georgetown. They argued the arrangement was little more than a basketball transaction, that Thompson risked tarnishing the school's image in exchange for boosting his NCAA results. Thompson never denied that he benefited from Iverson's enrollment—the Hoyas returned to the Sweet Sixteen and Elite Eight with Iverson in the lineup—but during his 2016 Hall of Fame induction speech, Iverson also made clear what the coach did for him. "I want to thank Coach Thompson for saving my life," Iverson said.

"I never worried about Allen the two hours when he was on the court," Thompson says. "I worried about the others."

Ray Allen grew up in a world as structured as Iverson's was unstructured. The son of an Air Force mechanic, he traveled the world, raised on military bases from Oklahoma to Great Britain. When he finally put down roots in South Carolina, he was the odd man out, the Black kid who "talked like a white boy," thanks to the British accent he carried across the pond.

Raised with discipline, he approached the sport the same way. Allen honed his game for hours on the court, playing against grown men to get tougher, and practicing his shooting stroke until it became almost an art form. Basketball earned him legitimacy and entry among the teenagers, but by then he didn't much care for acceptance. Allen was comfortable being different, hyperfocused on his craft and content with solitude. He became a reader, and would grow into one of the most thoughtful conversationalists in the NBA. He led his South Carolina high school to a state title, drawing interest from across the country. He boiled his choices down to Kentucky, then coached by Rick Pitino, and UConn—opting for the Huskies, he said years later, because he felt like Calhoun was more vested in his future.

The two players' games were as distinctly opposite as their upbringings. Iverson was basketball unscripted, his game honed on the playgrounds and based on instinct and almost a complete disregard for his own well-being. Often the smallest guy on the court, he was always the toughest and the fastest. "So fast, ridiculously fast," Villanova All-American Kerry Kittles says. "You couldn't stay in front of him. You. Could. Not. Stay. In. Front. Of. Him." Allen, on the other hand, was a basketball purist's dream. Fundamentally sound, his shot was near textbook perfection, his game predicated on doing things the right way. Though their time in the league was fleeting (both would be gone by 1996, Iverson, a sophomore, drafted first that year and Allen, a junior, taken third), they left behind indelible legacies, cemented in one fateful game at Madison Square Garden in 1996.

By 1995–96, league membership was in a state of flux. Notre Dame joined for all sports save football, while other schools, originally added for just football, began competing in all sports, including hoops. It was, to say the least, messy. In so many ways, UConn carried the Big East through that pivotal transition. Once the team no one wanted, the Huskies became the picture of consistency. On the heels of that 1990 Elite Eight run, they would go to two more Sweet Sixteens and another regional final. But Calhoun was damned by his own success. For all UConn had achieved, it had yet to reach a Final Four, and when the Huskies arrived in New York for the 1996 tourney, they were greeted by tabloids accusing their coach of underachieving. Calhoun played it cool, but anyone who knew the man knew the criticism ate at him.

Thompson, too, arrived with critics sniping at him, the Hoyas equally victims of their own success. For all he had achieved, Thompson still had only one national title to show for it.

On the eve of the tournament, Ray Allen earned Big East Player of the Year honors, winning the award even though Iverson led the league in scoring and steals and, in the only head-to-head meeting between the two teams, doubled Allen in scoring as Georgetown won the game. Iverson never said he was fueled by the snub, but he certainly played like a man with something to prove. In a quarterfinal waxing of overmatched Miami, he finished with 38 points, 2 shy of the Big East Tournament scoring record at the time, and then dropped 28 against Villanova to advance Georgetown to the title game.

On the other side of the bracket, Allen did not initially wear his Player of the Year crown well, shooting just 4 of 17 and scoring 11 as his teammates carried the Huskies to a romp over Seton Hall. He rediscovered his groove quickly, though. In a semifinal against Syracuse, Allen finished with 29 points, 19 in the first half and 10 in the final seven minutes as the Orange threatened an upset.

The Garden buzzed as the lights dimmed for that first Saturday night final, the stage set with two great teams, led by two great players. "You know, sometimes you walk into a building and you can feel it," Calhoun says. "It was magical"—at least until the game started.

The matchup between the two stars at first failed to ignite, Iverson dogged by UConn guard Ricky Moore and plagued by foul trouble, and Allen unable to find his shooting stroke. The game, in fact, belonged more to Georgetown's Victor Page, a player from the Barry Farms projects in D.C., brought in as the backcourt complement to Iverson. Page would score 20 in the game, win tourney MVP, and help push the Hoyas to an 11-point lead with four minutes to play. Up comfortably, Thompson turned again to Iverson, subbing him in for Page. "I followed the philosophy of Red Auerbach, that regardless of how poorly your best players are playing, when it comes down to the end, you put them in the game," Thompson says. "I put our best player back in the game and it stopped some of [Page's] momentum. That's one of the biggest mistakes I ever made."

Not that the coach could have seen what was coming. No one could. Kirk King, a junior from Louisiana and role player for UConn, scored 8 of his 20 points in the final four minutes, launching the Huskies on an offensive assault against one of the best defensive teams in the country. When King threw down a putback dunk with a minute to play, the Huskies trailed by just 1, and the pro-UConn crowd worked itself into a frenzy.

Back in the game after the Huskies rallied, Page missed the front end of a one-and-one, giving UConn a chance to win with 45 seconds left. As the shot clock wound down, Moore handed off to Allen, who dribbled at the top of the arc. Though the logical person to take the big shot normally, Allen didn't seem the smart choice at the time—he'd failed to make a single bucket in the entire second half and had missed 14 consecutive shots. Allen pulled up, his legs scissoring, looking as if he was going to pass the ball. Instead, at the last minute he tossed an off-balance shot at the rim.

And in that moment, all of the work on the military bases and in the quiet of seclusion paid off. The man who had perfected his jumper found the reward for his diligence: The ball glanced off the front of the rim, up and over, and through the net. Iverson wasn't going to go down without a fight, but the guard's pull-up jumper came up short, as did the layup rebound from teammate Jerome Williams.

Suddenly there stood UConn, the team no one had wanted in the league, hoisting a trophy as the Big East Tournament champion. "Magical," Calhoun reiterated. "Just magical."

The Huskies, though, failed to take the pixie dust with them to the NCAA Tournament. Awarded a number one seed, they were upset by Mississippi State in the Sweet Sixteen.

Not that the Big East's run was over.

No, instead unheralded Syracuse carried the Big East's water in March. After they'd dropped to 14–6 on the heels of an overtime loss to Villanova in January, no one thought much about the Orange. Boeheim tinkered with his lineup, inserting Queens kid and junior college transfer Jason Cipolla into the starting lineup. Known then for his lack of defense, Cipolla became a frequent late-game hero, joining with leading scorer John Wallace to lead Syracuse on an unexpected 7–1 charge to finish the regular season.

Ousted by Allen and UConn in the Big East Tournament, the Orange earned the fourth seed in the NCAA Tournament. And while the Huskies were sent packing early, Syracuse kept marching. In a game that would endear that 1995–96 team to the Orange faithful for life, Wallace and Cipolla combined for some serious March drama to oust Georgia in the Sweet Sixteen. Wallace found Cipolla with an inbounds cross-court desperation pass, and Cipolla sank the baseline jumper to force overtime at the buzzer. With 2.8 seconds left in the extra period, Wallace, who would finish with 30 points and 15 rebounds, drained a leaning 3-pointer, and the Orange advanced to the Elite Eight.

A roster that included only one player destined for the NBA then topped Kansas, a team with four future NBAers, 60–57, to advance to the Final Four. When the team returned to Syracuse that night, Wallace paraded around the downtown watering holes with the net draped around his neck.

No one would claim that this was Boeheim's finest team, but it was arguably his feistiest. The Final Four that year took place in the very familiar Meadowlands, just a few hours' ride from Syracuse. Joined by its orange-clad faithful in full throat, the Syracuse zone defense baffled Mississippi State, and the Orange advanced to the title game. Cipolla memorably strolled to the press table after the game ended, picked up the phone, and announced to the dial tone on the other end of the line, "I'm rolling to the championship."

But he and his teammates rolled into a brick wall. Kentucky, Syracuse's title-game foe, was loaded with so much talent that its apt nickname was "The Untouchables." Coached by the man Boeheim once wooed on his wedding night to be his assistant, Rick Pitino, the Wildcats had lost only two games all season, and throttled teams all throughout the NCAA Tournament. The coach who'd been labeled an upstart whippersnapper all those years ago by Massimino was now arguably one of the best in the game, rebuilding a Kentucky team that had been hit with devastating NCAA sanctions into a national force.

Given little chance to win, Syracuse offered much more fight than expected. But Tony Delk drained seven 3-pointers, puncturing the Orange zone just enough to lead Kentucky to the title. Rightly praised for leading a team of overachievers, Boeheim nonetheless concluded his twentieth year as head coach without a title.

He became the latest coach dogged by his inability to win the big one, an unfair tag that virtually every successful coach carries at one time or another. At least Boeheim had a colleague to carry the albatross: Calhoun, despite a 223–72 record from 1989 to 1998, hadn't yet reached a Final Four.

Calhoun did a little reassessing, trying to figure out what was preventing his team from making the final step. He thought maybe his relentless pursuit of perfection wore out players mentally. "Tired minds, tired legs," Calhoun says. He could not and would not change entirely, but he worked to strike a better balance. He demanded the same intensity, but dialed back on the hours. He made time for fun, scheduling more movie nights or team meals—little things he thought would lessen both the physical and mental grind of the long season.

Rejuvenated after star Rip Hamilton elected to return to school rather than go pro, the Huskies started the 1998–99 season on a summer tour of London and Tel Aviv, Calhoun letting down his guard even more, relaxing with his team as they toured the sights. They returned to the States ranked second in the nation. El-Amin, though just a sophomore, established himself as a leader. The Minneapolis native was drawn to UConn by basketball, but also by the East Coast rap culture, and brought that attitude and verve to practice. Confident and at times comical, he had one mission that year: "Put UConn on the map for good," he says.

For the entirety of the season, the Huskies and Duke swapped spots in the polls, but the Blue Devils, already owners of two national titles, always seemed to rank ahead of the Huskies in the court of public opinion. That didn't sit well in Storrs, especially as the Huskies plowed through their season, gobbling up the Big East regular-season title and the Big East Tournament crown while losing just two games all year. "Duke, always Duke," El-Amin says. After steamrolling through the opening weekend of the NCAA Tournament, Calhoun and UConn torched Iowa by 10 and finally got over their perceived barrier, beating an upstart program by the name of Gonzaga to reach the Final Four.

Having achieved a goal that had eluded the program for so long, the Huskies could barely enjoy the view. They were too good to merely get to the national semifinals now. Stealing a page from Thompson's handbook, Calhoun squirreled his team in a hotel away from the Final Four hub in Tampa, hoping to defuse some of the pressure. The plan worked, with the businesslike Huskies beating Ohio State to reach the national championship.

Naturally, only one team could be on the other side—Duke, the Huskies' nemesis from nine years ago and the thorn in their side all season. The Blue Devils owned a 37–1 record and possessed a huge edge in big-game experience. At 33–2, there was nothing especially plucky about the Huskies, but they nonetheless were labeled the underdogs, both in people's opinions and in Vegas, where oddsmakers made Duke the 9.5-point favorite. "We were both ranked one and two the whole season," El-Amin says. "We thought it was really disrespectful." It was and it wasn't. El-Amin is right that UConn hung practically in lockstep with Duke that season, but those particular Blue Devils, with four players who months later would be first-round NBA draft picks, seemed unbeatable. Always looking for an edge, Calhoun used the perceived slight to his advantage and employed a little mental gamesmanship with his team. "The most important thing was our kids thought we were underdogs," he says. "I might have played that up a little bit."

Fueled by the disrespect, perceived or real, the Huskies dogged the Devils for the entire game. The game featured eight ties and fourteen lead changes, neither team able to get any breathing room from the other. As the game headed toward the final minute, El-Amin drained a baseline floater, giving UConn a

3-point lead, 75–72. Moore fouled William Avery on the next Duke possession, and Avery sank both free throws, putting Duke back within one. El-Amin missed a pull-up jumper, giving the Blue Devils a chance to take the lead with less than 30 seconds to play. But UConn, a team built all those years ago by Calhoun on the reliability of defense, won it on that end of the floor. Moore, who years earlier had dogged Iverson in that Big East Tournament final, guarded Trajan Langdon, who already had 25 points, as he tried to make his way toward the basket. Moore refused to give Langdon an inch or allow him to spin, and Langdon wound up being whistled for traveling. Forced to foul, the Devils sent El-Amin to the line. The guard sank the two freebies with 5.2 seconds to go.

Langdon pushed the ball ahead as quickly as he could for Duke, but tripped as he tried to split two defenders. He lay sprawled on the floor as the clock expired, UConn the 77–74 winner and national champion.

El-Amin ran in circles, eventually finding his way toward the TV crew, his voice ringing clearly across the CBS telecast: "We shocked the world!" Years later, he doesn't back down from his claim. "I'm sorry, we did," El-Amin says. "If you weren't a UConn fan, you didn't see us winning. But Coach always told us, 'This is why you play the game.' We were the better team that night. We deserved to win."

At twenty years old, the Big East now owned three national championships. And by the time he retired, Calhoun would bring two more trophies to the league's case, more titles than any single coach in league history. "The Big East gave Connecticut a forum, but Jimmy ran with it," Tranghese says. "What he did, that's just remarkable, the most remarkable story. Go back and look at the entire Big East—what Jim Calhoun did is mind-boggling at times."

That night, while his players celebrated in the team hotel,

Calhoun went to his room and sat the championship trophy on his dresser, facing his bed. The man who all those years earlier had told his wife, Pat, that she might not see much of him as he worked to build UConn woke up the next morning laughing. He nudged Pat, telling her to take a peek at the dresser. "It was still there," he says. "I couldn't believe it. I wanted it to be Ground-hog Day."

Alas, the world had to keep spinning. As the Big East pushed into the next millennium, it headed into a decade of yet more incredible moments . . . and devastating changes.

CHAPTER 11

THE LAST OF THE ORIGINALS: BOEHEIM FINALLY GETS HIS RING

"We're going to get it right this time"

Back when the Carrier Dome debuted, two students met at the Alvord House, a family-owned restaurant in the Syracuse suburb of Marcellus, New York. One was a theater major, the other an idea man. In 1978, Syracuse had decided to stop using the Saltine Warrior, a student dressed up as a Native American, as its mascot, recognizing the insensitivity in the portrayal. But the school did not provide an alternative mascot that year. Which is where the two students, the Alvord House, and a few beers came in.

Deciding it was high time their school came up with something, the two started playing word association, trying out different rhyming schemes. Of course, nothing rhymes with *orange*. "So we tried *dome. Home, phone, lone.* Whoa, the Lone Ranger," says Dennis Brogan. "That was it." A quick trip to a nearby Sears for a cowboy outfit, a dye kit to turn the pants and vest orange, and a can of blue spray paint to alter ordinary boots, and lo and behold, the Dome Ranger was born.

For ten years Brogan, the theater major, patrolled the Dome, eventually becoming an unofficial official mascot. Granted a courtside seat, he enlivened the crowd, cajoled fans out of their seats, and antagonized coaches. Upon his retirement in 1990, Thompson gifted his longtime antagonist a towel. "To the Dome Ranger, thanks for all the great memories," he wrote.

By the dawn of the new millennium, there was reason to fear the Big East soon would become just that: a memory. Dogged by coaching changes and forced to stretch its boundaries even farther because of football, the league spent the early part of the 2000s creating some of its most unforgettable moments, all the while trying to outrun its own demise.

But as much as people look at that 2000-to-2013 span as the beginning of the end of the league, the Big East did not go quietly into the night. Syracuse and UConn each would win national championships, and the two schools would parry in an unforgettable instant classic of six overtimes in the Big East Tournament quarterfinals. John Thompson III would lift Georgetown to another Final Four, as would Jay Wright at Villanova. In 2011, as it swelled to its fullest girth of sixteen teams, the league would send a record eleven teams into the NCAA Tournament field, and in 2013, before it all came undone, Louisville would send the league out with yet another championship. "It wasn't the same, of course, but in my humble opinion the league then was as good in terms of its dominance as it was in the glory years," Thompson III says. "During that second wave, even when it got bigger, kids grew up knowing that the Big East was a basketball league."

That was the thing about the Big East. Bastardized and bloated in geography and size, it still owned the identity Gavitt had constructed all those years earlier. It was gritty and tough, its epicenter still in New York, its personality unchanged. West Virginia, Notre Dame—these teams didn't fit the original mold geographically, but they suited the way the league played.

Above all else, great players still wanted to be a part of it, as Boeheim found out when one of them committed to Syracuse. In the summer of 2001, Mike Hopkins, Boeheim's associate head coach, was hot on the recruiting trail of Matt Walsh, a Philly-area sharpshooter, heading down to Lewes, Delaware, to watch Walsh play in the Slam Dunk to the Beach. But his fellow assistant, Troy Weaver, suggested Hopkins check out another player while he was there, insisting that this other kid was head and shoulders above Walsh. "He had his braids, his headband around his neck, and he was in the layup line," Hopkins says. "I probably watched four layups and I looked at Weav and said, 'Oh my God.' I hadn't seen him play yet, but I knew."

The player was Carmelo Anthony. In a nearly endless list of greats to come through Syracuse, others such as Pearl might be more beloved, but none did what Melo did for the city, the program, and Boeheim. And Anthony did it in just one season, delivering to Syracuse the final prize missing from the trophy case—a national championship.

It's fitting that Boeheim earned his championship when he did. By 2003, he was the last man standing, the final coach from the original group of seven still coaching in the Big East. A man universally praised for his fierce loyalty, Boeheim stayed true to both his alma mater and his league, refusing to budge. Yet as his tenure continued and his resume grew thicker and thicker with successes, the last step remained elusive. Boeheim did not need a national title to validate him, but no one doubted how badly he wanted one, dating all the way back to that Keith Smart dagger shot in the 1987 title game. "He never talked about it, never said anything about it," Hopkins says. "But his body language, seeing him slumped in the chair after Indiana . . . he deserved it."

It is not a fair measure of a man's worth that only he who wins titles is considered among the best. The NCAA Tournament requires luck as much as skill, and the best team isn't always the last one standing. But such is the judgment of sports—only ultimate winners are considered ultimate successes. And despite all that Boeheim had accomplished, he managed only the rather backhanded compliment of being the best coach to never have won it all.

Naturally, for a man who waited twenty-seven seasons to get there, the final mountaintop couldn't be summited easily. The 2002–3 team wasn't his best team, or even necessarily his most talented. They were young—Kueth Duany was the lone senior—and had to figure things out before they could find their stride. Along with Anthony, the Syracuse roster included two other quality freshmen in Gerry McNamara and Billy Edelin, as well as long and lanky sophomore Hakim Warrick. But they needed to learn to work together. "Carmelo's trust in his teammates evolved as the season went on," McNamara says. "He was so good, early on it may have been frustrating for him at times, to be able to play at the level he can but not many else can. Eventually he started to understand, 'Hey, Gerry can make that shot,' or 'Hakim can isolate.' He started to understand the value of having good players around him." Like most young teams, especially those used to scoring in bunches, the Orange struggled when a team took them off their offensive game.

Not surprisingly, the one team that could really match wits with Boeheim was the one team still with stability at the top. By 2003, Calhoun ranked as the second-longest-tenured coach in the conference, and on the heels of his own first championship, he found the sweet spot of success. Once an outpost, Storrs became a basketball destination. No one confused UConn with Yukon anymore. The once undesirable Huskies reigned as a flagship team in the best conference in the country. UConn played for the league title in 2000 and won the Big East Tournament again in 2002.

But defense remained Calhoun's calling card, and though his 2002–3 team was young, relying on sophomores Ben Gordon and Emeka Okafor, they were less susceptible to the fickle whims of offense. In February, they ground the Orange to a near halt, taking a team that had scored 94 points a game earlier against West Virginia and holding it to just 61. Later that year, they knocked the Orange out of the Big East Tournament with the same defensive grind. Syracuse shot just 23 of 80, and 2 of 18 from the 3-point line, in the loss. Though Anthony had 29 points, he needed 28 shots to get them, and the league's rookie sensation wound up leaving New York empty-handed.

Instead a wizened member of the old guard reminded everyone that year how the Big East was done. For years Pitt existed on the outskirts of the league's elite, good but never quite as good. In 1988, coach Paul Evans led the Panthers to their apex, a regular-season league title and a number two ranking, but they were bounced from the NCAA Tournament in the second round by Vanderbilt. Unable to match that zenith, Evans was forced to resign in 1994, and his replacement, Ralph Willard, did not fare much better. Amid lousy results and a player arrest, Willard resigned in 1999.

When the school hired Ben Howland out of Northern Arizona that year, it did not exactly win the press conference. Area reporters questioned what they deemed a small-minded hire, convinced Howland didn't have the stuff for the big time. But he grew the Panthers into a classic Big East team. Aesthetically they weren't always pleasing, what with their grind-it-out style, but a program that never had a Big East niche suddenly had an identity. Pitt was tough, and maybe even a tinge nasty.

As the league grew and had to separate into divisions, twice Howland led the Panthers to the West Division title. But in 2002,

UConn beat Pitt in double overtime for the league championship. Guard Brandin Knight reentered the game with an injured knee but was unable to connect on a would-be winner from 40 feet out for the Panthers.

A year later, in 2003, Pitt and UConn met again for the title. This time Knight already was injured. He'd badly sprained his ankle the night before, in the semifinal against Boston College. Already a lock for an NCAA Tournament bid, no one would have blamed Howland if he'd opted to bench his star for the championship game. No one except Knight, that is. He played 37 minutes, scored 16 points, and dished out 6 assists as the older Panthers (with three seniors and two juniors) effectively beat the snot out of Connecticut, 74–56, giving the Big East yet another new tournament champion. "Do you really think there's any way in the world I would have been able to keep him out?" a giddy Howland said afterward. "He would have killed me."

Four league teams (Pitt, Syracuse, UConn, and Notre Dame) earned NCAA bids that Selection Sunday. All four made it to the Sweet Sixteen, but Dwyane Wade and Marquette ousted Pitt, top-seeded Arizona took care of Notre Dame, and Texas quite literally stuck it to UConn—the Huskies' hope for tying the game with 20 seconds left was dashed when Marcus White's putback shot got stuck between the backboard and the rim and the Longhorns retained possession. Disappointed as he was with the loss, Calhoun sent a letter to the Texas head coach, his old league rival Rick Barnes. Barnes was nine years and two jobs removed from his days at Providence, but Calhoun still felt the Big East kinship, and wrote to congratulate Barnes on all he had accomplished. "I always remembered that," Barnes says.

That left Syracuse, which ironically nearly didn't even make the Sweet Sixteen. A game earlier, in the second round against Oklahoma State, the Orange trailed 14–2 to start the game, and

31–25 at the half. In the locker room, Boeheim didn't rant or rave; he simply challenged his young team. "We're going to see what you're made of," he told his players. "You've got 20 minutes to figure it out. You're either going to get run out of this gym, or you're going to get back in this game." The message from that speech would carry the Orange not only through the second half, where they'd rally to go from down 12 to win by 12, but as they marched through March. Challenged by a late-surging Auburn in the Sweet Sixteen, Syracuse dug deep and won again, then thumped Oklahoma by 16 in the Elite Eight.

Sixteen years after his heart was broken by Keith Smart and Indiana, Boeheim returned to New Orleans for yet another Final Four. Upon arrival at the airport, the coach boarded the bus that would squire the Orange throughout the weekend, and was greeted by the man who would serve as the team host. "We're going to get it right this time," the man said. Boeheim did a double take, only then realizing it was the same man who had hosted the Orange in 1987. "I was glad to see him," the coach says, "I took it as a good sign."

Odds are Anthony had slightly more to do with the results than the old-timer. The phenom poured in 33 against Texas in the national semifinal, and his rookie backcourt mate McNamara added 19 as Syracuse advanced to the national title game. As Anthony exited the floor, the orange-clad fans chanted "One more year," hoping Melo would defy the odds and stay in college rather than turn pro.

At least they knew they had him for one more game, against Kansas for a national title. The pregame story lines were easy. On one side sat Roy Williams, the man with the best winning percentage of any D-I coach without a title; on the other sat Boeheim, hoping to exorcise the Keith Smart demon in the same place he'd had his heart broken in 1987. At the time, Boeheim's record more than spoke for itself. He was 652–226, his .742 winning percentage second only to Williams's, and twenty-five times led Syracuse to 20 wins or more. He also was 0 for 2 in title games.

As Syracuse gave back all of an 11-point halftime lead to the Jayhawks, history seemed hell-bent on repeating itself, the Orange implosion resembling the disaster in 1987 against Indiana. Boeheim had little time to think about ghosts of Final Fours past, his thoughts occupied with the yo-yo battle between Syracuse and Kansas in the second half.

Finally, as time whittled down, Kansas's sharpshooter Kirk Hinrich had an open look at what would have been a game-tying three, the ball mercifully rattling out. "I contested late," Gerry McNamara admits. "I saw Coach out there, waving his Gumby arms around, telling me to contest it." After forward Hakim Warrick secured the rebound and got fouled, Boeheim subbed McNamara out for Edelin. McNamara had a bird's-eye view of what happened next.

Just a 67 percent free-throw shooter, Warrick missed both of his freebies, giving the Jayhawks, still down 81–78, another chance with 13.5 seconds to play. Hinrich swung the ball around to the corner, finding Michael Lee, another great Kansas shooter. At the last second Warrick came from nowhere, stretching his long arms to get a piece of the ball, blocking the shot. The officials reviewed the play, then put 1.5 seconds left on the clock—and taking twenty-five years off every Syracuse fan's life, especially those who'd endured Smart's magic all those years earlier. "All weekend, all we heard about was Keith Smart," McNamara says. "I remember thinking, 'Of course it's going in. That's what happens.'"

In the final 1.5 seconds, Hinrich did manage to get off a shot, but there would be no last-second miracle. This time the ball fell to the floor, and Boeheim finally had his national championship.

The players collected in a dogpile on the court—"The side of Kueth's shoe kicked me in the face," McNamara says with a laugh—while their coach gave one of his patented smirks before casually going over to shake Williams's hand. Though elated, Boeheim managed to keep his emotions in check until he finally boarded the bus to return to the team hotel. As he climbed the steps, the team host greeted him with a grin and a bear hug. "You were right," Boeheim told him.

While the players celebrated at the hotel, the coach and about twenty others gathered for a late-night dinner at the Smith & Wollensky steak house with close friends and longtime colleagues, including Tranghese and P.J. Carlesimo. The ex–Seton Hall coach couldn't let his buddy off without a dig. "I can't believe it took you this long to win," he said as the dinner crowd roared with approval.

Later, in the wee hours, they all journeyed to Bourbon Street, where the Syracuse faithful still celebrated. "He had on his trench coat, the one he always wears, but he also wore the hat—the national championship hat," Hopkins says of Boeheim. "That was it. The hat was the symbol of his outward celebration. Boosters are crying, but he's not out there like, 'I just won a national championship.' Just Cool Hand Luke with his hat, that's it."

There was no holding back the tidal wave of joy among the fans, especially the soused ones on Bourbon Street. They soon spied their coach and rushed over to greet him, the crowd eventually growing so thick that the police came along, offering Boeheim a ride back to the hotel. He left reluctantly, moved by the outpouring of kindness he'd experienced. "That was, honestly, that was the best," he says. "It was a great moment. A really great moment."

If he'd known then what he knows now, maybe Boeheim would have lingered there on the street even longer. In ten years' time, Boeheim, the last original conference pillar, would be forced into a new conference alliance. Syracuse's departure would eventually crack the Big East's very foundation. Yet even as it headed toward a tumultuous end, the Big East kept delivering great moments.

CHAPTER 12

SIX OVERTIMES AND THE END OF AN ERA

"My final gift to you"

On the surface, the Big East indeed looked perfect. Though its borders now stretched practically nationwide, the essence of the league—combative, combustible, and dominant basketball—remained. In its last decade, from 2004 to 2013, the conference would win two more national titles and claim seven Final Four berths, five unique teams winding their way to the national semifinals. And in 2011, the league would break its own record, earning 11 NCAA Tournament bids.

But behind closed doors the conference meetings, once collegial if hot-tempered, turned tempestuous. With more money than just the chump change of ball deals at stake and football causing a rift between the schools that sponsored the sport and those that didn't, the rancor and ill will hit a tipping point when founding member Boston College announced it was departing for the ACC in 2005. A furious Tranghese, angered at how the school handled its departure, practically Italian-hexed the Eagles. "I told Boston College people, 'If you go, you're going to get your money, but you're never going to win,'" he says. "'You'll never win at football and you'll never win at basketball.' And I was right."

Yet not even the chaos of that decade, one that created a fissure so deep that it would ultimately force the conference to disband in order to be reborn, could keep the league from shining. The might of the Big East was too strong. A year after Syracuse finally hoisted a national championship trophy, UConn delivered the Big East's second run of back-to-back title winners, capturing the whole thing in 2004.

The Huskies that year were loaded. "The guys coming off the bench were lottery picks," Calhoun jokes. He wasn't far off. Six of those Huskies wound up first-round picks, and the only team to challenge UConn was their Final Four nemesis, Duke, in the national semifinals. In yet another classic between the two, UConn rallied from down 8 with a little more than 3 minutes left in the game to win, and then waxed Georgia Tech, 82–73, for the championship. "We were better because we played in the Big East," Calhoun says. "In that era it was incredibly difficult to win games in our league, and that prepared you for the tournament. It was a great, great benefit."

No doubt, when expanded to its fullest, the Big East presented an impossible gauntlet to manage, especially in New York. Though the league grew to sixteen teams for the 2005–6 season, it didn't invite all of its members to their own postseason tourney until 2009. Only the top twelve earned a spot in New York, teams nine through twelve starting play on Wednesday night, everyone else earning a bye until Thursday.

In 2006, the first year of full expansion, Syracuse limped to the Garden on a three-game losing skid. Only three years removed from the national title, the Orange were seeded ninth with a lousy 7–9 Big East record. Worse, Gerry McNamara, their star player, quite literally limped into New York, still suffering from what he'd later learn was a stress fracture in his pelvic bone. But at first neither McNamara nor anyone else knew what the injury was, even though the pain at times was unbearable. Everyday tasks such as tying a pair of shoes proved impossible, and a simple sneeze sent him into a spasm of agony. Boeheim rationed McNamara's practice time and the player lived in the training room, but he refused to skip a game or even complain, even as his shooting percentages dipped to the worst of his four-year career.

The statistical slide did not diminish his adoration in Syracuse. Born and raised just down I-81 in Scranton, Pennsylvania, McNamara is the only Syracuse player to finish with 2,000 points, 600 assists, and 250 steals, and his blue-collar approach rendered him one of the most beloved Orange players of all time. His senior night that year became a downright spectacle, with the Carrier Dome actually selling out for the first time in its twenty-six-year history. Fans streamed in from Scranton, sixty buses enjoying a police escort out of his hometown, to watch their favorite son play. Some sat in what would be considered the opposite end zone were it a football game, so far away that they had no choice but to watch the action on the big screens. Many didn't even stay for the game; they came just to say goodbye and thank you to Gerry. During the pregame festivities, schoolchildren actually sang a song dedicated to McNamara. The whole thing was such high emotion that at one point Jay Wright, whose Villanova team served as Syracuse's opponent that day, turned around and spied his wife, Patty, crying in the seats just behind his bench. "What are you doing?" he yelled. "Why are you crying?"

As it turned out, Wright and Villanova would ruin McNamara's last stand, much as Georgetown had spoiled the last game at Manley. "Yeah, nobody from Villanova was crying afterward," McNamara says. The Wildcats won, 92–82, and the NCAA on-campus record crowd of 33,633 left dejected and worried about what Syracuse could accomplish in New York.

On the eve of the Big East Tournament that year, the Syracuse *Post-Standard* ran an anonymous poll of league assistant coaches. By an overwhelming vote, McNamara earned the "honor" of Most Overrated. The next night, the senior guard drove the length of the court and launched a buzzer-beating 3-pointer to beat Cincinnati in the first round of the Big East Tournament, and an enraged Boeheim unleashed his fury about the poll in an expletive-laced tirade. "I have to laugh a little bit when our own paper is calling him . . . overrated," he said in the postgame press conference. "They actually listened to a couple of assistant coaches who I guarantee will never be head coaches if they think Gerry McNamara is overrated." He went on to say, "Without Gerry McNamara we wouldn't have won ten fucking games this year. OK? Not ten . . . That's the most bullshit thing I've seen in thirty years."

Thus began a run that even long-standing Broadway shows would envy for its drama. Fueled by McNamara's heroics, Syracuse became the first team to win four games in four nights and capture the Big East Tournament title. It was an epic run made all the more improbable as McNamara played through his pelvic injury. After each game, he'd ease himself into a cold tub, or in this case into a Marriott Eastside hotel bathtub that a courteous bellboy filled with water and ice nightly. The next day he'd tie up his sneakers and play another game.

After hitting the hero shot against Cincinnati on Tuesday night, he turned around for a noon quarterfinal tip against Connecticut, the number one team in the nation, sinking a three to send the game into overtime. Syracuse won that one as McNamara scored 17 points, dished out 13 assists, and somehow played 41 minutes. Another evening in the cold bath, another tip-off against a great team, this time rival Georgetown in the Friday night semifinals.

By then the pain was nearly unbearable, and McNamara remembers telling his athletic trainer he wasn't sure if he could play. He lasted just 12 minutes in the first half, his absence evident—Syracuse trailed by 15 at the break, scoring just 21 points. Like Willis Reed, who decades earlier limped onto the same Garden court to inspire the Knicks in a Game 7 NBA Finals showdown with the Lakers, McNamara somehow managed to play in the second half, rallying Syracuse all the way back to a 58–57 win, setting up teammate Eric Devendorf for the go-ahead layup.

That left just one more game, against Pittsburgh, for the Big East Tournament title. The building that night actually felt alive, as if its nerve endings were firing with anticipation. Jamie Dixon, a Howland assistant, had followed in his former boss's footsteps after Howland left for UCLA, maintaining Pitt's identity as a nasty defensive team. Though the Panthers recruited players from New York and boasted a heavily local roster, the Garden remained Syracuse territory, the orange-clad faithful flocking to the building for McNamara's Big East curtain call. His final bow: 38 minutes, 14 points, and 6 assists; a 65–61 win and a Big East Tournament title. As he went out to grab the championship trophy and his hardware for MVP, McNamara slipped an orange T-shirt over his jersey. "Overrated?!!" it read.

The injury ultimately would be too much for McNamara. Unable to function in the NCAA Tournament, he played only 23 minutes and scored 2 points in a loss to Texas A&M. The loss stung, but the memories from New York helped ease them. "I had played in so many great games, beginning with my freshman year when we won the national championship, but this was mine," he says. "This was my team, and after all the criticism and adversity I had gone through all year—I don't know. A lot of people ate their words that week." McNamara did not go on to NBA glory—he's now an assistant with Boeheim at his alma mater—but in that New York snapshot, he became as famous as any player in college basketball. Thanks again to the bright lights of ESPN and the aura of the Garden, people tuned in to watch, convinced they would see a little more magic each night. That McNamara delivered elevated him beyond just the Syracuse annals and into Big East lore.

Three years later, the old hero of New York had a front-row seat to what was arguably the greatest game in Big East history and, to many, one of the most engrossing college basketball games of all time. To fans of that era, it is a where-were-you-when moment. Those who watched the whole thing wear their commitment like a badge of honor, and those who retired early still kick themselves for their lack of fortitude.

For the Big East, the six-overtime game between Syracuse and Connecticut in the 2009 Big East Tournament quarterfinal served as a very loud rejoinder that though the league's identity had been threatened by football, basketball remained its soul.

Sports often are told by statistics, and there is one number that says everything about that marathon game: 226. That's how many minutes it took to complete. The game began at 9:36 p.m. and ended at 1:22 a.m. It lasted so long that the Philly reporters who left after filing their game stories off the earlier Villanova game took the local NJ Transit train to Trenton, drove the forty minutes from the station to their homes, and still saw the end of the game. It lasted so long that P.J. Carlesimo, in Indianapolis to call the Big Ten Tournament on the radio, started and finished a steak dinner at St. Elmo's Steak House, and wound up watching the end at the bar with the waitstaff and cooks after the restaurant closed. It lasted so long that Leo Rautins, in Toronto after working a Raptors game, listened on the other end of his wife's phone for more than an hour as his son, Andy, played on. "At one point I heard them playing 'Oh What a Night' over the loud-speaker," Rautins says. It lasted so long that when two reporters exited the Garden onto the streets of New York, one looked around at the empty city streets and remarked, "The city sleeps."

"I was exhausted just watching it," says McNamara, who sat beneath the basket. "I kept thinking, 'So this is what people are talking about when they watch a game as a fan? The anxiety? Yeah, this sucks.'"

Had it ended in regulation, it would have made the Big East highlight reel. With 1.1 seconds left, freshman Kemba Walker grabbed a rebound and laid it in for UConn, knotting the game at 71, setting up Devendorf for what he thought was his hero moment, when he corralled that Paul Harris pass for the quick three at the buzzer.

Except . . . except in the middle of the mayhem, referee John Cahill went to the monitor to review the play. With assistant coaches hovering over his shoulder, he asked the video coordi-nators to enlarge the replay as much as they could, trying to fig-ure out if the ball left Devendorf's fingertips before the clock expired. After looking at it over and over, Cahill knew the game was not, in fact, over. "I turned around and said to Bob [Donato], 'Bob, that's no good,'" Cahill says. Donato immediately volun-teered to share the good news with Calhoun, while Cahill was tasked with informing Boeheim. "He looks at me with that Jim Boeheim look, no emotion," Cahill says. "And he just says, 'You better be fucking right.'"

Denied a fabulous finish, instead the two teams delivered a game for the ages, with one big shot begetting the next, ulti-mately ending just one OT shy of the all-time NCAA record for a game. Rick Jackson's lay-in for Syracuse tied the score at 81 and forced overtime number two. Jonny Flynn missed a jumper late for the Orange, and the game went on to the third extra period.

Rautins drained a three to knot the score again, and UConn's A.J. Price and Jeff Adrien both missed to stretch the game into OT number four. Syracuse missed at the end, Harris failing to connect on two chip shots as the buzzer sounded, and the game went into the fifth.

With each extra period, the fans—those who didn't leave—somehow grew louder. Refusing to sit down, they yelled as if they were torn between rooting their own team to victory and hoping the game might never end. Gassed players doubled over and tugged on the hems of their shorts, while the officials guzzled Gatorade in an attempt to stave off cramps. "I think it was about the fifth overtime that Syracuse put in walk-on Justin Thomas, who hadn't played much," says Bill Raftery, who was on the TV call. "Everybody in that game is just dead. He's out there doing jumping jacks at the top of the zone. We were dying laughing."

Maybe the only person more exhausted than the players was Lisa Zanecchia. Unbeknownst to almost everyone in the building, Tranghese had decided to retire. This would be his last Big East Tournament, and his longtime assistant, with the help of Tranghese's wife, Susan, had planned a little surprise party following the game. They'd invited staff, plus friends from Providence, to join them at their favorite Italian haunt, owned by good friends. Only the game wouldn't end, and Zanecchia had to keep calling the owners, asking if they'd stay open. "I just kept calling and calling," she says.

Tranghese, who had no clue that he would be the guest of honor at a dinner later, watched the game in awe, amazed at the send-off his beloved tournament was giving him. Just before the fifth overtime, he slipped a note to the broadcasting team of Raftery, Jay Bilas, and Sean McDonough. "This is my final gift to you," he wrote. Of the note, Raftery says, "Now I never keep anything, but I had Jay and Sean sign that and I put that note with the final box score and had it framed. It still hangs in my office."

The commissioner, though, was premature in his footnote. The game was not yet over. Flynn, who would play 67 of the 70 minutes, sank two free throws with 20 seconds left in the fifth OT to tie the game at 110, using a little body language to coax the second rattler through the net. Price missed on a long three, and Adrien's rebound jumper swirled around the rim before falling off, sending the game to the sixth OT. A weary security guard, charged with standing on the court between sessions, took his post during the break and joked, "I say we just go to a shootout," suggesting hockey's sudden-death solution.

Finally, 15 seconds into that sixth OT, Rautins popped off a screen and drained a three, giving Syracuse its first lead in any overtime period. The Orange never gave it back, extending their advantage over the equally exhausted Huskies. A game with so much drama eventually ended with a whimper, Syracuse pulling away to win, 127–117.

The exhausted players spent extra time in the handshake line, even rivals finding reasons to hug. For the better part of their careers together, Devendorf and Price engaged in a constant chatter of trash talk. On that night, though, they smiled and shook their heads before embracing. "People ask me all the time, 'Are you glad that shot in regulation didn't count?' And yeah, I am," Devendorf says. "That shot was the setup to everything that came after." It was, of course, easier for Devendorf to wax eloquent. His team won. It was not so easy for the Huskies, especially for one of the sport's notorious bad losers. In the postgame press conference, no amount of prompting could get Calhoun to speak to the magnitude of what he'd just been part of. He was too angry he'd lost. "People always ask me how I felt because it was historic," Calhoun says. "That's like being shot at Gettysburg and being happy about it. I got shot."

The game ended at 1:22 a.m., but the night was hardly over for those involved. Cahill and his officiating crew went back to the hospitality suite at the Hyatt to eat and go over the assignments for the next day's semifinals. He doesn't remember exactly what time he left the suite, but it was late enough—or, perhaps more accurately, early enough—that when he got back to his room, the morning's papers were waiting at his doorstep. After he'd gotten a few hours of sleep, his phone rang. His boss, Art Hyland, was on the other end, asking if he'd recovered. "Not really," Cahill says. "And then he says, 'OK, good. You have the Villanova-Louisville game at seven.'"

Devendorf and his roommate, Arinze Onuaku, found a late-night diner and grabbed some food. They returned to their rooms and switched on the TV. Their game already was an instant classic, replaying on ESPN. "I think I went to bed around four," he says.

McNamara went to the team hotel, where he bumped into Mike Hopkins in the lobby. The associate head coach asked the ex-player if he wanted to help break down game film of West Virginia, Syracuse's semifinal opponent. The two worked until the sun came up.

When he finally got out of the Garden, after congratulating Boeheim and trying to console the inconsolable Calhoun, Tranghese headed to his party. Thirty years earlier, he'd helped Gavitt launch his brazen idea, never imagining the wild ride he'd take with the Big East. From a jack-of-all-trades sidekick negotiating TV deals in a muddy field, he'd become one of the most powerful men in college athletics. His last TV deal with ESPN, a seven-year agreement made in 2006, was worth $250 million.

He had watched the conference swell from its original seven members, including plenty of reluctant and cynical head coaches, to a sixteen-team beast spilling over with future Hall of Famers. By the time it reached its thirtieth birthday that summer of 2009, the conference had sent seven different teams to the Final Four in the NCAA Tournament modern era, dating to the bracket expansion in 1985. Only the Big Ten, older by seventy-three years, could match the Big East's diversity. In that same era, the league claimed four unique national champions. No one else had more than three.

But Tranghese was ready for a change. He had shepherded the league through the departure of Boston College, and created a separate football division. He felt good about the Big East's future.

Thanks to Zanecchia, the restaurant staff waited up, even though the guest of honor didn't arrive until two in the morning. They laid out the food and drink and then departed, asking only that the last person to leave lock the door on the way out. Nostalgic but not melancholy, Tranghese reveled in the memories, and the old stories were embellished in the retelling. There were a few tears, but mostly there was laughter. This was something to be celebrated, a success story grander than even Dave Gavitt, the ultimate dreamer, could have envisioned.

Somewhere around six in the morning the party broke up, everyone spilling onto the city streets, the sun just starting to rise.

Tranghese did as he was asked, and locked the door behind him.

A LEAGUE REBORN, BUT NEVER DUPLICATED
"Once in forever"

Dave Gavitt died on September 16, 2011. A day later, Syracuse and Pittsburgh announced they would leave the Big East and join the ACC, essentially laying the league to rest alongside its founder. As Lou Carnesecca might say, they finally took the chandeliers.

The news of their pending departure had been brewing for some time, and the breakup had been threatened for even longer. Tranghese thought he'd left his conference in good standing; instead he'd left it sitting on a fault line. The football and basketball interests were too disparate to reconcile, the possible profit too large to walk away from. "I think everyone knew it wasn't sustainable for a long time," says Vince Nicastro, a former Villanova athletic director and the current Big East deputy commissioner and chief operating officer. "It was going fine for a while, and in large part, our association with football really helped us, not only with competitiveness, but we had a seat at the governance table, and it helped with year-round exposure. But it couldn't last."

In May 2011, just a month after Kemba Walker led UConn on an unbelievable run that ended with the Huskies' national title, the league agreed in principle to a new nine-year TV package with ESPN worth $1.4 billion, or $11 million per school. Members were haggling over how to split the money when things all but stalled. Pushed hard by Pitt officials to not take the deal—at the time the Pac-12 also was negotiating a deal that would set the market value—the league followed their lead and gambled it could score better if it waited things out, maybe even finding a more lucrative payday with NBC or Fox. "I think that was the stupidest decision ever made in college athletics," a source told CBSSports.com at the time. Indeed, it proved to be the conference's undoing. ESPN, unable to secure a commitment from Big East football schools that they'd stick around for the long haul, essentially yanked its offer.

Wooed by other suitors and less confident in their own home, football-playing schools started to eye other league affiliations. By then, conference realignment had taken over college athletics, the shifts all driven by football. Basketball, once the lone player in the development of the Big East, became an afterthought in the conference's demise.

Pitt and Syracuse took the bait first, going public with their decision before even telling their longtime colleagues.

Nicastro, getting ready to head to a Villanova football game, learned of the news when he saw it on the sports ticker on TV. Georgetown president Jack DeGioia doesn't remember the particulars of how he found out, just that he was "shocked, completely and totally shocked." In Providence, still reeling from the death of his lifelong friend, Tranghese was disgusted. "I said to [Gavitt's wife] Julie, 'I'm glad he's not alive to see this,'" Tranghese recalls. "I couldn't bear to watch this with him."

In a week's time, they all gathered at the Cathedral of Saints Paul and Peter in Providence, Jim Boeheim and Jim Calhoun sharing one pew, John Thompson, Jr., and DeGioia directly behind them, to say goodbye to the man who had brought them together. Gavitt's Final Four players served as his pallbearers, escorting their coach one final time. "At one point, Ernie [Di-Gregorio] says to Marvin [Barnes], 'No, over here, Marvin,'" says DeGioia, a Providence native who grew up seeking out Friars games on his transistor radio. "He was still the point guard. It was lovely."

As Gavitt was laid to rest, so, too, was the Big East. Though exit strategies had to be negotiated and the rest of the dominoes would need time to fall, the Big East, as fans knew it, was over.

Pitt's exit stung the conference. Syracuse's gutted it. Years earlier, Tranghese had invited Miami into the fold in order to prevent Syracuse from leaving. It didn't matter. The Orange were leaving anyway, taking the very essence of the Big East with it. The Orange are woven into the very fabric of the Big East, from the Manley Field House moment to six overtimes, from the Louie and Bouie Show to the Pearl to Melo, and Boeheim above all. Synonymous with Syracuse, Boeheim was, by extension, synonymous with the Big East. And now it was all over, the basketball history felled by football. "They took our song and changed it," John Thompson, Jr., said of the demise of the league he loved.

Boeheim, caught between loyalty to his alma mater and loyalty to his league, grieved especially hard. Though he understood the business, he expressed his disappointment and, even after years in the ACC, laments the decision. "It wasn't once in a lifetime," he says of the Big East. "It was once in forever."

The dam broken, other schools headed to the exits. After West Virginia bolted for the Big 12 in October, the Big East was forced to Band-Aid its existence, offering invitations to an Ellis

Island–like list of schools—Boise State, San Diego State, Navy, Temple, and East Carolina as football schools; Memphis, Central Florida, Houston, SMU, Tulane, and Loyola as basketball members. It became absolute chaos, schools agreeing to join and then changing direction before ever playing a game.

In September 2012, Notre Dame left for the ACC, Rutgers joined the Big Ten a month later, and Louisville headed for the ACC in November. Months of haggling and even lawsuits over exit fees and withdrawal dates ensued as the league desperately tried to scramble for its existence, but in doing so it sacrificed its very identity. This wasn't Gavitt's vision; this was a mess. "We're going to bring in SMU?" Thompson said at the time. "What the hell? They're nice people, but they don't belong here."

Eventually the original core of the league agreed on the path to take. With decisions being made with little regard for them and the boundaries of the Big East stretched to comical lengths, the leaders of the non-football schools met privately. Years earlier, back when Boston College had created the first fissure, Tranghese and the league presidents added a clause to the by-laws—"a prenuptial agreement," Nicastro says. It provided that if the seven basketball-playing members (Villanova, Providence, Georgetown, Seton Hall, St. John's, DePaul, and Marquette) exited together, they could do so without paying exit fees and retain whatever NCAA Tournament money they earned.

That served as the out the basketball schools needed, and in December 2012, the leaders of the Catholic 7, as they came to be known, met at St. John's, agreeing essentially to secede. "We felt like what was required to sustain the commitment to football had made the conference something that was no longer recognizable," DeGioia says. "It was impossible to sustain a coherence of the original vision of the Big East."

It's funny how history repeats itself. The Catholic 7's decision to leave the Big East together and re-form as another conference was nearly as daring a move as the one Gavitt made in 1979. At the time, basketball schools did not rule the roost. Even bluebloods such as Kansas were hanging on for dear life as their universities negotiated landing places based solely on the financial whims of football. Now seven people—and not exactly seven sports power brokers, either: one president was a philosopher by trade (DeGioia), one was a mathematician (Seton Hall president Gabriel Esteban), and the others were priests—were turning the world onto its backside. They had little choice, of course, but that didn't mean it wasn't a little crazy.

Yet with almost warp speed, they made decisions that were both difficult and necessary. Going all in on basketball, they parted ways with UConn, which was still in need of a football home; added Butler, Xavier, and Creighton; and negotiated to keep the name Big East, retain the Garden for their postseason tournament, and establish a TV deal with Fox for $500 million— less than what football schools were getting, but more than enough to sustain the conference. They also announced they would declare their official arrival in July, and begin competition in the fall of 2013.

Watching from afar, Val Ackerman, who was teaching a leadership course at Columbia University, used the league's rebirth as a case study for her students. A pioneering player at the University of Virginia herself and the first president of the WNBA, Ackerman loved the idea of a conference geared wholly toward basketball, but thought the presidents' timeline seemed a tad ambitious. "These guys can't possibly be starting this year," she remembers thinking. "No way. It has to be next year."

When those same presidents called Dan Beebe, he thought the same as Ackerman. "July?" he remembers thinking. A former Big 12 commissioner who lost his job after his league went through realignment, Beebe came on as a consultant in April 2013, asked to sign a thirty-day contract. "I said, 'Uh, you're going to need a little longer than that,'" Beebe says. "They wanted to put the key in the ignition and go. No, no—the car doesn't have an engine yet, or a steering wheel." He wound up staying six months, assisted eventually by Ackerman herself. A search firm led the presidents to Ackerman, who went from studying the league to becoming its commissioner.

It was, in so many ways, a total throwback. Ackerman wasn't out in a muddy field negotiating a TV deal in a trailer, but it was nearly the same mom-and-pop start as the Big East in 1979. There were modern twists to the tale—without a Big East email account, for instance, Ackerman used her Gmail account for months—but it was the same by-the-bootstraps story, equally comical in its shoestring beginnings.

Georgetown managed the league's checking account, since it didn't have one of its own, and Ackerman hired people with a promise more than a contract—"I kept saying, 'I don't have a benefits package just yet, but trust me, I will,'" she says with a laugh. The skeleton crew she brought in spent more than a year working out of the Manhattan-based Proskauer law offices. Joe Leccese, the firm's chairman, who also headed up their sports group, represented the Catholic 7 in the critical early negotiations, gave Ackerman an office, and then eventually extended an entire hallway to the Big East. They stayed there until September 2014, the firm's administrative assistants doubling as Big East administrative assistants.

Beebe worked on developing a schedule not just for men's and women's basketball, the flagship sports, but for all twenty sports that would now be housed under the league umbrella. He targeted John Cahill, recently retired, as the league's new supervisor of officials. "To be honest, it was exhausting, and I don't know if I could survive another year like that," Ackerman says. "It was memorable and a great story, but it was really, really hard."

What buoyed Ackerman—really, what lifted everyone involved in the resurrection of the Big East—was a refusal to let the league die. It was a commitment that went far deeper than just loyalty to a job or trying to make a buck. The Big East—its identity, its tradition—meant something to so many people, and so it became about more than just self-preservation; it was about preserving history. "There is kind of an integrity, but I don't mean in an honest or dishonest way," DeGioia says. "I mean consistency, coherence, alignment. The Big East knows what it is."

And what the Big East is, even its reconfigured status, is what it always was: a powerful basketball league. In its first seven years as a reestablished league, the Big East already has produced two national players of the year (Creighton's Doug McDermott and Villanova's Jalen Brunson) and eight first-round NBA draft picks. The ten-member conference has never earned fewer than four NCAA Tournament bids, and in 2017 seven of its ten teams went to the tourney.

The most telling statistic, though, is the simplest and most obvious: Two new national championship trophies now sit in the Big East cases. Villanova, national title winner in 2016 and 2018, has proven that not only is it possible for basketball-centric programs to survive without the boost of big-money football, but they can thrive. If people wanted to write off the Wildcats' first championship, won on an epic buzzer-beating 3-pointer, as a fluke, there was no dismissing the Cats as a national power when they won again in 2018, dominating the tournament field.

By extension, then, there was—and is still—no dismissing the Big East. It is not the same. Nothing could be. That era of college basketball, of wildly combustible coaches and dominant players, is gone. There is too much money involved for coaches, too many images to protect, and too little time for players, who rarely stay in college for four years.

But once doomed by comparisons to what was, the Big East

now is strong enough to be judged for what it is. "We may not have the personalities, but there's still an understanding like there was then, that we're part of something special," Jay Wright says. "Those guys, they were all larger than life. But nothing is bigger than the Big East."

ACKNOWLEDGMENTS

The email arrived in my inbox on February 21, 2019. *Literary agent reaching out,* the subject line read. Two days earlier, I'd written a story for *The Athletic* about the chaos inside the old Big East coaches' meetings, and the story caught Matt Carlini's eye. He'd always believed the Big East deserved a book, he said in his email. Might I be interested in writing it?

So if I'm going to start off these acknowledgments accurately, this is where I have to start. Matt not only saw the idea for a book and believed I could do it, he shepherded me through the entire process. I am indebted to him.

Matt also introduced me to a fabulous editor, Mary Reynics. The story of the Big East is complicated, and without Mary there's no way I could have maneuvered through its history. She kept me on course, helped me drill down on what was truly important, and with gentle suggestions made the words better.

I cannot adequately express my gratitude to those who provided the nuts and bolts for this book by sharing their stories. No one person is more or less important, but a few deserve a mention. Before the world shut down, Michael Tranghese spent hours in a hotel conference room with me, reliving the league's history. Dan Gavitt, Jim Boeheim, Jim Calhoun, P.J. Carlesimo, Gary Williams, Jay Wright, Steve Lappas, Rick Pitino, and Rick Barnes answered repeated calls and text messages. I had the true honor of spending hours with Lou Carnesecca and Jack Kaiser in a small office on the St. John's campus as they bantered back and forth and shared their memories, and I am so incredibly grateful that I spoke with John Thompson, Jr., before he passed away.

For all of the names you read in the book, there are dozens whose names don't appear but who helped me chase down phone numbers or set up the interviews that made the stories come alive: John Paquette at the Big East, Pete Moore at Syracuse, Tom Chen at Seton Hall, Phil Chardis and Mike Enright at Connecticut, Mike Laprey at Boston College, Diana Pulupa at Georgetown, and Michael Sheridan at Villanova all merit a nice bottle of wine, and my friends Mike Waters, of the Syracuse *Post-Standard,* and Kevin McNamara, of KevinMcSports.com, get a double. My niece/transcriber extraordinaire, Kelly Pennett, has a lifetime supply of whatever she chooses.

I am fortunate to work at a place that wholeheartedly endorsed this undertaking, and I thank *The Athletic*'s Alex Mather and Adam Hansmann for their support; my editor, Hugh Kellenberger, for making me a better writer; and Seth Davis for walking me through the how-tos of book writing.

We sportswriters tend to overthink, so I appreciate my best friends in the business, Pat Forde, Shannon Ryan, and Brian Hamilton, for their patience, and my mentor, Dick Jerardi, for basically directing my entire journalism career.

From the deck at the Shore to the screened-porch clubhouse,

the good humor of my friends Bill and Karen Eng, Matt and Meg Bingham, Kris Cauda, Peggy Meurer, MaryLou and Pete Sienko, Matt and Lynne Coulter, and Sandy and Pete Borowsky was a welcome escape.

Finally, I teased my family that I was going to dedicate my book to my dogs, since they were constantly underneath my chair as I typed. The canine companionship was welcome, but there's simply nothing more important than the love and support (and tolerance) of George, Madigan, and Kieran.

BIG EAST NAISMITH MEMORIAL HALL OF FAME MEMBERS

RAY ALLEN
University of Connecticut player, inducted 2018

JIM BOEHEIM
Syracuse University head coach, inducted 2005

JIM CALHOUN
University of Connecticut head coach, inducted 2005

LOU CARNESECCA
St. John's head coach, inducted 1992

PATRICK EWING
Georgetown player, inducted 2008

DAVE GAVITT
founder and commissioner, inducted 2006

ALLEN IVERSON
Georgetown player, inducted 2016

ALONZO MOURNING
Georgetown player, inducted 2014

CHRIS MULLIN
St. John's player, inducted 2011

DIKEMBE MUTOMBO
Georgetown player, inducted 2015

JOHN THOMPSON, JR.
Georgetown head coach, inducted 1999

GARY WILLIAMS
Boston College head coach, inducted 2014

BIG EAST TIMELINE

MAY 31, 1979

League announces formation. Boston College, Connecticut, Georgetown, Providence, St. John's, Seton Hall, and Syracuse are original members. Dave Gavitt is named commissioner.

MARCH 1, 1980

Georgetown defeats Syracuse, 87–81, and wins the first Big East Tournament, played in Providence.

1980

Villanova joins the Big East.

1982

Georgetown is the first Big East team to reach the Final Four. The Hoyas defeat Louisville, 50–46, in the national semifinals but lose to North Carolina, 63–62, in the championship game.

1983

The Big East Tournament moves to Madison Square Garden. St. John's wins the title, and Chris Mullin is named tournament MVP.

1984

Georgetown defeats Houston, 84–75, to become the first Big East team to win a national championship.

1985

The Big East is the first (and still only) conference to place three teams in the Final Four. Georgetown, St. John's, and Villanova all advance to the national semifinals, played in Lexington, Kentucky. Villanova upsets Georgetown, 66–64, to win the championship.

1986

The Big East becomes the first conference to sign an exclusive TV deal with ESPN.

1987

Syracuse and Providence reach the Final Four. The Orange defeat the Friars in the national semifinals, 77–63, but lose to Indiana, 74–73, in the national championship game.

1989

Seton Hall is the sixth Big East team to reach the Final Four, losing in overtime, 80–79, to Michigan in the national title game.

1990

Dave Gavitt leaves the Big East to become the head of basketball operations with the Boston Celtics. Mike Tranghese is named commissioner.

1991

The Big East adds an eight-team football division. Miami wins the football national championship.

APRIL 13, 1992

Lou Carnesecca announces his retirement from St. John's.

1995

Rutgers and West Virginia are added as full-sports members. Notre Dame joins for all sports but football.

1996

The Big East is the first conference to place three players on the Associated Press All-American first team—Connecticut's Ray Allen, Georgetown's Allen Iverson, and Villanova's Kerry Kittles. Syracuse reaches the Final Four, losing to Kentucky in the national championship game, 76–67.

JANUARY 9, 1999

John Thompson, Jr., announces his retirement from Georgetown.

1999

Connecticut beats Duke, 77–74, to win the Big East's third national title.

2000

Virginia Tech becomes a member in all sports.

2003

Syracuse defeats Kansas, 81–78, to win the Big East's fourth national championship.

2004

Connecticut defeats Georgia Tech, 82–73, to win the league's fifth national championship.

2005

The Big East adds Cincinnati, DePaul, Louisville, Marquette, and South Florida to grow the basketball league to sixteen teams. Boston College announces it will depart the Big East for the ACC.

2006

The Big East earns a record eight NCAA Tournament bids.

2007

Georgetown advances to the Final Four, losing to Ohio State, 67–60, in the national semifinals.

2009

Syracuse defeats Connecticut, 127–117, in a six-overtime Big East Tournament quarterfinal. The Huskies and Villanova advance to the Final Four. UConn loses to Michigan State in the national semifinals, 82–73, and the Wildcats lose to North Carolina in the national semifinals, 83–69.

2010

West Virginia advances to the Final Four, losing to Duke, 78–57, in the national semifinals.

2011

The Big East breaks its own record, earning eleven NCAA Tournament bids. UConn, winning a record five Big East Tournament games in five nights, defeats Butler, 53–41, to wins its third national championship and the sixth for the conference.

SEPTEMBER 2011

Syracuse and Pittsburgh announce they will leave the Big East for the ACC, eventually agreeing to depart in 2013.

OCTOBER 2011

West Virginia announces it will leave the Big East for the Big 12, eventually agreeing to depart in 2012.

2012

Notre Dame announces it will leave the Big East for the ACC.

2012

Louisville advances to the Final Four.

DECEMBER 15, 2012

The basketball-playing schools DePaul, Georgetown, Marquette, Providence, St. John's, Seton Hall, and Villanova (dubbed the Catholic 7) announce they will separate from the football-playing schools and form a new conference.

2013

Syracuse and Louisville reach the Final Four. Syracuse loses to Michigan in the national semifinals, 61–56. Louisville defeats Michigan, 82–76, to win the league's seventh national championship.

MARCH 20, 2013

The Catholic 7 announce they have retained the Big East name, and have negotiated to continue the tournament in Madison Square Garden. Butler, Creighton, and Xavier are added as members, and the new Big East announces a TV deal with Fox Sports.

JUNE 26, 2013
Val Ackerman is appointed Big East commissioner.

2016
Villanova defeats North Carolina, 77–74, to win the Big East's eighth national championship.

2018
Villanova defeats Michigan, 79–62, to win the Big East's ninth national championship.

JULY 1, 2019
The Big East announces Connecticut will return to the conference.

INDEX

ABOUT THE AUTHOR

DANA O'NEIL has been a sportswriter and national college basketball reporter for over three decades, covering eighteen Final Fours. A senior writer at *The Athletic*, she has worked at ESPN and the *Philadelphia Daily News*, and has been honored with multiple writing awards. She served as the president of the U.S. Basketball Writers Association, only the second woman to lead the organization. A graduate of Penn State, she lives in Newtown, Pennsylvania, with her husband and two children.

Twitter: @DanaONeilWriter